Taking Aim at Attack Advertising

Taking Aim At Attack Advertising

Understanding the Impact of Negative Campaigning in U.S. Senate Races

KIM L. FRIDKIN

PATRICK J. KENNEY

OXFORD
UNIVERSITY PRESS

OXFORD
UNIVERSITY PRESS

Oxford University Press is a department of the University of Oxford. It furthers
the University's objective of excellence in research, scholarship, and education
by publishing worldwide. Oxford is a registered trade mark of Oxford University
Press in the UK and certain other countries.

Published in the United States of America by Oxford University Press
198 Madison Avenue, New York, NY 10016, United States of America.

Library of Congress Cataloging-in-Publication Data
Names: Fridkin, Kim L., author. | Kenney, Patrick J., author.
Title: Taking aim at attack advertising : understanding the impact of
negative campaigning in U.S. Senate races / Kim L. Fridkin, Patrick J. Kenney.
Description: New York, NY, United States of America : Oxford University Press, [2019] |
Includes bibliographical references.
Identifiers: LCCN 2018046853 (print) | LCCN 2018059876 (ebook) |
ISBN 9780190947583 (Universal PDF) | ISBN 9780190947590 (E-pub) |
ISBN 9780190947606 (Oxford Scholarship Online) |
ISBN 9780190947576 (pbk. : alk. paper) | ISBN 9780190947569 (hardback : alk. paper)
Subjects: LCSH: Political campaigns—United States. | Advertising,
Political—United States. | United States. Congress. Senate—Elections. |
Voting research—United States.
Classification: LCC JK2281 (ebook) | LCC JK2281 .F74 2019 (print) |
DDC 324.70973—dc23
LC record available at https://lccn.loc.gov/2018046853

1 3 5 7 9 8 6 4 2

Paperback printed by Sheridan Books, Inc., United States of America
Hardback printed by Bridgeport National Bindery, Inc., United States of America

Contents

Preface

WE HAVE HAD the good fortune of working together for a very long time. In fact, our collaborations constitute a significant portion of our collective careers. This specific project represents the culmination of work we began almost 20 years ago, when we published an article in the *American Political Science Review* showing different types of negativity alter people's likelihood of participating in elections. In the two decades since, we have developed additional aspects of our theory, including our contention that people vary in their tolerance of negative campaigning. In this book, we develop our theory more fully, and we test the validity of the theory with a series of data sets across several years. We believe the *tolerance and tactics theory* will shed light on the two central questions motivating a great deal of work on negative campaigns: Do negative messages depress evaluations of candidates under attack? And is it possible negative campaigns shape the likelihood citizens will go to the polls on Election Day? The results described in our book empirically support the veracity of our theory, suggesting our work over the past two decades has been fruitful. We hope scholars will think the culmination of our efforts add up to a significant contribution to the study of how negative campaigning influences the beliefs and behaviors of America's citizens in elections.

To test the tolerance and tactics theory of negativity, we compiled divergent data sets collected in 2014, 2015, 2016, and 2017, focusing primarily on the 2014 U.S. Senate campaigns. We utilized different methods, including surveys, experiments, content analyses, and focus groups. We have been helped and aided by a wonderful group of talented graduate and undergraduate students. We thank, especially, Jillian Courey and Manny Gutierrez, who helped with running the experiments, focus groups, and content analyses. Josh Thompson collected political advertising data early in the project, and Sammy Goldenberg helped with our early focus groups. Our wonderful crew of undergraduate assistants in the School of Politics and Global Studies Laboratory has been instrumental in our data collection efforts; we owe a debt of gratitude to Joshua Galvan, Ryan Deutsch, Ryan Haddad, Micah Kyler, Kerry Morris, Maddy Sutton, Kelly Morris, Jasmyn Kamal, and Zachary Arlington. We would also like to thank Erika Franklin Fowler for her helpful comments on an early version of chapter 6 presented at the American Political Association meetings in 2016. Erika encouraged us to utilize the Wesleyan Media Project data and to merge respondents with the advertisements aired in their Senate election. It was a great suggestion and yielded a better set of findings. Finally, we would like to thank Pat Crittenden, as always, for her expert editing of the manuscript.

We are pleased to have our book published at Oxford University Press. Dave McBride has been supportive of the project since our initial discussions at the American Political Science Association meeting in San Francisco in August 2017. We have benefited a great deal from his guidance. We have had a wonderful experience at Oxford University Press.

We dedicate this book to our families. Kim is grateful to her husband, Bob, her daughters, Jennifer and Melissa, and her mom, Barbara, for their love, support, and inspiration. Pat is thankful to his ever-increasing family. First and foremost, his wife, Sally, has provided constant support of all his projects across 38 years of marriage. Sally and Pat are grateful for their family, Jessica and Matt, Sean and Amanda, Michael and Derrick, Mary and Ryan, and three wonderful grandkids, Joseph, Eleanor Grace, and Mason. Simply hosting Thanksgiving dinners for the Kenney family will require Pat to coauthor with Kim for many decades to come.

I

Untangling the Impact of Negative Campaigning on Citizens

OUR STORY BEGINS with two women from Iowa, mother and daughter, who witnessed, participated in, and voted in political campaigns collectively for nearly a century. Mary was born two years after women were granted suffrage and lived her entire life within a few miles of where she was born in Iowa. She graduated from high school in the spring of 1941 and was working as a "Rosie the Riveter" by the summer of 1942. Like so many people of her generation, she embraced her civic responsibility across many decades doing such things as working at the polling booth on Election Day, volunteering in a Head Start preschool, serving on the board of a small elementary school, and raising money for a women's shelter. She never missed voting in an election— federal, state, or local. She studied the candidates' backgrounds, experience, and issue positions when deciding whom to support. She often fretted about her choice all the way to the voting booth.

The importance of the Iowa presidential caucuses exploded in the 1970s, when Mary's state became the epicenter of presidential politics for the 12 months preceding the caucus vote in January or February of the presidential election year. It is impossible to live in Iowa in the months leading up to the caucuses and not notice the teams of aspiring candidates, thousands of campaign workers, and hundreds of national and international reporters running to and fro across the state. Mary embraced the excitement. She never missed a caucus, irrespective of how cold the January night. In the months preceding the night of the caucuses, pamphlets arrived at her door, and campaign workers and sometimes the candidates themselves called her home, cajoling her to caucus for them. Campaign advertisements blitzed the small media markets of Iowa, especially as the caucuses neared; the number of political ads, the percentage of allotted advertising time, and the negativity of the campaign messages have all increased across the past four decades (e.g., Geer, 2006). Mary grew weary of the scope, incivility, and content of the negative campaign messages. She found the incessant nature of these advertisements off-putting, unnecessary, unpleasant, and, by the end of the long campaign, annoying. To be sure, she still caucused, but she felt that the level of negativity was too high and her tolerance for this type of campaigning was low.

Rita, Mary's daughter, was born and raised in Iowa and lives a few miles from where she grew up. Like Mary, Rita has a strong sense of civic duty and loves following political campaigns. She began tracking politics in earnest in the late 1980s and now is a veteran of eight caucuses. She attends campaign rallies and finds her way to small venues where candidates are visiting with a couple of dozen people. She's bumped into more than one presidential hopeful in grocery stores and restaurants. The retail nature of campaigning in Iowa in the months preceding the caucuses suits her well. She receives a lot of attention from eager campaign staffers pursuing her to support their candidates. In fact, she's been called by and has talked directly to one president and one vice president of the United States—both men were checking to be certain she was caucusing for them.

Rita is nearly unfazed by the negative campaign messages and rhetoric exemplified in many of the television commercials. Withering attacks, especially against the rival party, are expected. She views harsh critiques of candidates as part and parcel of contemporary campaigns. She thinks that clear comparisons need to be drawn and highlighted between rival candidates because much is at stake in presidential elections. According to Rita, attacks need to be pointed, especially if they are true, harsh if necessary, and repeated over time. Rita, in contrast to Mary, has a much higher tolerance for negative campaigning.

Although the variability in levels of tolerance is pronounced between Mary and Rita, they are both strong partisans and support the same team. They place themselves on the same side of the ideological scale but are not rigid ideologues. They follow issues related to the "nature of the times" and routinely focus on the personality traits of the candidates. They have similar levels of civic responsibility and believe that government and politicians react to the broad concerns of the American electorate, sometimes successfully but often not. Amid similarities in attitudes about candidates, campaigns, and the role of government, they vary considerably in their acceptance of negative campaign messages.

The presidential caucuses pique the interest of large numbers of Iowans, and although nonpresidential contests draw less attention, Mary and Rita follow dutifully and participate in those contests as well. Nonpresidential campaigns in Iowa, similar to House, Senate, and gubernatorial campaigns across the nation, have become increasingly intense and negative, especially since 1994 (e.g., Fowler, Franz, and Ridout, 2016; Jacobson and Carson, 2015).

Iowans were served by the same two senators for over 30 years. Senator Chuck Grassley, Republican, was elected in 1980, and Senator Tom Harkin, Democrat, was elected in 1984. Senator Harkin's retirement created an open seat for the 2014 senatorial election cycle, a highly polarized period in this traditional swing state. The stakes were high, and Iowans, predictably, were in for a donnybrook.

Republicans nominated State Senator Joni Ernst, and the Democrats countered with U.S. Congressman Bruce Braley, who represented Iowa's first congressional district. Pre-election polls indicated that the race would be close; in fact, the highly respected YouGov poll from late October 2014 had the race essentially tied. This was not surprising—after all, Iowans had elected a Republican and a Democrat to represent them in the U.S. Senate for over 30 years. Both candidates raised enough resources to conduct aggressive statewide campaigns. They repeatedly canvassed the tiny, small, and medium-size towns in Iowa across the summer and during the fall harvest. The state's local newspapers followed the campaign carefully, and the venerable *Des Moines Register* endorsed Braley. The candidates participated in televised debates, and, as expected, they both produced dozens of different campaign advertisements that appeared constantly in the relatively affordable Iowa television markets.

Campaign messages delivered from the podium, during debates, and in 30-second television commercials contained a mix of positive and negative themes. But as the campaign moved into the fall, the messages grew increasingly negative, with each candidate attacking the other frequently. The content of the candidates' criticisms followed familiar themes found in many campaigns conducted during the early years of the 21st century, bouncing along a continuum from highly relevant to surprisingly trivial. For example, each candidate focused on the voting record of the other. Ernst criticized Braley on a number of his votes in the U.S. House on key issues, including health care. Ernst also emphasized Braley's missed roll call votes, denying Iowans a voice on important policy issues. Braley attacked Ernst for votes cast during her tenure in the Iowa legislature, suggesting her voting record did not align with her campaign rhetoric. In the midst of discussing such highly relevant topics for assessing legislative candidates running for office, the candidates sometimes lapsed into topics far less germane to governing. For example, they debated the use and meaning of a baby "chick" in a television commercial. They also squabbled over the fact that Senator Grassley, elected to the U.S. Senate since 1980 and not up for reelection, did not hold a law degree while serving on the Senate Judiciary Committee.

In addition to the variability in the relevance of their campaign rhetoric, the tone of the candidates' negative commercials varied dramatically. Their messages, mirroring patterns of attack advertising across the nation in highly competitive races, fell along a continuum from civil dialogue to uncivil attacks characterized by harsh and shrill criticisms. For example, some of their messages were courteous and respectful, while stressing differences between their candidacies. However, in other messages, the candidates' rhetoric was bitter and strident, with ad hominem attacks. Several of these commercials were literally dark in presentation, with menacing music accompanying the voice of the unknown spokesperson making alarming claims. The number of attack advertisements aired on television was high, especially for Iowa. More than 22,000 negative advertisements targeted Ernst during the course of the campaign, while more than 30,000 commercials attacked Braley in the months leading up to Election Day (Fowler, Franz, and Ridout, 2017). It was almost impossible for Iowans to avoid the heated debates, name-calling, endless commercials, and discussions about the candidates among friends, sometimes even strangers, either in person, on the phone, or online.

On Election Day, after many months of back-and-forth between the candidates and their surrogates, Iowans cast more votes for Ernst than for Braley, thereby making Ernst the first woman in Iowa history to be elected to the U.S. Senate. This campaign captures the combustible mix of the content and tone of negative political advertising frequently on display in America's competitive campaigns. And citizens like Mary and Rita, varying in their ability to tolerate negative messaging, find themselves enmeshed in these campaigns while trying to carry out their civic responsibility on Election Day. Most likely, Mary and Rita voted for the same candidate. However, after months of harsh and uncivil attacks, often centered on messages unrelated to governing, Mary was undoubtedly tired of the candidates and wearily filled out her ballot, thankful for the end of the campaign. Rita, armed with lots of reasons for supporting one candidate over the other, was energized and looked forward to voting on Election Day.

This project is partly about discovering differences in people's tolerance for negative campaigning during electoral contests. We believe that Rita and

Mary are not unique. Instead we will show that people's level of tolerance for negativity is explained by a series of basic social, demographic, and political factors. However, identifying variability in people's tolerance for negative rhetoric is only part of the story. The tactics employed by the candidates in shaping the content and tone of their negative attacks are equally important. We know that candidates will produce a mix of messages and that voters will view some of these messages as far more relevant and civil than others.

In this book we develop what we call "the tolerance and tactics theory of negativity." We demonstrate empirically that the marriage of citizens' tolerance for negativity, on the one hand, with the tactics employed by candidates, on the other hand, will sharply advance our understanding of how negative campaigning affects the beliefs and behaviors of citizens during U.S. campaigns. The combination of knowing how citizens feel about negativity and identifying the specific content and tone of negative messages opens a new path for understanding the impact of negative advertising. We have high hopes that this analytical framework will yield some clarity for students, scholars, journalists, commentators, and pundits who study, cover, investigate, and worry about the increasingly negative nature of contemporary U.S. elections.

Understanding the impact of negative campaigning is crucial because it is an ever increasing and pervasive force in the United States (for a review of recent trends see Fowler, Franz, and Ridout, 2016: 50–65). During the final days of the 2016 presidential election, about $110 million were spent on television advertising, with about 70,000 different political advertisements disseminated across the nation (Wallace, 2016). The overwhelming majority of these advertisements, 92% in fact, criticized Democrat Hillary Clinton or Republican Donald Trump. Only 3% focused on positive messages about Clinton, and 5% were built around positive messages about Trump.

The amount, scope, creativity, and accessibility of negative campaign information has increased and is especially common in competitive elections (e.g., Brooks and Murov, 2012; Geer, 2006, 2012; Fowler et al., 2016; Fowler and Ridout, 2011; Mattes and Redlawsk, 2015). There is little chance that the pace of negative advertising will slow anytime soon, given protections provided in the First Amendment to the U.S. Constitution as well as recent U.S. Supreme Court decisions on fundraising and spending (e.g., *Citizens United v. FEC*). Political commentators and scholars have grown increasingly concerned that the nature and conduct of political campaigns dampens people's optimism about the democratic process (e.g., Gabriel, 2016; Massaro and Stryker, 2012; Phillips, 2016; Rogowski, 2014).

The ubiquitous nature of negative campaigning has produced a significant amount of sophisticated scholarly research that continues to accumulate at an impressive rate. The relationship between campaign negativity and citizens' attitudes and actions have motivated two central questions: (1) Do negative advertisements persuade voters to form negative impressions of competing candidates? (2) Do negative campaign messages affect citizens' willingness to go to the polls on Election Day? These questions have long been a central focus for the study of representative democracies, as they are crucial for understanding the attitudes and actions of citizens. However, clear and unequivocal answers have been less than forthcoming. In fact, two extensive and thoughtful meta-analyses reviewing the extant literature demonstrate that the impact of negative advertising on persuasion and participation is inconsistent and elusive (see Lau et al., 1999; Lau, Sigelman, and Rovner, 2007). Furthermore, Lau and Rovner (2009), writing for the *Annual Review of Political Science,* updated the literature but continue to find inconclusive effects regarding the impact of negative campaigning.

Scholarly research, however, has not subsided in the face of inconsistent findings in the decade since these meta-analyses were conducted (e.g., Banda and Windett, 2016; Hassell and Oeltjenbruns, 2016; Ridout et al., 2018; for a review, see Ridout and Holland, 2017). Recent work suggests the impact of negative advertising on people's beliefs and behaviors varies across citizens, messages, and candidates, and these forces often condition one another (e.g., Henderson and Theodoridis, 2017; Krupnikov, 2011, 2014; Mutz, 2015). We turn first to the question haunting the managers of all political campaigns: Do negative messages depress impressions of candidates?

Put simply, Lau, Sigelman, and Rovner's (2007: 1182) summary from over a decade ago holds up well: "The picture is mixed, with the bulk of the evidence pointing to a modest tendency for negative campaigns to undermine positive affect for the candidates they target." To be sure, a number of studies over three decades demonstrate that candidate evaluations decline when the candidate is under attack (e.g., Merritt, 1984; Kaid and Boyson, 1987; Franz et al., 2008; Freedman and Goldstein, 1999; Goldstein and Freedman, 2000; Lau and Pomper, 2002; Gerber et al., 2011; Banda, 2014; Cassese and Holman, 2017).

Nevertheless, the impact of negative advertisements on impressions of candidates is conditioned by a number of factors. For example, attack advertising sponsored by interest and advocacy groups is more influential than negative commercials sponsored by political parties (Dowling and Wichovsky, 2014). In addition, the timing of negative advertisements matters, with criticisms delivered late in the campaign being more effective because negative critiques decay sharply over time (e.g., Gerber et al., 2011; Hill et al., 2013). Banda (2014) shows attacks on candidates are more influential when political issues are used to make rivals appear more ideologically extreme.

Negative advertising can have intended and unintended consequences on people's impressions of competing candidates. In particular, when a candidate launches an attack on a rival, the negative message may "backfire" or "boomerang," creating more negative views of the candidate sponsoring the negative advertisement (Skaperdas and Grofman, 1995). Researchers have documented the backlash effects of negative advertising with experimental methods (e.g., Garramone, 1984; Hill, 1989), aggregate data (Jasperson and Fan, 2002; Lau and Pomper, 2002), and survey designs (Kahn and Kenney, 2004; Lau and Pomper, 2002). Negative advertising can backfire because voters feel sympathetic toward candidates under attack, especially when these candidates have not initiated the critiques (e.g., Hitchon and Chang, 1995; Haddock and Zanna, 1997; Pinkleton, 1998).

More recently, scholars have shown that the size of the backlash effect is conditioned by specific characteristics of citizens and candidates. For example, Dowling and Wichowsky (2015) found backlash effects are less likely when advertisements are sponsored by outside groups rather than by parties or candidates. In addition, Krupnikov and Bauer (2014) found women candidates who initiate negative attacks are more likely to be punished by voters since these women are viewed as violating standard gender stereotypes by acting aggressively during campaigns. Similarly, Krupnikov and Piston (2015) found the size of the backlash against African American candidates is significantly larger among whites who hold more negative views of African Americans. Also, incumbents are more likely to suffer from backlash effects, compared to challengers (e.g., Fridkin and Kenney, 2011; Lariscy and Tinkham, 1999).

Finally, isolating the impact of negative messages on citizens' views of the candidates is complicated during elections because campaigns are highly dynamic affairs with constant interactions between the candidates and voters (e.g., Banda and Windett, 2016; Box-Steffensmeier, Darmofal, and Farrell, 2009; Hassell and Oeltjenbruns, 2016).[1] Panel data, including multiple

---

1. The dynamic nature of campaigns, with candidates often simultaneously attacking each other, along with attack messages delivered by campaign surrogates and third-party groups, makes it difficult to isolate the direct (i.e., persuasion) and indirect (i.e., backlash effects) impacts of negative advertisements during an ongoing campaign. Instead, experimental designs (see Druckman et al., 2006) offer scholars the control necessary to manipulate who is under

interviews with the same voters over the length of the campaign, can help scholars identify the impact of negative advertisements on evaluations of the competing candidates. In fact, researchers utilizing these kinds of research designs do indeed find negative attacks on rivals lead to lower evaluations of the targeted candidates (e.g., Hillygus and Sheilds, 2004; Box-Steffensmeier, Darmofal, and Farrell, 2009).

In the end, existing research suggests that attack advertising can influence impressions of candidates under certain conditions. However, careful theorizing is needed in order to identify the most important factors likely to condition the impact of negativity on citizens' views of the competing candidates. Furthermore, in order to successfully measure the influence of negative campaign messages during elections, it is necessary to employ diverse research designs, including examining the messages of candidates and the reactions of voters in real time during actual campaigns.

Although the main objective of negative advertising is to depress citizens' evaluations of targeted candidates, negative campaigning may influence people's likelihood of participating in elections. In particular, if negative attacks are vicious and pervasive, citizens may become disgusted with the candidates and campaigns and decide to stay home on Election Day. This outcome raises broader questions and concerns regarding the quality and health of elections to produce legitimate outcomes in representative democracies. Consequently, exploring the link between negative campaigning and electoral turnout has motivated a significant amount of scholarly attention.

Ansolabehere and Iyengar (1996), employing an impressive multimethodological research design, were the first scholars to look at the relationship between negative advertising and turnout. They conducted a series of experiments and examined the relationship between the tone and turnout of Senate campaigns by using an aggregate analysis of the 1992 Senate elections. Results from both the aggregate analysis and the experiments suggested that negative information decreases turnout.

In the more than two decades since Ansolabehere and Iyengar (1996) published their book, a number of studies have looked at the relationship between negative campaigning and turnout. The vast majority of these studies cast doubt on the strength and direction of Ansolabehere and Iyengar's original findings. Many studies suggest that negative information either has no

---

attack and who is initiating the attacks (e.g., Mutz, 2015). Nevertheless, it is often difficult for experimentalists to make generalizations about actual campaigns where millions of dollars are spent on negative commercials and millions of voters are viewing these messages.

effect on levels of turnout or that negative advertising may actually stimulate turnout. Brooks (2006), reexamining Ansolabehere and Iyengar's aggregate analysis of Senate elections, finds no relationship between the tone of Senate campaigns and turnout in elections. Finkel and Geer (1998), looking at presidential elections from 1960 to 1992 with contextual and survey data, show that increases in exposure to negative advertising do not lower turnout. Krasno and Green (2008) show that the amount of negative advertising aired during the final weeks of the 2000 presidential election had a negligible effect on voter turnout.

Several researchers have identified a positive relationship between negative information and the likelihood of voting. The logic for these findings is grounded in the idea that negative information often delivers important information about candidates' issue positions, political experiences, and personal traits and voters are looking for information to help guide their vote choice (e.g., Geer, 2006). Freedman and Goldstein (1999), Goldstein and Freedman (2002), and Freedman, Franz, and Goldstein (2004) find exposure to negative rhetoric is related to higher turnout in the 1996 and 2000 presidential elections as well as in the 1997 Virginia gubernatorial campaign. Geer and Lau (2006), Clinton and Lapinski (2004), and Hillygus (2005), also looking at presidential campaigns, find turnout increases with negative campaigning, although the authors differ in their assessments of the size of that relationship.

Lau and Pomper (2001, 2004) examine U.S. Senate races from 1988 to 1998 with both aggregate and individual-level data and find a curvilinear relationship between negative information and turnout in U.S. Senate elections. In particular, Lau and Pomper find that negative information stimulates turnout until negative campaigning becomes very intense, and then participation declines. Jackson and Carsey (2007) and Kahn and Kenney (1999a) examine the relationship between negative advertising and turnout in U.S. Senate campaigns in 1998 and 1990, respectively. Jackson and Carsey find exposure to negative campaigning produces a strong mobilization effect, while Kahn and Kenney find evidence for both mobilizing and depressive effects of negative information on turnout, depending on the content and tone of the negative messages.

Similar to the findings on the persuasive effects of negative advertising, a closer look at the impact of negative campaigning on turnout demonstrates the importance of conditional effects. First, certain types of citizens are more likely to be demobilized by negative advertising. For example, people who are less sophisticated about politics, less attached to the political parties (e.g., independents), or less interested in politics are more likely to stay home on Election Day when confronted with a flood of negative advertisements (e.g., Kahn and Kenney, 1999a; Jackson and Sides, 2006; Niven, 2006). Second, certain types of negative messages are more likely to increase citizens' likelihood of heading to the polls. For example, negative information focused on issues tends to be more effective at increasing turnout, compared to other topics (e.g., Brooks and Geer, 2007; Stevens, 2012). Third, how negativity is measured (i.e., proportion of negative information versus absolute amount of negative information disseminated during a campaign) and when negative information is disseminated (e.g., late in a campaign, before or after citizens make decisions about whom to support) can influence the mobilizing or demobilizing impact of negative campaigning (Krupnikov, 2011; Stevens, 2009).

In summary, a number of researchers have examined whether negative advertising depresses or increases citizens' likelihood of casting a vote on Election Day.[2] Looking at different types of campaigns, with different types of data, in different years, and with different measures of negativity, the results of these studies have been inconsistent. However, a key conclusion of the literature is that the relationship between negativity and turnout is conditioned by characteristics of the citizens, the campaigns, and the types of negative messages.

The extant literature examining the impact of negative campaigning on turnout as well as investigations into the relationship between negative messages and assessments of candidates demonstrates the importance of considering variation across different types of negative messages as well as different types of citizens. This is precisely where we intend to situate our contribution to the study of negative campaigning. We present a theoretical framework where we identify central dimensions of negative messages (i.e., the relevance and civility of negative advertisements) as well as key characteristics of citizens (i.e., citizens' intolerance of negative campaigning) to explain when negative

---

2. Some researchers have examined the relationship between negative campaigning and people's political efficacy and political trust. Again, the results have been equivocal. While Ansolabehere et al. (1994) and Finkel and Geer (1998) find that increases in negative advertising are associated with decreases in political efficacy, other scholars fail to find a negative relationship (e.g., Brooks and Geer, 2007; Goldstein and Freedman, 2002; Jackson, Mondak, and Huckfeldt, 2009; Pinkleton, Um, and Austin, 2002; Wattenberg and Brians, 1999). Looking at political trust, Brader (2005), Brooks and Geer (2007), and Leshner and Thorson (2000) identify a negative relationship between increases in exposure to negative advertising and decreases in political trust. However, Geer (2006) and Lau and Pomper (2004) report no relationship between negative advertising and levels of political trust, and Martinez and Delegal (1990) report trust in government actually *increases* after exposure to negative advertisements.

messages will influence assessments of the candidates as well as people's propensity to participate in elections. We utilize a multimethodological approach, with surveys, experiments, content analysis, and focus groups, to test empirically the veracity of our theory. Furthermore, we test our theory in the context of an ongoing campaign where people's partisan proclivities as well as their prior history with the candidates are likely to influence their views of campaign messages. We turn now to a more extensive discussion of the theoretical framework guiding our investigation.

A Theoretical Framework for Understanding When Negative Messages Matter

We rely on theoretical work in social psychology, political science, and communication, in tandem with a growing set of empirical findings, to understand how negative information shapes voters' actions and attitudes during elections. As earlier illustrated by the example from the 2014 Iowa senatorial campaign, we advance the tolerance and tactics theory of negativity to broaden and improve our understanding of the impact of negative messages during political campaigns. The theory has two core components. First, citizens vary in their tolerance for negative campaigning. Put simply, some people tolerate and even enjoy negative attacks on candidates far more than others who find sharp and shrill criticism inappropriate and tiring. The variance in voters' tolerance for negative campaign rhetoric is the starting point for understanding how voters respond to negative stimuli during campaigns.

Second, we believe the tactics employed by candidates and campaign strategists is crucial to understanding the effectiveness of the messages. We have argued that negative messages are arranged along two dimensions: (1) the relevance of the content and (2) the civility of the tone (e.g., Fridkin and Kenney, 2008, 2011). Relevant messages are related directly to candidates' governing activities (e.g., issue positions salient to voters, legislators' voting records, ideology), personal traits linked to success in politics (e.g., experience in politics, expertise in policy matters), and pertinent personal characteristic (e.g., connections to the state). Irrelevant messages are less obviously connected to candidates' abilities to govern (e.g., positions on issues long off the nation's agenda, contentious divorces decades earlier, drug use in college).[3]

---

3. The relevance of messages may differ across time and across individuals. For instance, a candidate's religious upbringing may be considered more relevant to a socially conservative voter than to another voter. Similarly, certain types of personal misbehavior in a candidate's

We have shown that citizens are not only capable of distinguishing between messages varying in their relevance, but they also place more weight on relevant messages when choosing between candidates (Fridkin and Kenney, 2008, 2011).

In addition, the civility of messages is important for understanding the impact of negative criticisms. The tone of messages ranges along a continuum from nasty and harsh to more even-tempered and courteous. A number of researchers have begun to measure civil and uncivil political content as well as to explore how the civility of messages influences citizens' attitudes toward candidates, government, and policy matters (e.g., Anderson et al., 2014; Avery, 2009; Brooks and Geer, 2007; Haselmayer and Jenny, 2014; Hill, Capella, and Cho, 2015; Mutz, 2007, 2015; Mutz and Reeves, 2005; Stevens et al., 2015; Sydnor, 2018). The consensus from these studies is that incivility in negative campaign messages is prolific; however, researchers disagree about the impact of uncivil messages on voters' views of candidates.

We theorize that the variance in the relevance and civility of negative messages influences the effectiveness of these messages (Fridkin and Kenney, 2008, 2011). In particular, we contend that uncivil but relevant negative messages powerfully shape citizens' views about candidates. This combination is particularly potent because harsh (i.e., uncivil) attacks are more likely to be noticed by potential voters (e.g., Lau, 1985; Mutz, 2015), and negative critiques on relevant topics provide important information about the risks of supporting certain candidates. In contrast, irrelevant messages, whether delivered in a civil or an uncivil manner, are unlikely to influence voters' impressions of candidates.

In addition, we hypothesize that the relevance and civility of negative messages can determine people's likelihood of voting in electoral campaigns (e.g., Kahn and Kenney, 1999a). We argue that when negative messages focus on a relevant topic and employ a courteous tone, voters will be mobilized for two reasons. First, negative messages focusing on important topics point out the potential risks associated with specific electoral choices (e.g., Lau, 1985). Second, motivating people to action, like going to the polls, is often associated with positive encouragement and grounded in ideas of civic responsibility embedded in a range of institutions, such as family, church and schools

---

distant past may have been considered irrelevant by large swaths of voters a decade ago, but the same misbehavior in the wake of the #MeToo movement may be viewed as more relevant. In chapter 6, we explore how differences in people's political predispositions influence their views of the relevance of political messages.

(Verba, Schlozman, and Brady, 1995). Useful criticisms of candidates delivered in a respectful manner helps nudge people to take the time to vote and fulfill their civic duty. However, when negative messages center on questionable topics and are presented in an overly strident matter (i.e., mudslinging), we expect that voters will become alienated with the electoral process and will be less likely to participate in the election. In other words, when campaign messages become increasingly shrill and nasty and focus on petty and irrelevant topics, citizens will become disgusted with the mudslinging and will be more likely to stay home on Election Day. We argue that considering both the relevance and the civility of negative campaign messages will clarify the relationship between negative campaigning and political participation.

According to the tolerance and tactics theory of negativity, it is not enough to focus on the relevance and civility of the campaign messages. To understand when negative campaigning will be consequential, we also need to consider citizens' tolerance for negative messages (Fridkin and Kenney, 2011). We theorize that people's predispositions regarding the appropriate nature of political discourse determines their receptivity to negative messages that vary in civility and relevance. People who are least tolerant of negativity are most likely to be affected by negative messages. We believe that the tolerance and tactics theory of negativity provides a better understanding of how negative information affects citizens' beliefs and behaviors on Election Day. We turn next to a more extensive discussion of the two components of our theory: (1) people's tolerance of negativity and (2) the relevance and civility of negative messages.

Understanding the Importance of Tolerance

We have argued and demonstrated empirically that people have an underlying tolerance for negative messages (Fridkin and Kenney, 2011). We know from fields as disparate as business, medicine, and psychology that people differ in their tolerance for ambiguity (Furnham and Marks, 2013), their tolerance for risk (Grable, 2000), and their tolerance for distress (Simon and Gaher, 2005). More relevant to the political domain, researchers have shown that people vary in their tolerance for disagreement or conflict (Mutz and Reeves, 2005; Sydnor, 2015; Teven, McCroskey, and Richmond, 1998; Ulbig and Funk, 1999). The common denominator across these diverse literatures is that people vary in their willingness to accept unpleasant situations or behaviors.

Just as some people are more comfortable with conflict or risk, we expect that people also differ in their tolerance for negative campaign messages.

Some people do not mind that a negative commercial is delivered in a strident fashion or focuses on trivial topics. These individuals are comfortable with candidates using whatever means necessary to attack their opponents during campaigns. For other people, certain types of negative messages are unacceptable and cross the line of common decency.

We contend that people's tolerance for negativity will influence their receptivity to negative messages delivered during campaigns. For people who have a high tolerance for negative messages (i.e., people who think any type of attack advertising is appropriate), the attack advertisements will be less influential. In contrast, citizens who have a low tolerance for negativity will be more influenced by negative messages.

Some researchers have begun to measure differences in tolerance to negative messages. For instance, Muehling, Vijayalakshmi, and Laczniak (2016) examine people's responsiveness to comparative attacks in product commercials (e.g., a Pepsi commercial saying that Pepsi tastes better than Coke). They find that people with low levels of tolerance toward negativity view comparative product commercials as less fair and less useful than people with higher tolerance to negativity. Stryker, Danielson, and Conway (2015), looking at negative political messages, develop a measure of people's tolerance for political incivility. They find women are less tolerant of political incivility than men, Democrats are less tolerant of political incivility than Republicans, and students who watch certain types of political programming (e.g., NPR, Fox News, *The Daily Show*) differ in their tolerance for political incivility.[4]

Scholars have looked at a variety of factors that influence people's receptivity to negative messages. For instance, Craig and Rippere (2014) find that people's levels of trust affect their responsiveness to negative messages. They find that levels of trust yield a "meaningful, if limited, role in shaping citizens' reactions to negative campaign appeals" (Craig and Rippere, 2014: 19). Specifically, negative appeals are more influential among people with higher levels of trust in leaders and institutions. Similarly, Neuman, Marcus, and MacKuen (2013) show that people's feelings of anxiety, enthusiasm, and aversion are related to their attentiveness to negative political information in news stories. Finally, Molders, Van Quaquebeke, and Paladino (2015) demonstrate that citizens with a communion orientation (i.e., people who place a higher value on cooperation, relationships with others, sense of belonging)

---

4. The cross-sectional nature of their design makes it difficult to sort out whether tolerance was shaped by media consumption or variability in tolerance leads to different levels of media consumption.

view disrespectful political discussions more negatively than people with an agency orientation (i.e., people who place a higher value on striving for power, competence, and achievement). This collection of studies validates our contention that people differ in their receptivity to negative messages.

In our earlier work, we demonstrated that people's level of tolerance toward negative political messages varies in systematic ways. Democrats, women, and older Americans, for example, are less tolerant of negative campaign rhetoric than Republicans, men, and younger citizens (Fridkin and Kenney, 2011; Fridkin, Kenney, and Wintersieck, 2015; Fridkin et al., 2016). In addition, we have shown that citizens' tolerance toward negative campaign messages are orthogonal to partisanship and ideology (Fridkin and Kenney, 2011). In other words, people's tolerance of negativity is something more than partisan or ideological reactions to rival candidates and political parties.

A crucial tenet of the tolerance and tactics theory of negativity is that people's level of tolerance toward negativity influences how negative messages affect people's evaluations of political candidates as well as people's level of engagement in political campaigns. Most generally, we hypothesize that people with less tolerance toward negative campaigning (i.e., greater sensitivity to negative messages) will be more affected by negative advertising. We can also derive more specific expectations from the tolerance and tactics theory of negativity. For example, we expect that people who are least tolerant of uncivil and irrelevant negative appeals will be more susceptible to messages delivered in an overly strident fashion and focused on a topic of questionable relevance. Compared with people who are more tolerant of negativity, those with less tolerance are more likely to be demobilized when the political landscape features a great deal of uncivil and irrelevant negative advertisements.

Understanding the Importance of the Relevance and Civility of Negative Appeals

Over a half-century of research demonstrates that citizens worry about some political issues and topics far more than others. Issues related to peace and prosperity, for example, often top the public agenda regarding the most pressing national problems (e.g., Abramson et al., 2015). Also, models predicting vote choice show that certain issues are weighed more heavily by voters as they choose between candidates, and these topics often change with the "nature of the times" (e.g., Fiorina, 1981). With regard to the content of campaign messages, certain topics will be considered far more relevant to potential voters than other topics. For example, Freedman, Wood, and Lawton (1999) found that people believe it is fair for candidates to criticize their opponents for their roll call votes, their business practices, and for taking money from special interest groups, but people view attacks on the candidate's family or past extramarital affairs as out of bounds.

Consider the following advertisements aired in Iowa. An advertisement entitled "Obamacare Is Hurting Iowa Families" chastised Bruce Braley for voting for Obamacare as a member of the U.S. House of Representatives. The advertisement claimed Obamacare has limited the choice of insurance plans and doctors for Iowans and has produced skyrocketing premiums for Iowa families. The focus on Obamacare was likely to be viewed as relevant by many voters in Iowa, since affordable health care is often a salient issue for voters. In contrast, in another advertisement entitled "So Slick," the narrator ties Braley to Michael Bloomberg's agenda and explains that in Iowa, Braley tries to hide his connections to Bloomberg. The commercial continues with video of Braley saying that he has never met Bloomberg, but in the next clip, Braley and Bloomberg are shown attending the same event. We believe that this commercial focusing on Braley's connection to Bloomberg will be viewed as less relevant to Iowans than the advertisement highlighting Braley's position on Obamacare.

The relevance of the topic to the voters is only one component of negative messages. In addition, negative attacks are presented with a tone or spirit of civility ranging along a continuum from quite nasty and harsh to more moderate or tempered. The civility of negative messages has garnered a significant amount of scholarly attention.[5] Coe, Kenski, and Rains (2014: 358) define civil discourse as the "free and respectful exchange of different ideas," while Sapiro (1999) describes civility as constructive engagement with others through argument, deliberation, and discourse. Herbst (2010) adds to Sapiro's definition, arguing that reciprocity is an element of civility as well as emotional self-control and a sense of good feeling.[6]

Studies of the tone of negative advertisements note that uncivil attacks use terms such as "hypocrites," "reckless," liars," and "immoral," while messages with a more civil tone employ far more moderate descriptors, such as "career politicians," "Washington insiders," "inexperienced," and "ineffective." Researchers exploring civility do find a relationship between the

---

5. There is also a great deal of discussion by political journalists, pundits, and scholars regarding the health of America's democracy in the face of highly uncivil political dialogues (e.g., Nagourney, 2016; Mattes and Redlawsk, 2015).

6. See also Jamieson and Hardy (2013).

civility of the campaign messages and citizens' attitudes, but these findings vary by research methodologies (e.g., survey vs. experimental vs. content analyses), thereby making it difficult to identify a clear set of conclusions.[7] The general consensus emerging from these studies is that incivility in negative campaign messages is increasing with each campaign cycle; however, the nature, frequency, and influence of uncivil messages varies across campaigns, mediums, and topics (e.g., Anderson et al., 2013; Avery, 2009; Brooks and Geer, 2007; Haselmayer and Jenny, 2014; Hill, Capella, and Cho, 2015; Jamieson and Hardy, 2013; Mutz, 2007, 2015; Mutz and Reeves, 2005; Stevens et al., 2013).

In the race for Iowa's seat in the U.S. Senate in 2014, advertisements varied dramatically in terms of civility. A prime example of an uncivil advertisement was "The Gang of Five" spot sponsored by Conservative War Chest. The commercial portrays Bruce Braley as a "puppet" for the Gang of Five. The narrator explains:

> Just as the Obama administration uses federal agencies to suppress dissent and violate civil rights of their political opponents, these extremist liberals are smearing Republicans like Joni Ernst because they have a hidden hard left agenda. Braley is loyal not to his constituents but to Washington liberals. He gets a free ride from the elite media because he's being propped up by the Clintons, Obama, and the Gang of Five. The Gang of Five are smearing Republicans to protect their faithful allies like Bruce Braley. Tell the Gang of Five that you can't have a puppet senator. . . . Tell the Braley puppeteers that this is Iowa and we won't let you Detroit America with taxes and debt and no jobs.

The narrator's script is delivered in an ominous tone, with threatening music in the background and with unflattering and dark pictures of Braley along with President Obama, Nancy Pelosi, and other "extremist liberals" (e.g., Rachel Maddow, Michael Moore, Alec Baldwin, Chuck Shumer). In addition, phrases, like "health-care rationing," "assaults on religious freedom,"

---

7. In addition, there is an emerging literature placing contemporary uncivil political discussion in historical perspective (e.g., Geer, 2006, 2013; Jacobson, 2013; Shea and Sproveri, 2012; Shea and Fiorina, 2013; Sobieraj and Berry, 2011). Overall, the findings indicate incivility is not new; it tends to be episodic depending on the contentious nature of politics, issues, and ideology, but its reach in contemporary campaigns is broad, reflecting the cheap availability of information.

and "lawless federal judges" are flashed on the screen. This advertisement, with the over-the-top language (e.g., "smearing," "puppet," "suppress dissent"), the foreboding music, and the menacing tone of the narrator, embraces many of the features of uncivil negative messages.

In contrast, another negative advertisement in Iowa, "Iowa Values," sponsored by the Sierra Club and aimed at Joni Ernst, utilized a more civil tone. This advertisement begins with a video of Ernst saying "I have Iowa values" at a campaign event. Then the narrator asks, "What is really behind Joni Ernst's 'values'?" Cutting to a video of Ernst saying that she would close the doors to the Department of Education, the narrator says that Ernst's education plan would threaten Pell grants for 213,000 Iowa students. Then the advertisement shows a video of Ernst at a debate saying, "Let's shut down the federal EPA," and the narrator says that Ernst would cut clean air and water protections. The commercial concludes with the narrator saying, "Joni Ernst's values aren't for Iowa." While this is clearly an attack advertisement, it does not use unflattering pictures of Ernst, does not utilize dark images, and does not engage in ad hominem attacks. We expect that differences in the civility of negative messages, along with variation in the relevance of such messages, will alter their impact on voters.[8]

We believe that the tolerance and tactics theory of negativity will improve our understanding of the power and pitfalls of negative campaigning. In this chapter we have presented illustrative examples, along with theoretical reasoning and a review of existing empirical studies, demonstrating our theory's utility for understanding how negative advertising shapes people's actions and attitudes during political campaigns. We intend to test the veracity of our theory in the remaining chapters of this book. In the next few pages, we present the plan of our book.

---

8. During an ongoing campaign, voters' partisan proclivities, their policy views, and their feelings about competing candidates will influence their impressions of the civility and relevance of negative messages. For example, a strong Democrat viewing a negative commercial attacking a Democratic senator running for reelection is likely to view the commercial as less civil than a strong Republican viewing the exact same commercial (e.g., Gervais, 2014, 2015). In the language of motivated reasoning, Democrats will be more motivated to view such a commercial as uncivil, while Republicans are more likely to see the same advertisement as civil (e.g., Redlawsk, 2002; Redlawsk, Civettini, and Emmerson, 2010; Taber and Lodge, 2006). Similarly, people's political views will influence their evaluations of the relevance of negative messages. For instance, people with strongly negative views about Obama's signature health care law may view a negative advertisement attacking a Democratic candidate for supporting Obamacare as highly relevant. In comparison, people who care less about the issue of Obamacare or individuals who are favorable toward Obamacare are less likely to see the relevance of criticizing a candidate for voting for the health care reform package.

Chapter 2: Data, Measurements and Methodology

We compile divergent data sets collected in 2014, 2015, 2016, and 2017, focusing primarily on the 2014 U.S. Senate campaigns, to test the tolerance and tactics theory of negativity. We utilize different methods, including surveys, experiments, content analyses, and focus groups, to measure the key aspects of our theory: (1) people's tolerance for negativity; (2) the relevance and civility of negative advertisements; (3) people's reactions to negative commercials varying in civility and relevance; (4) the impact of negative advertisements on people's assessments of candidates and on their decision to participate in Senate elections.

We rely on four original datasets to examine voters' intolerance toward negativity. These include the 2014 Cooperative Congressional Election Survey (CCES), the 2016 CCES, as well as two surveys of Arizona State University students - an internet survey conducted in 2015 and an in-person survey conducted in 2016. Second, we utilize political advertising data collected by the Wesleyan Media Project (WMP) to examine the amount and content of negativity disseminated during the 2014 Senate elections. We also conduct an original content analysis of the relevance and civility of all the negative advertisements included in the WMP dataset. Third, we employ focus groups to examine people's reactions to negative commercials disseminated during the 2014 Senate elections. In one of the focus group studies, we ask respondents to rate the civility and relevance of several advertisements from 2014. In the second focus group study, we utilize state-of-the-art software (*Emotient*) to analyze people's emotional reactions to negative advertisements that vary in their civility and relevance (based on the original content analysis of the negative advertisements). Fourth, we rely on a survey experiment embedded in the 2014 CCES to examine how people's tolerance for negativity affects their response to negative campaigning during the course of an ongoing campaign. Finally, we combine the CCES 2014 survey data with the data from the WMP to connect people's attitudes toward candidates with the specific advertisements aired in their media markets during the campaign. With these two datasets, we examine how negative campaigning shapes citizens' assessments of competing candidates and their likelihood of going to the polls.

Chapter 3: Citizens' Tolerance of Negative Campaigning

We uncover systematic differences in people's tolerance toward negative messages. Women and older people are less likely to tolerate uncivil and irrelevant negative advertisements, while people who are more engaged in politics and who place themselves to the right on the ideological scale are more likely to tolerate these same messages. Furthermore, we find that people's tolerance of negative campaigning is dynamic and changes over the length of the campaign. We also show people's tolerance for negativity decreases when exposed to a greater dose of negative political advertisements during campaigns for the U.S. Senate.

Chapter 4: An Examination of the Amount, Substance, and Tone of Negative Commercials in Senate Elections

In the 2014 senatorial elections, negative advertisements were most pervasive in competitive races, during the last weeks of the campaign, on local news broadcasts, and during early morning and afternoon programming. The bulk of negative advertisements are sponsored by interest groups, while parties and candidates are much less likely to sponsor attack advertisements. We also examine the relevance and civility of the 2014 negative commercials and find that more than one-third of the advertisements were categorized as very uncivil, while only one in ten commercials was seen as focusing on an irrelevant topic.

Chapter 5: Reactions to the Civility and Relevance of Negative Advertisements

Relying on two different focus groups, we look at people's reactions to negative commercials aired during the 2014 Senate campaigns. In our first focus group, we find that people are able to distinguish between advertisements varying in their civility and relevance. In addition, when people are asked what they like and dislike about specific commercials, participants mention the relevance of the topic about 20 percent of time, while citing the civility of the advertisement 10 percent of the time. In the second focus group, we rely on emotion analysis software to gauge people's emotional reactions to negative advertisements aired during the 2014 Senate elections. With the aid of the *Emotient* software, we examine whether people with different levels of tolerance for negativity have different emotional reactions to messages that vary in civility and relevance.

Chapter 6: Examining Citizens' Impressions of Negativity during U.S. Senate Campaigns

Utilizing a survey experiment embedded in the 2014 CCES study, we find that people are sensitive to relatively modest changes in the tone of advertisements. In addition, people judge commercials differently depending on whether the advertisement is attacking candidates who share an individual's partisan pro-file. For instance, people view advertisements as harsher in tone and less rel-evant when aimed at their partisan favorites. Also, and consistent with our theory, tolerance for negativity consistently alters people's impressions of the relevance and civility of negative commercials.

Chapter 7: How Negative Campaigning Influences Citizens' Evaluations of Candidates and Likelihood of Voting

In this chapter we test the culmination of the tolerance and tactics theory of negativity. We demonstrate how the relevance and civility of negative messages disseminated during campaigns, along with people's tolerance for negativity, influence people's evaluations of the competing candidates as well as their eventual decision to vote in the election. Combining the 2014 CCES survey data with information about the airing and content of nega-tive advertisements disseminated during the Senate campaigns, we are able to connect people's attitudes and actions about their Senate contest with their campaign environment.

Chapter 8: The Consequences of Negative Campaigning

In this final chapter, we review our findings on the impact of negative campaigning in U.S. Senate races and we evaluate the evidence for the toler-ance and tactics theory of negativity. We also discuss how our theory helps clarify several debates in American politics (e.g., the effectiveness of nega-tive advertisements, the (de)mobilizing impact of negativity in campaigns). Furthermore, since the bulk of negative advertisements are sponsored by outside groups, we consider how the increased role of outside money, and dark money, in particular, shapes political campaigns. Finally, we conclude with some thoughts about the role of contemporary campaigns in America's democracy.

2

Data, Measurements, and Methodology

TESTING THE TOLERANCE and tactics theory of negativity requires extensive data on how people feel about negative campaigning, the tactics candidates deploy when criticizing opponents, and how the interplay between these two concepts shapes citizens' evaluations of candidates and their likelihood of engaging and voting in campaigns. We rely on four original data sets to examine the antecedents of citizens' tolerance of negativity. These include the 2014 Cooperative Congressional Election Survey (2014 CCES), the 2016 Cooperative Congressional Election Survey (2016 CCES), and two surveys of Arizona State University students (i.e., an internet survey conducted in 2015 and an in-person survey conducted in 2016). Political advertising data collected by the Wesleyan Media Project (WMP) enable us to examine the amount and type of negativity disseminated during the 2014 Senate election (Fowler, Franz, and Ridout, 2017). In addition, we conduct an original content analysis of the relevance and civility of all the negative commercials included in the WMP data set.

We then combine the 2014 CCES survey data with the WMP analyses to connect people's attitudes toward the Senate candidates with the specific advertisements aired during the campaigns. In summary, we utilize a pre-election survey experiment, content analyses, focus groups, a postelection survey, and new technology using facial recognition software to monitor people's emotional reactions to negative campaign advertisements. We move now to a detailed discussion of the data sets and describe how key concepts are measured.

Why U.S. Senate Campaigns?

Presidential campaigns receive the lion's share of attention by the national news media as well by political scientists (e.g., Clinton and Lapinski, 2004;

Geer, 2006 Goldstein and Freedman, 2002; Martin, 2004); however, examining negative campaigning at the presidential level is challenging. Each presidential general election typically features the two major party candidates facing off against each other. Therefore, it is difficult to untangle the impact of negative advertising from the idiosyncrasies of the candidates. U.S. House races are problematic for different reasons. While each race for the U.S. House of Representatives is contested every two years, the vast majority of these races are noncompetitive affairs where the incumbent cruises to victory and negative campaign messages are rare. For example, in 2016, fewer than 10% of all House races were competitive (Collins, 2016). Furthermore, even in these competitive districts, the impact of negative advertisements is likely to be limited given the poor fit between the congressional district and the media market (e.g., Prinz, 1995; Stewart and Reynolds, 1990). House races are often low-information campaigns where voters rely on such cues as incumbency and partisanship when casting their ballots, so campaign advertising is less influential (e.g., Ansolabehere and Snyder, 2002; Cox and Katz, 1996; Prior, 2006).

We argue that U.S. Senate elections are the ideal laboratory for exploring the impact of negative advertising for a number of reasons. First, U.S. Senate campaigns vary much more dramatically in their competitiveness, compared with U.S. House contests (Jacobson and Carson, 2015), and many senatorial contests feature a great deal of political advertising. For instance, a study published by the WMP in August 2016 reported that more than $247 million had been spent to air more than 280,000 advertisements in U.S. Senate races across the country (Wesleyan Media Project, 2016a). Second, every two years, one-third of the seats in the U.S. Senate are contested, thereby allowing us to examine about 33 contests between the two major party candidates. This provides a great deal of variation in the quality of candidates, the types of campaigns messages, the intensity of the campaigns, and the amount of negativity (e.g., Abramowitz and Segal, 1992; Kahn and Kenney, 1999b; Westlye, 1991). Third, by examining off-year elections for the U.S. Senate, we eliminate the confounding factor of the high-profile presidential contest. In senatorial races contested during presidential election years, it is often difficult to disentangle the effects of the presidential campaign (e.g., the themes of the presidential election, the political advertisements emanating from the presidential candidates, the negativity of the presidential campaign) from the impact of the U.S. Senate races. For these reasons, we believe that the 2014 U.S. Senate elections provide an ideal laboratory for exploring the role of negative campaigning. We turn now to an extensive discussion of the data sources developed and utilized to test the tolerance and tactics theory of negativity in the U.S. Senate.

2014 Cooperative Congressional Election Survey

The 2014 CCES, conducted by YouGov, is an internet-based survey using a matched random sample methodology to create a nationally representative sample. Specifically, YouGov identifies a target population using demographic information, develops a target sample through a random draw of respondents, and then matches the target sample to the target population using a matching algorithm (Ansolabehere and Schaffner, 2015).[1]

The 2014 CCES includes a "common core" section of survey questions along with individual modules administered to subsets of the full sample. We obtained a sample of 2,000 respondents for our individual module, with the pre-election wave conducted during October 2014 and the postelection wave conducted during the two weeks following Election Day. In our pre-election survey, we asked respondents to indicate their level of interest in politics and to rate the U.S. Senate candidates in their state on a standard feeling thermometer. We also asked respondents to assess the Senate candidates' competence and trustworthiness. In addition, we included a series of questions about negative campaigning. For instance, we asked respondents to assess the tone of the Senate campaign in their state, and we included an index assessing people's tolerance for negative campaigning.

In the postelection survey, we repeated many of the questions from the preselection survey, including the feeling thermometer and trait questions for the Senate candidates, the tone of the campaign question, and the index assessing tolerance toward negativity. In addition, we assessed respondents' level of civic duty as well as their external political efficacy. Finally, we asked respondents to evaluate the usefulness of various negative political messages disseminated during the 2014 U.S. Senate campaigns. For instance, we asked respondents, "During the 2014 election, Republicans ran negative ads criticizing Democratic incumbents for their support of Obamacare. How useful did you think it was to criticize Democratic incumbents for supporting Obamacare?" We include the pre-election and postelection survey in Appendix A.

---

1. Ansolabehere and Shaffner (2015) validate the sampling by comparing the state-level samples within the survey with the state-level election results. They find the partisan bias in the sample is less than one percentage point for both gubernatorial and senatorial vote estimates. In addition, Ansolabehere and Shafner report there is no evidence of systematic bias or of inflation of the precision of the estimates when they examine the relationship between the reported vote in the survey for governor and senator and the actual vote for these offices across the states.

We rely also on several questions included within the common core section of the study, including measures of the partisanship and ideology of the respondent, measures of media usage, and questions assessing the respondent's views on issues. We also utilize common core questions to develop a political knowledge index.[2] These questions were asked of the full sample of 56,200 adults in the pre-election survey and 48,853 in the postelection survey.[3]

Most important for our purposes, we conducted an original survey experiment as part of the 2014 CCES. In the survey experiment, we exposed respondents to the text of four actual negative advertisements aired during the 2014 senatorial campaign. The precise nature of the content of the advertisements varied depending on the Senate race. For example, respondents living in states where Republican incumbents were running against Democratic challengers were shown the text of four advertisements: two advertisements attacking the Republican incumbent and two attacking the Democratic challenger. Similarly, respondents living in states with Democratic incumbents for reelection were presented with the text from two advertisements attacking the Democratic incumbent and two advertisements criticizing the Republican challenger.

Respondents were randomly assigned to one of two versions of each advertisement: one advertisement relied on a civil tone, and the second version of same advertisement utilized an uncivil tone (see Appendix B for the text of the different advertisements). The differences in tone represented variability in the tenor of advertisements aired during the 2014 campaign.

We chose negative advertisements aired in multiple Senate races during the 2014 campaign in order to capture the common negative messages utilized during those campaigns. Negative advertisements attacking Democratic incumbents for their support of Obamacare were shown in more than 15 states during the election. These advertisements were created and aired by numerous outside groups, including Americans for Prosperity and Club for Growth. A second negative advertisement attacking Democratic incumbents focused on senators "going Washington." The National Republican Senatorial Committee and Crossroads GPS aired advertisements with this theme.

---

2. We utilize open-ended knowledge questions because Mondak and Anderson (2004) show that men's greater likelihood of guessing when responding to close-ended knowledge questions inflates the observed gender difference in political knowledge. Nevertheless, since we do not offer respondents an incentive for giving correct answers, we may underestimate people's overall level of political knowledge (Prior and Lupia, 2008).

3. The common-core content for the 2014 CCES study can be found at https://cces.gov.harvard.edu/pages/welcome-cooperative-congressional-election-study.

The negative advertisements attacking Republican incumbents focused on two topics: Republicans' ties to Wall Street and the shutdown of the federal government in 2013. Both of these themes were emphasized in advertisements developed and aired by the Senate Majority PAC and were shown in a number of states, including Arkansas, New Hampshire, Kentucky, and Louisiana.

Turning to challengers, Democrats running for the U.S. Senate were primarily criticized on two fronts: (1) the Democratic challenger would be a rubber stamp for Obama, and (2) the Democratic challenger was too liberal and out of step with the state. Advertisements focusing on the Democrat as a rubber stamp were created and run by disparate groups, including the National Republican Senatorial Committee, the Conservative Campaign Committee, and the Campaign for American Values PAC. Several groups, including Club for Growth and American Crossroads, aired the "too liberal" attack advertisement.

Finally, in several Senate races in 2014, Republican challengers were criticized for their extreme positions on abortion. The Senate Majority PAC, Planned Parenthood Action, and the Women Speak Out PAC criticized Republican challengers for their conservative positions on abortion in Colorado, Iowa, and New Mexico, among other states. In addition, Republican challengers in at least eight states (i.e., Colorado, Michigan, Iowa, New Hampshire, Kentucky, Oregon, Louisiana, North Carolina) were the subjects of attack advertisements highlighting the challengers' ties to the Koch brothers. Several groups, including the League of Conservation Voters, Moveon.org, Next Gen Climate Action, and the Senate Majority PAC, aired these negative commercials.

The 2014 CCES survey experiment allows us to see whether people respond differently to actual advertisements varying in civility during an ongoing election. These data provide the analytical leverage to determine how people respond to these types of advertisements and how such advertisements influence people's views of the candidates during the campaign.

2015 Arizona State University Online Survey

We conducted a supplemental survey experiment examining the impact of civil and uncivil negative advertisements. In the national survey experiment, respondents read the scripts of the negative advertisements. However, as we know, nearly all citizens watch political advertisements onscreen and do not read advertising scripts. To try to alleviate concerns that reading scripts instead of viewing advertisements may produce significantly different results, we conducted an online survey experiment with Arizona State University students. In this survey experiment, students were randomly exposed to civil or uncivil versions of the actual political advertisements aired during the 2014 campaign, not simply the scripts of these advertisements.

The ASU experiment was conducted in October 2015 with 530 respondents completing the survey. Respondents were asked the same battery of questions measuring intolerance toward negativity, as well as general political questions, such as party identification and ideology (see Appendix C for the questionnaire). Respondents were exposed to the following four commercials: (1) the Obamacare commercial, (2) the government-shutdown commercial, (3) the rubber-stamp advertisement, and (4) the advertisement tying the Republican candidate to the Koch brothers.[4]

The 2015 ASU online study enables us to see how people react to actual advertisements varying in civility. With the 2015 ASU survey, we also can assess the antecedents of people's intolerance toward negative campaigning. Finally, we understand that the ASU online study has limitations. First, participants were asked to respond to negative advertisements aired nearly a year after the election. Second, they were asked to rate advertisements about candidates running for Senate elections outside of their own states. Finally, the respondents in the ASU online study are students and are not representative of a nationwide sample.

2016 Arizona State University In-Person Survey

The experimental lab at ASU conducted a set of studies focused on the 2016 presidential campaign. In one of these studies, an in-person experiment with 320 subjects conducted on September 26, 2016, we inserted our standard measure of tolerance toward negative campaigning in the pretest questionnaire.[5] Given that tolerance toward negativity is central to our theory, we wanted to validate the determinants of people's intolerance toward negativity across different years and different campaigns.

---

4. Respondents were exposed to similar commercials for men and women candidates. We relied on advertisements that were aired against the following candidates: Mark Begich and Mary Landrieu (Obamacare: Civil and Uncivil), Corey Gardner and Terry Lynn Land (Abortion: Civil and Uncivil), Mark Pryor and Michelle Nunn (Rubber Stamp: Civil and Uncivil), Bill Cassidy and Joni Ernst (Koch Brothers: Civil and Uncivil). See Appendix D for the text of these advertisements, along with accompanying YouTube links.

5. These are the four questions assessing intolerance toward negativity: (1) Some negative advertisements are so nasty that I stop paying attention to what the candidates are saying.

2016 Cooperative Congressional Election Survey

The 2016 Cooperative Congressional Election Study (2016 CCES), similar to the 2014 CCES, is a nationally representative survey conducted by YouGov with common core questions asked of the entire sample, along with individual modules administered to subsets of the full sample. Our module included 1,000 respondents. This module was shared with several researchers at the School of Politics and Global Studies at ASU, with each researcher adding questions to the subsample of 1,000 respondents. We included our standard measures assessing people's tolerance of negativity. The common content included interviews with 117,316 respondents across all 50 states, and the survey was in the field from October 4 through November 6, 2016 (Ansolabehere and Schaffner, 2017).

We compare the demographic profile of respondents from each of the four survey samples in Table 2.1. The CCES samples are more diverse, with more strong Republicans and strong Democrats, compared to the student samples. In addition, the student's samples are somewhat more liberal than the more representative CCES samples. And, of course, the student samples are significantly younger and include more male respondents than the CCES samples. Nevertheless, including four different samples for four different years provides us with more confidence regarding the validity of our findings.

Content Analysis of 2014 Political Advertisements in U.S. Senate Races

In chapter 4 we examine the content and tone of negativity in the advertisements disseminated by the candidates during the 2014 campaigns for the U.S. Senate. We utilize data made available from the WMP. The WMP was established in 2010 to track advertising in federal elections, and it is a successor to the Wisconsin Advertising Project that tracked political advertising between 1998 and 2008. The source for the advertising data for the WMP comes from Kantar Media/CMAG, which provides detailed and real-time

---

(2) Hard-hitting commercials attacking the opponent are not helpful during election campaigns. (3) Negative advertisements discussing a candidate's personal misbehavior are fair game. (4) I find negative political commercials attacking a candidate for conduct occurring long before the candidate entered public life as uninformative.

Table 2.1 Comparison of CCES Samples and ASU Online Samples

	2014 CCES	2016 CCES	2015 ASU Online	2016 ASU On Campus
	(n=2,000)	(n=1,000)	(n=530)	(n=320)
Party Identification				
Strong Democrats	22%	25%	14%	19%
Democrats	12%	14%	9%	11%
Leaning Democrats	9%	7%	26%	26%
Independents	20%	17%	14%	10%
Leaning Republicans	10%	8%	16%	10%
Republicans	9%	14%	11%	11%
Strong Republicans	17%	13%	11%	13%
Ideology				
Extremely Liberal	8%	8%	7%	7%
Liberal	13%	12%	20%	21%
Somewhat Liberal	10%	12%	19%	16%
Moderate	27%	29%	24%	24%
Somewhat Conservative	13%	12%	17%	13%
Conservative	18%	18%	10%	17%
Very Conservative	12%	8%	3%	2%
Political Interest				
Not Very Interested	29%	17%	8%	
Somewhat Interested	38%	42%	36%	
Very Interested	33%	40%	55%	
Age[1]	47.1 (17.3)	46.7 (17.1)	24.3 (6.9)	20.7 (4.6)
Gender				
Men	48%	48%	56%	57%
Women	52%	52%	44%	43%

[1]We present the mean and standard deviation for the age of respondents.

tracking of advertisements, including when, where, and how often each advertisement aired. The data also include a video file for each unique advertisement. The WMP then processes and codes the advertisement tracking data from all 210 media markets in the United States.

Political advertisements were aired more than 1,025,000 times during campaigns for the U.S. Senate in 2014. Of these advertisements, WMP coded 46% as negative, 35% as positive, and 19% as "contrast" advertisements. Furthermore, the number of airings varied widely, with only 211 airings in the Idaho Senate race between Senator Jim Risch (R) and Nels Mitchell (D), compared with more than 110,000 airings in the North Carolina race between Senator Kay Hagan (D) and Thom Tillis (R).[6]

Negative advertisements were aired more than 400,000 times during the 2014 Senate elections. The vast majority of these airings (60%) were made by outside groups with names such as 60 Plus Association, Ending Spending Action Fund, and Freedom Partners Action Fund, representing the right side of the political spectrum, and NextGen Climate Action Committee, Senate Majority PAC, and Patriot Majority, representing the left.

Among the negative advertisements run by outside groups during the 2014 election was a spot sponsored by the Senate Majority PAC. It appeared nearly 2,000 times in the hard-fought North Carolina race between Kay Hagan and Thom Tillis. In the advertisement, a woman sitting in front of a television in her home says, "All these ads. It's hard to sort out this North Carolina Senate race. But what Thom Tillis did when running the state legislature makes it a little easier. He raised taxes on our retirement income, even when giving big tax breaks to corporations. Now he's got a plan to replace Medicare benefits we've been promised with a voucher. Premiums could go up as much as 50%. Tillis's record is crystal clear. Thom Tillis is not for us."

Also in North Carolina, Americans for Prosperity, an influential conservative issue-advocacy group founded by the libertarian activist David Koch, ran an advertisement attacking Kay Hagan. The advertisement, called "Exempt Me Too," ran on the airways in the Tar Heel State almost 1,700 times. The advertisement had an innocuous beginning: "Women are the driving force in the new economy. They balance the family checkbook. They start businesses, create jobs." Then the advertisement becomes more critical: "Kay Hagan just doesn't get it. Instead of listening to North Carolina, Hagan continues to push for Obamacare. Hagan supports waivers for friends of Obama and

---

6. Thom Tillis unseated incumbent Kay Hagan 49% to 47% in North Carolina. In Idaho, Jim Risch won reelection with 65% of the vote.

special treatment for Congress and their staff. And who gets stuck with the bill? Families and small businesses. Kay Hagan. Taking care of Washington insiders, not North Carolina families."

Beyond documenting when advertisements were aired, WMP conducted an impressive content analysis of each unique commercial. In 2014, 661 unique negative advertisements were aired during the general election cycle in contests for the U.S. Senate. The WMP codes the content of each advertisement using a web-based content analysis platform.[7] The coding categories include, among other things, the tone of the advertisement, what endorsements (if any) are mentioned, the sources cited, the type of music used, the mention of specific terms (e.g., "the middle class," "Wall Street," "special interests"), the narrator's gender, the specific issues discussed, and the major focus of the advertisement.

While we utilize a great deal of the information gathered by WMP, we conducted an original content analysis of all of the negative advertisements provided by WMP to code additional aspects of the tone and content of these messages. For example, we coded for the relevance and civility of each of the advertisements. Coders determined whether the advertisement was low, medium, or high in terms of the civility of the tone, as well as low, medium, or high regarding the relevance of the topic.[8] We provide detailed coding instructions in Appendix E. To demonstrate differences between advertisements rated low, medium, or high in relevance and civility, we present some examples in Table 2.2

In addition to coding the relevance and civility of each negative advertisement aired during the 2016 Senate campaigns, we also coded a wide variety of personal criticisms of candidates, such as the mention of the following terms: "inexperienced," "erratic," "not one of us," "not hardworking," "weak leader," "not smart," "dishonest," "lacks independence," "too liberal," "too conservative," "going Washington," "negative ties to Koch brothers," "rubber stamp on Obama." The original content analysis by WMP did not code for specific trait mentions. We added coding of negative traits in our

---

7. See Wesleyan Media Project (n.d.). For details of the coding of the advertisements, including assessments of reliability, see Wesleyan Media Project (2017).

8. We had five undergraduate students and one graduate student coding the advertisements. The coders were trained, reliability checks were conducted, and changes were made to the coding instrument (along with additional training) to ensure a high level of agreement among coders. Reliability checks were conducted between one of the authors and each of the research assistants several times during the coding process. Information on the training of the coders along with the presentation of reliability coefficients are detailed in Appendix E.

Table 2.2 Content Analysis Coding of Civility and Relevance of Negative Advertisements

Example of Advertisement Coded as Low in Civility. **Title**: "We Were There." **State**: Arkansas. **Candidate Attacked**: Democrat Mark Pryor. **Content of the Commercial:** The advertisement begins with an older male veteran saying, "When America needed us, we were there." A young woman veteran appears on the screen saying, "We proudly served." A series of veterans continue, "Our government promised veterans' health care; instead we got neglect, disrespect, and lies. It was Mark Pryor's job to protect us. Mark Pryor, you sat on the committee that oversaw the VA and let this scandal happen. His record clearly shows he votes with Barack Obama ninety percent of the time. Mark Pryor, you were supposed to have our backs and you failed us." The advertisement ends with these words in white against a black backdrop: "Mark Pryor: Failed Arkansas Veterans." (Note: the graveness of the veterans' narration along with terms like "neglect," "disrespect," and "lies" and "you failed us" contribute to the low civility rating.)

Example of Advertisement Coded as Medium in Civility. **Title**: "Good for the Goose." **State**: Arkansas. **Candidate Attacked:** Democrat Mark Pryor. **Content of the Commercial**: The advertisement begins with a video of a goose and a gander squawking, with silly music. The squawking and music continue throughout the commercial, with a narrator saying, "What's good for the goose ought to be good for the gander. Not in Washington. Mark Pryor cast the deciding vote to make you live under Obamacare. But Pryor votes himself and everyone in Congress special subsidies so they're protected from Obamacare. Exemptions and special subsidies for Mark Pryor; higher premiums for you. Mark Pryor: Voting with Obama. Voting against Arkansans like you." (Note: the upbeat music, the squawking of the geese, and the use of cartoonish graphics contribute to the medium civility rating.)

Example of Advertisement Coded as High in Civility. **Title**: "Leap of Faith." **State**: Arkansas. **Candidate Attacked:** Democrat Mark Pryor. **Content of the Commercial:** The commercial begins with a woman (co-owner of "Small Town Tours") explaining, "My husband and I started this business on a leap of faith. We have everything from the body shop guy to mechanics, to a cleaning crew, to the dispatch, to the drivers. Our dream now is survival. Obamacare has already raised the premiums. It's already costing us a fortune. It not only hurts our business, but it's hurting our employees. I wish Senator Pryor had listened to us when we told him how Obamacare would affect our business. And I wish he would have voted against it, but he didn't." (Note: the narrator—the small business owner—is discussing her struggles with Obamacare, but she doesn't use strong terms to criticize Senator Pryor.)

Table 2.2 Continued

Example of Advertisement Coded as Low in Relevance. **Title**: "Isn't One of Us." **State**: Kansas. **Candidate Attacked**: Democrat Greg Orman. **Content of the Commercial**: The advertisement begins with a picture of Greg Orman boarding a private plane and the narrator saying, "Greg Orman sure isn't one of us. Orman has a million-dollar mansion in Johnson County." (A chorus of people off-camera ask in unison "Johnson County?" and a picture of a mansion is shown with a picture of Orman superimposed on it.) "Another in Idaho." (A chorus of people ask "Idaho?" and a picture of the back of a man playing golf is shown.) "And he had another in Florida." (A chorus of people ask "Florida?" and a picture of a mansion on an island appears). "And Orman's firm got over a one hundred thousand dollars in tax breaks to do business near Las Vegas." (A chorus of people ask "Las Vegas?" and a picture of a Las Vegas casino is shown.) "Multimillionaire Greg Orman even invested in a partnership with the Chinese government." (A chorus of people ask "China?") "Greg Orman sure isn't one of us." (A picture of Orman is superimposed in front of a flying private jet.) (Note: most of the commercial suggests Orman is not a true Kansan because of his wealth, even though one of his houses is in Johnson County, Kansas. The advertisement also points out that Orman does business with Las Vegas and China, but it's not clear why business dealings with China and Las Vegas are problematic.)

Example of Advertisement Coded as Medium in Relevance. **Title**: "Mystery." **State**: Kansas. **Candidate Attacked**: Democrat Greg Orman. **Content of the Commercial**: The commercial begins with the camera panning a corn field at dusk with threatening clouds; the narrator says, "There's a mystery in Kansas and its Greg Orman. Orman sides with the liberal Democrats. But now he's hiding." (A picture of a red farm house on a prairie appears on the screen.) "The press says that Orman's game plan seems to be to run out the clock and avoid taking tough stands. Deceptive. But there's one place that Orman did take a stand: gun control." (A picture of Orman is superimposed on a field under a threatening sky.) "Orman supports the Obama-Bloomberg gun control agenda. You can't trust Greg Orman with your rights or your freedom." (Note: The first part of the advertisement discussing Orman "hiding" does not seem to be focusing on an important topic. However, the second part of the advertisement says that Orman supports gun control, although no evidence supporting the claim, such as citing a newspaper article or an Orman speech, is provided, and such a position is likely to be relevant to the average voter in Kansas.)

(continued)

Table 2.2 Continued

Example of Advertisement Coded as High in Relevance. **Title**: "Attendance." **State**: Kansas. **Candidate Attacked:** Republican Pat Roberts. **Content of the Commercial**: The commercial begins with a video of Senator Pat Roberts from 2004 saying, while pointing his finger, "It is very, very important. Attendance is where you gain the experience and expertise to do the job." A narrator says, "That was ten years ago. This year Roberts has missed seventy percent of his committee hearings and missed almost eighty percent of his agriculture committee hearings. But Roberts managed to find time to vote for a pay raise five times, while missing hearing after hearing. Pat Roberts: missed hearings, salary increases, not working for Kansas anymore." (Note: the juxtaposition of the video of Roberts saying that attendance is "very, very important" with evidence of his dismal attendance record at committee hearings makes the issue of his attendance relevant in his reelection campaign.)

supplemental content analysis because mentions of personal traits are often an important element of negative advertisements (e.g., Benoit, 2000; Johnston and Kaid, 2002), and information about the personal traits of candidates may influence people's impressions of the candidates as well as overall vote choice (e.g., Funk, 1999; Hayes, 2010; Markus, 1982).

Focus Group Assessing Variations in the Civility and Relevance of Negative Commercials

We conducted a focus group study relying on students at ASU to see whether people distinguished between negative messages that vary in terms of the relevance of the content and the civility of the tone. This focus group study allows us to validate the coding of relevance and civility in the supplemental content analysis. While the implementation of the focus group took place before the supplemental coding of the negative advertisements, we purposely chose advertisements for the focus group that varied in terms of the civility of the tone as well as the usefulness of the content.

For example, we chose an advertisement aired in the North Carolina Senate race aimed at Thom Tillis that appears to focus on an irrelevant topic. The advertisement, called "The Apartment," criticized Tillis, who was sharing a Washington, D.C., apartment with his chief of staff, because his chief of staff was caught having an affair with a lobbyist and was forced to resign. The narrator in the advertisement says, "Thom Tillis's reaction: he claims he was surprised by his roommate's affair." In contrast, we also include an advertisement emphasizing a more useful topic for voters: an advertisement detailing a candidate's extreme stand on abortion. This advertisement, titled "Backwards," discusses Republican Cory Gardner of Colorado's record on abortion, including "Gardner's support for harsh anti-abortion laws. Even sponsoring a bill to make abortion a felony, including cases of rape and incest," as well as "Gardner's eight-year crusade that would ban birth control."

We also included advertisements varying in their tone. For example, an uncivil advertisement attacking Republican Joni Ernst that aired in Iowa suggested that she received money from shady out-of-state interests in exchange for her pledge to support outsourcing of jobs to China and Mexico. This advertisement, titled "Dark Money," begins with two men in suits sitting in a smoke-filled room laughing at a picture of a U.S. senator on a screen in front of the room. One of the men asks, "Who's next?," and the other man changes the picture to Ernst and says, "Iowa. Joni Ernst." The first man asks, "We got her to pledge?," and the second man confirms, saying, "Joni signed on the line," and takes a piece of paper out of a manila folder and shows the paper to his colleague. The second man continues, "The tax breaks that pledge protects are gold. Green light. More outsourcing. China, Mexico, all the way." The first man asks, "She isn't worried about Iowa jobs?," and his colleague takes out a briefcase, puts it on the table, says, "Never mind that," opens up the briefcase, looks inside, and says, "Joni Ernst is with us."

While the "Dark Money" advertisement is strongly suggesting that Ernst sold her votes for cash, an uncivil claim, we also included advertisements employing a more courteous tone. For instance, an advertisement running in New Hampshire opens with a girl standing behind a microphone on a large stage at a spelling bee with a picture of Jeanne Shaheen behind her. One of the three teachers running the spelling bee from the front row of the auditorium says, "Your next word is Shaheen." The little girl asks, "May I have a definition please?" A second teacher answers, "Shaheen: a Washington liberal out of touch with New Hampshire, voted for the Obama agenda ninety-nine percent of the time." The little girl asks, "May I hear it in a sentence?" A third teacher responds, "Jeanne Shaheen was the deciding vote for Obamacare." The little girl gives her answer, "Shaheen: O-B-A-M-A." The three teachers look at each other and say in unison, "Close enough." The message of the advertisement was clearly that Shaheen supports Obama's agenda, but the humorous delivery increases the civility of the message.

In addition to choosing advertisements varying in their civility and relevance, we also chose advertisements attacking Democrats, Republicans, incumbents, nonincumbents, and women and men candidates. The texts of the advertisements used in the focus group are displayed in Appendix F, along with YouTube links to the actual advertisements. We recruited more than 300 students to participate in our online focus group. The students were randomly assigned to one of two groups. In each group, students watched seven advertisements and answered a series of questions about each. The advertisements examined by each group were different; therefore, we have assessments of 14 different negative advertisements disseminated during the 2014 campaign.

Students were asked to rate the civility and relevance of each advertisement on a scale ranging from 1 (not hostile at all; not useful at all) to 5 (very hostile; extremely useful). They were also asked to rate how much they liked each commercial on a scale ranging from 1 (dislike the advertisement a great deal) to 5 (like the advertisement a great deal). Finally, participants were asked, in an open-ended format, to name one thing they liked and one thing they disliked about each of the commercials.[9] In Table 2.3 we provide a demographic description of this focus group sample of ASU students.

Measuring People's Emotional Reaction to Negative Commercials

We utilized state-of-the-art software to analyze people's emotional reactions to negative campaign advertisements that aired during the 2014 senatorial elections. More specifically, we relied on an automated facial action coding system (FACS) that measures emotions displayed in facial expressions. FACS examines a set of facial muscle movements that corresponds to a displayed emotion. The system was developed by Ekman and Friesen (1976) and updated in 1997 (Ekman and Rosenberg, 1997). FACS identifies different action units corresponding to different emotions. For example, "disgust" is expressed by nose wrinkling and the raising of the upper lip. FACS enables the measurement and scoring of facial activity in an objective, reliable, and quantitative way. It is often used to measure the effectiveness of media content, especially product advertising (McDuff et al., 2013).

Several software packages have been developed to code facial expressions automatically, including Emotient FACET, Affectiva AFFDEX, and Noldus

9. See Appendix G for a copy of the questionnaire used in the focus group studying people's assessments of the relevance and civility of negative advertisements.

Table 2.3 Demographic Profile of the Focus Group Assessing Civility and Relevance of Negative Advertisements

Party Identification	
Strong Democrats	20%
Democrats	13%
Leaning Democrats	25%
Independents	10%
Leaning Republicans	11%
Republicans	12%
Strong Republicans	9%
Ideology	
Extremely Liberal	10%
Liberal	25%
Somewhat Liberal	15%
Moderate	18%
Somewhat Conservative	12%
Conservative	14%
Very Conservative	3%
Political Interest	
Not Very Interested	10%
Somewhat Interested	43%
Very Interested	47%
Age[1]	22.2 (3.92)
Gender	
Men	57%
Women	43%
N	332

[1] We present the mean and standard deviation for the age of respondents.

FaceReader. In the present study, we relied on Emotient FACET. This software tracks 20 action units (e.g., inner brow raiser, upper lid raiser, nose wrinkle), allowing the extraction of overall sentiment (i.e., positive, negative, or neutral streams) as well as seven basic emotions (joy, anger, surprise, fear, contempt, sadness, disgust) and two advanced emotions (frustration and confusion) (Teixeira, Wedel, and Pieters, 2012). In Figure 2.1 we show a

FIGURE 2.1 Emotient FACET display of a subject watching a negative political commercial.

screenshot of the Emotient FACET display of a subject watching a negative political commercial. (All figures were created by the authors.)

We chose to examine eight advertisements from the 2014 Senate elections based on the coders' assessments of the relevance and civility of the advertisements in the supplemental content analysis. In particular, we stratified the population of advertisements by the civility and relevance ratings and the gender of the candidate targeted in the advertisement. We chose two advertisements that received the lowest civility (i.e., a score of 1) and relevance ratings (based on the content analysis), two advertisements receiving a medium rating on both dimensions (i.e., a score of 2), and two advertisements receiving the highest civility and relevance ratings (i.e., a score of 3). In addition, we chose two advertisements that were rated as very uncivil (a score of 1) but highly relevant (a score of 3).[10] For each category of advertisements, we chose one advertisement attacking a woman candidate and one advertisement attacking a man candidate. We present the text of the eight advertisements, the civility and relevance ratings, and YouTube links to the advertisements in Appendix H.

The focus group measuring emotional reactions convened on the ASU campus in September 2017. Participants were recruited from a pool of students

---

10. We do not include any advertisements high in civility (i.e., a score of 3) and low in relevance (i.e. a score of 1) because these types of advertisements are quite rare, occurring only twice in the data set of 661 advertisements.

taking political science courses in the fall of 2017. Participants were assigned a day and time to come to the School of Politics and Global Studies laboratory to take part in the focus group. Once subjects arrived at the laboratory, they sat down at a laptop computer. When all (between 20 and 30 participants) were seated, the purpose of the study was explained, and they were instructed to put on the headphones provided to begin.

Table 2.4 Demographic Profile of the Focus Group Examining Emotional Reactions to Negative Advertisements

Party Identification

Strong Democrats	25%
Democrats	16%
Leaning Democrats	19%
Independents	9%
Leaning Republicans	11%
Republicans	13%
Strong Republicans	8%

Ideology

Extremely Liberal	9%
Liberal	26%
Somewhat Liberal	18%
Moderate	20%
Somewhat Conservative	13%
Conservative	10%
Very Conservative	4%

Political Interest

Not Very Interested	8%
Somewhat Interested	37%
Very Interested	55%

Age[1]   22.2 (3.41)

Gender

Men	53%
Women	47%
N	276

[1] We present the mean and standard deviation for the age of respondents.

The study was delivered via Qualtrics, and participants answered a series of general questions about politics. They then clicked on the link to each advertisement, answered a series of questions, and then proceeded to do the same for the next advertisement. The webcam on the laptop recorded each of the participant's facial expressions during the focus group session. After viewing all the commercials, the participants answered several more general questions about politics, as well as standard demographic questions. The full questionnaire utilized with this focus group is presented in Appendix I; we also present a demographic description of the focus group participants in Table 2.4.

Summary

We have presented a detailed discussion of the distinct and extensive data sets required to test the tolerance and tactics theory of negativity. Our data-gathering efforts cover more than one election year, employ multiple methods of inquiry, involve several thousand citizens spread across the 2014 U.S. Senate campaigns, and are singularly focused on providing several measures of the key concepts of our theory. It is now time to assess the data we gathered to determine whether the tolerance and tactics theory of negativity provides insight into how negative information affects the beliefs and behaviors of U.S. citizens during U.S. Senate elections.

As we discussed in chapter 1, understanding people's level of tolerance is the starting place for sorting out the impact of negative campaigning on citizens as they wind their way toward Election Day. Chapter 3 provides the first crucial test of our theory as we show that people vary systematically in their tolerance of negativity during campaigns and that we can predict and understand individual variation across citizens, across time, and across campaigns.

3

Citizens' Tolerance of Negative Campaign Messages

DURING THE 2014 Iowa Senate race, Mary and Rita reacted differently to the ubiquitous negativity of the campaign. They are a mother and daughter with the same political affiliation and background but with different opinions about the appropriateness of uncivil and irrelevant negative messages. When viewing attacks on Bruce Braley and Joni Ernst, Rita's attitude was "Bring it on," while Mary preferred the candidates to stay focused on the important issues of the day and to deliver their messages with a courteous and measured tone. We believe that Mary's and Rita's distinctive responses to negativity are not unique. Instead, the tolerance and tactics theory of negativity contends that people differ systematically in their tolerance of negativity. Some, like Rita, are tolerant of messages delivered in a strident fashion or focused on topics only tangentially related to governing. For others, like Mary, some negative messages "cross the line" and insult their sensibility regarding public decency and fairness.

In this chapter we will show that we can predict people's level of tolerance for uncivil and irrelevant negative messages. In addition, we will demonstrate that people's tolerance for negativity changes over the length of the campaign and in response to the tone of the campaign. In later chapters, we will validate the tolerance and tactics theory of negativity by illustrating that people's level of tolerance for negativity shapes their beliefs and behaviors toward candidates during campaigns. We turn now to a discussion of how we measure people's tolerance toward negative campaigning.

Measuring People's Tolerance
of Negative Information

To estimate people's underlying levels of tolerance for negativity, we create measures assessing people's tolerance for different types of negative messages presented during campaigns. As we argued in chapter 1, candidates' messages vary along two dimensions: content (the relevance of the message) and tone (the civility of the message). Relevant messages are likely to resonate with people's worries and concerns (Fridkin and Kenney, 2008), such as negative information about how an incumbent voted on matters of public policy, while messages focusing on a candidate's behavior in college may be viewed as less helpful. Messages vary in their civility as well as in their relevance. Some negative messages are delivered in an uncivil and strident manner, whereas other negative commercials embrace a more measured and courteous tone (e.g., Brooks and Geer, 2007; Geer, 2006; Hill, Capella, and Cho, 2015; Mutz and Reeves, 2005).

To measure people's tolerance for irrelevant and uncivil messages, we asked them to indicate their level of agreement with four statements. The first two questions assess people's intolerance to incivility, and the second two measure people's intolerance to irrelevant messages.[1]

1. Some negative advertisements are so nasty that I stop paying attention to what the candidates are saying.

---

1. We have used this battery of questions in previous work; see Fridkin and Kenney (2011) and Fridkin, Kenney, and Wintersieck (2015). To assess the reliability of the measure, we calculated the Cronbach's alpha across the four items composing the intolerance index: Cronbach's alpha is .67 for the 2014 CCES data, .72 for the 2016 CCES data, and .64 with the 2015 ASU data. In the ASU 2016 survey, we altered the wording of two of the four questions in the battery to eliminate the negative wording and to see if the reliability of the battery was enhanced. In particular, we changed "Hard-hitting commercials attacking the opponent are *not helpful* during election campaigns" to "Hard-hitting commercials attacking the opponent *are helpful* during election campaigns," and we changed "I find negative political commercials attacking a candidate for conduct occurring long before the candidate entered public life as *uninformative*" to "I find negative political commercials attacking a candidate for conduct occurring long before the candidate entered public life as *informative*." Making these changes to the wording of the items does not enhance the reliability of the four-item measure of tolerance for negativity. Finally, for the 2014 CCES data, we can assess the reliability of the intolerance index by examining the correlation between the preelection and postelection intolerance measures (i.e., the test/retest method of measuring reliability). While the ongoing campaign may alter people's tolerance for negativity (see our examination later in this chapter), we nevertheless find a strong correlation (.66, p<.01) between preelection and postelection measures of intolerance to negative information. Overall, the test/retest assessment of reliability as well Cronbach's alpha's measure of reliability gives us confidence in the reliability of the four-item index of intolerance to negativity.

2. Hard-hitting commercials attacking the opponent are not helpful during election campaigns.
3. Negative advertisements discussing a candidate's personal misbehavior are fair game.
4. I find negative political commercials attacking a candidate for conduct occurring long before the candidate entered public life as uninformative.

According to the 2014 CCES results, people do not like incivility in campaigns (see Figure 3.1). For example, half of the respondents "agree

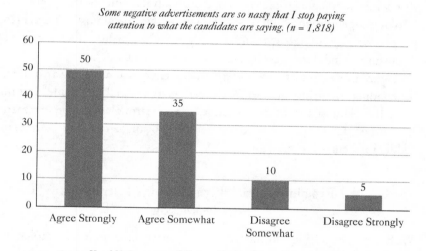

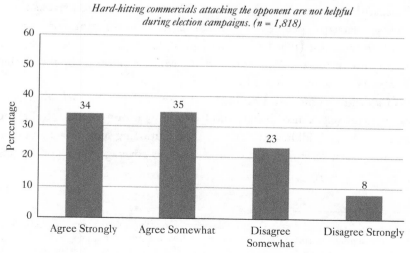

FIGURE 3.1 Measures of tolerance for incivility (2014 CCES).

strongly" and about one-third of the sample "agree somewhat" that campaign advertisements are "so nasty that I stop paying attention." Similarly, a little more than one-third of the respondents "agree strongly" and another one-third "agree somewhat" that "hard-hitting commercials attacking the opponent are not helpful during election campaigns." Overall, respondents overwhelmingly dislike harsh negative advertisements.[2]

Turning to the relevance of certain types of attacks, respondents are evenly split on whether negative commercials discussing "a candidate's personal misbehavior are fair game." Thirty percent of the sample "disagree somewhat" about the appropriateness of criticizing an opponent's personal behavior, while 36% "agree somewhat" that such advertisements are appropriate. Looking at people who hold stronger opinions, we find almost twice as many people "strongly disagree" than "strongly agree" regarding the relevance of discussing a candidate's personal misconduct (23% vs. 12%).

Figure 3.2 shows that 80% of respondents agree that "attacking a candidate for conduct occurring long before the candidate entered public life" is uninformative. Almost 50% of the respondents agree strongly with the statement. In contrast, fewer than 20% considered such prior behavior to be relevant fodder for a current campaign.

Explaining Variability in People's Tolerance of Negative Messages

We begin by exploring why men and women have different levels of tolerance for negative messaging during elections. Prior work has demonstrated a consistent gender gap in people's reactions to negative campaigning. For instance, both Kern and Just (1997) and King and McConnell (2003) find negative campaigning is more likely to produce unfavorable views of the sponsoring candidate for women, but not for men.

In addition, women are more likely to be demobilized by attack advertising than men are (e.g., Ansolabehere and Iyengar, 1996; Brooks, 2010; Kahn and Kenney, 1999a). Fridkin and Kenney (2004), utilizing survey data and content analysis of television advertising and news coverage, find mudslinging

---

2. To be sure, Mattes and Redlawsk (2015) demonstrated that the mere use of the phrase "negative campaigning" in survey questions yields negative responses from people. In a series of survey experiments, they demonstrated that the number of people reporting that they dislike negative campaigning varies predictably with the use of the phrase "negative" in the prompts.

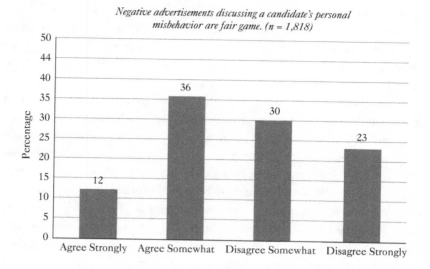

Negative advertisements discussing a candidate's personal misbehavior are fair game. (n = 1,818)

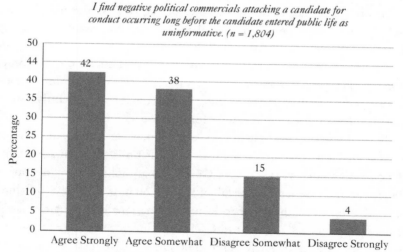

I find negative political commercials attacking a candidate for conduct occurring long before the candidate entered public life as uninformative. (n = 1,804)

FIGURE 3.2 Measures of tolerance for irrelevance (2014 CCES).

during Senate campaigns demobilizes women citizens but does not influence turnout levels among men. More recently, Brooks (2010), relying on an experimental design, demonstrates women are more likely than men to be demobilized by uncivil negative advertisements.

To explain why women are less receptive or less tolerant of negativity, we turn to the disparate fields of evolutionary psychology, communication, and political science. Numerous studies across these fields show women are more likely than men to dislike or avoid negative stimuli.[3] These differences in avoidance of negativity may be explained initially in evolutionary terms (Kamhawi and Grabe, 2008; Soroka et al., 2016) but are likely to be reinforced by gender differences in social learning and social roles (e.g., Bandura, 1977; Eagly, 2013; Wood and Eagly, 2002).

More closely related to negativity in politics, research examining gender differences in attention to negative news indicates women report greater anxiety than men in response to negative news. Women prefer positively framed news stories, while men prefer negatively framed stories (Galician, 1986; Kamhawi and Grabe, 2008; Pew Research Center for the People and the Press, 2004). For example, Kamhawi and Grabe (2008) exposed subjects to different combinations of positive and negative news stories and found male viewers report the highest arousal levels and better memory for negative stories. Women, in contrast, show signs of an avoidance response to negative news, rating positive stories as more arousing and demonstrating greater recall for positive stories.

Finally, our earlier work on tolerance of negative campaigning has consistently found that men are more tolerant of negative campaign messages compared to women (Fridkin and Kenney, 2011; Fridkin, Kenney, and Wintersieck, 2015; Fridkin et al., 2016). Stryker, Danielson, and Conway (2015), using an alternative measure of political tolerance for negative campaigning and surveying more than 20,000 students, also identify a significant gender gap in level of tolerance for negative messages.

To validate the gender gap in tolerance of uncivil and irrelevant messages, we examined four distinct data sources: (1) the national representative sample of 2,000 respondents via the 2014 CCES; (2) an online survey of approximately 500 ASU students in the fall of 2015; (3) an in-person survey of almost 250 ASU students in the fall of 2016; and (3) a national representative sample of 1,000 respondents via the 2016 CCES. We include the same measures of citizens' intolerance to uncivil and irrelevant negative messages in each of these surveys.

The data in Figure 3.3 illustrate a consistent gender gap in people's level of tolerance for negativity. Women are significantly less tolerant of incivility

---

3. The differences in preference for negative messages among men and women may be explained by sex differences in aggressiveness (for reviews, see Eagly and Steffen, 1986; Frodi, Macaulay, and Thome, 1977; Hyde, 1984). While scholars disagree about whether sex differences in aggression are explained by human evolutionary history (sometimes called sexual selection theory) or by gender differences in social roles, the evidence is clear that aggression is higher among men than women (e.g., Bettencourt and Miller 1996) and that aggression is more acceptable for men than women (Eagly 2013).

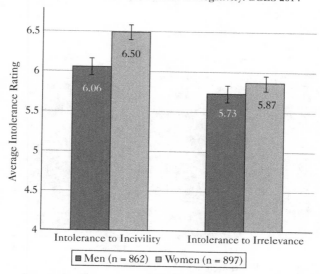

Gender Differences in Intolerance to Negativity: CCES 2014

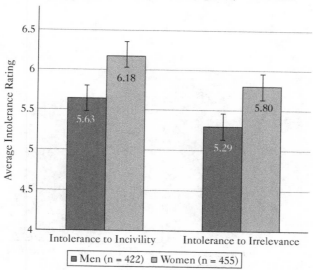

Gender Differences in Intolerance to Negativity: CCES 2016

Note: The means, with 95% confidence intervals, are displayed.

FIGURE 3.3A Gender gap in intolerance to negativity: CCES.

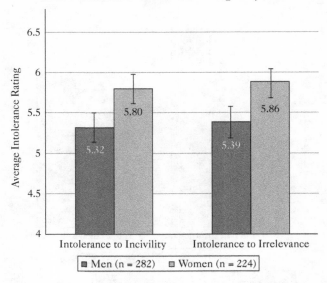

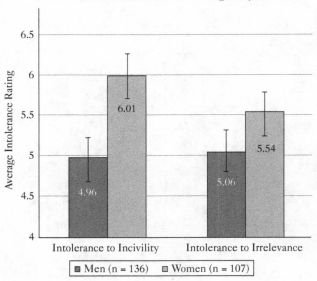

Note: The means, with 95% confidence intervals, are displayed.

FIGURE 3.3B Gender gap in intolerance to negativity: student samples.

than men. Regardless of whether we are looking at a large national sample of respondents or a smaller number of college students, women are consistently less likely to endorse uncivil negative messages compared to their male counterparts.

We see a similar pattern for tolerance of irrelevant messages in negative advertisements. Across the four distinct data sets over three different years, women are less tolerant than men of irrelevant messages. While the differences are less substantial for the relevance dimension of negativity, the gender gap does indeed reach statistical significance in two of the four comparisons (2016 CCES, 2015 ASU).

These data demonstrate that women across different election years (off-year elections, presidential elections, nonelection years) consistently score higher on levels of intolerance for both irrelevant and uncivil negative messages. Men, on the other hand, are bothered less by communications that cross the bounds of incivility and irrelevance.

Beyond gender differences, we found in our earlier work that older citizens are less tolerant of negativity compared to younger citizens (Fridkin and Kenney, 2011). To understand the reasoning underlying the empirical relationship between age and tolerance for negativity, we turn to the fields of psychology and gerontology. Psychologists and gerontologists have shown that older adults, compared to their younger counterparts, prefer to attend to positive information. This preference for positivity has been interpreted as reflecting older adults' motivation to optimize their current feelings about the stage of their lives. In particular, the socio-emotional selectivity theory explains that age-related shifts in goal priorities increase the salience of emotionally gratifying information for older people (e.g., Isaacowitz et al., 2009; Reed and Carstensen, 2012). In other words, as people age, they are more motivated to seek out positive stimuli because their time perspective and horizons are shorter.

We contend, echoing the predictions derived from the socio-emotional selectivity theory, that as people get older, they may be less tolerant of negative political information simply because they want to optimize positivity in their lives. We rely on the 2014 and the 2016 CCES data to examine the relationship between age and tolerance to negative campaigning.[4] In Figure 3.4, we look at

---

4. We do not utilize the ASU studies for this test since the variance in age in our student samples is understandably restricted. For instance, the 2015 ASU study has a mean age of 24 and a standard deviation of 7 years. The 2016 ASU study has a mean age of 21 and a standard deviation of 5 years.

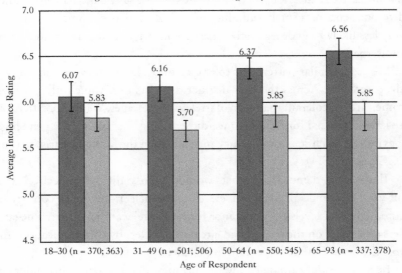

Age Differences in Intolerance to Negativity: CCES 2014

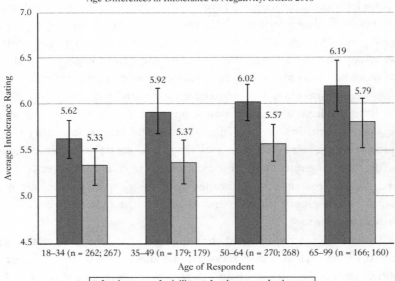

Age Differences in Intolerance to Negativity: CCES 2016

■ Intolerance to Incivility   □ Intolerance to Irrelevance

Note: The means, with 95% confidence intervals, are displayed.

FIGURE 3.4 Changes in intolerance to negativity over the life cycle.

the relationship between age and tolerance for irrelevant and uncivil messages. The data reveal a linear relationship between age and intolerance to incivility in both years. As people age, their tolerance for uncivil negative messages declines. We see, for instance, that the youngest people in both CCES samples (i.e., less than 35 years old) are significantly more tolerant of uncivil messages than the oldest people surveyed (i.e., 65 years old and older).

In contrast, the relationship between age and tolerance for irrelevant messages is less clear. In the 2014 CCES data set, people's level of tolerance for irrelevant negative campaigning is basically static across the different age groups. In the 2016 CCES data set, we see a slight increase in intolerance for irrelevant messages as people age. These results suggest that the relationship between age and tolerance for negative messages is stronger for uncivil compared to irrelevant messages.

In addition to age and gender affecting people's level of tolerance to negativity, political factors may also be consequential. We contend that people who are more engaged and interested in politics will be more tolerant of negative campaigning since negative messages are often a mainstay of intense electoral battles. Indeed, scholars have found strong partisans are less likely to be demobilized by negativity compared to weak partisans and independents (e.g., Lau and Redlawsk, 2015; Wolf, Strachan, and Shea, 2012). Similarly, people with more interest in politics and more attachment to a political party are often more receptive of uncivil and irrelevant negative messages (e.g., Fridkin and Kenney, 2011).

Some scholars have found Democrats and Republicans (and liberals and conservatives) react differently to negativity, with Republicans and conservatives more tolerant of negativity than Democrats and liberals (e.g., Ansolabehere and Iyengar, 1997; Lau and Redlawsk, 2015; Stryker, Danielson, Conway, 2015). For instance, Wolf, Strachan, and Shea (2012) found that Democrats were more likely than Republicans to say the 2010 campaign was the most negative campaign they had ever seen, and Democrats were also more likely to believe the tone of the campaign was bad for democracy.

We hypothesize that the connection between ideology and tolerance for negative campaigning may reflect differences in the type of media consumed on both ends of the ideological spectrum. For instance, Sobieraj and Berry (2011) found news content on the right contained more "outrage" speech than news on the left.[5] In a content analysis of talk radio, television news,

---

5. See Mutz (2015) and Herbst (2010) as well.

political blogs, and newspaper columns for a 10-week period in 2009, the authors examined the frequency of "outrage" speech, including insulting language, name-calling, verbal fighting and sparring, character assassination, misrepresentative exaggeration, mockery, belittling, and obscene language. They found that "outrage" speech was significantly more likely to occur from news sources on the ideological right, compared to the left. We hypothesize conservatives may be more tolerant of negative messages because they are more frequently exposed to uncivil speech via media outlets they pay attention to, like *Fox News* and the *Rush Limbaugh Show*.

To examine the impact of people's ideological views, interest in politics, and attachment to the political parties on people's level of tolerance for negative campaigning, we develop a series of multivariate models to predict tolerance for uncivil and irrelevant messages. We include people's gender and age in these models since we expect women and older people to be less tolerant of negative messages.[6]

Relying on data from the 2014 and 2016 CCES, we estimate OLS models predicting an individual's tolerance toward irrelevant messages and an individual's tolerance toward uncivil messages.[7] The results, presented in Table 3.1, show that certain people are significantly more tolerant of uncivil and irrelevant messages. We find people who are more interested in politics are more tolerant of uncivil and irrelevant messages. Regardless of whether we are looking at presidential or senatorial campaigns, we find that interest in politics is associated with greater tolerance of negative messages.

The results in Table 3.1 reinforce the bivariate relationships identified earlier. That is, men and women differ systematically in their tolerance of negative messages: women are significantly less likely than men to tolerate uncivil negative messages, even when controlling for people's engagement in politics

6. Strength of party affiliation is measured by recoding the 7-point party identification scale into 3 points (strong partisans = 3, weak partisans = 2, and Independents =1). Respondent's ideology is measured on a 7-point ideological scale (where 1 is extremely liberal and 7 is extremely conservative. Political interest is measured with a 3-point scale ranging from very interested (3), to somewhat interested (2), to not very interested (1). Gender is coded 1 = female, 0 = male; age is an interval measure.

7. We combine the two measures of tolerance toward irrelevant messages into a single relevance index, and we combine the two measures of tolerance toward uncivil messages into a single civility index. Both indices range from a low of 2 (very tolerant) to a high of 8 (very intolerant). The correlation between these two civility items is .44 (p<.01) in the 2014 CCES data set and .48 (p<.01) in the 2016 CCES data set, and the correlation between these two relevance items is .33 (p<.01) and .39 (p<.01) for the 2014 and 2016 CCES data sets, respectively. We rely on the Spearman's reliability rho to calculate the correlation between the measures because of the ordinal nature of the tolerance measures.

Table 3.1 OLS Regression Predicting CCES Respondents' Intolerance of Irrelevant and Uncivil Commercials

	Intolerance of Irrelevant Commercials		Intolerance of Uncivil Commercials	
	2014	2016	2014	2016
Political Characteristics				
Strength of Party	−.07 (.03)**	.03 (.05)	−.04 (.07)	−.08 (.05)
Ideology	−.10 (.02)***	.18 (.03)***	−.05 (.02)***	−.001 (.03)
Political Interest	−.19 (.05)***	−.48 (.07)***	−.26 (.05)***	−.32 (.06)***
Demographics				
Age	.006 (.002)***	.009 (.003)***	.02 (.002)***	.02 (.003)***
Gender	.08 (.07)	.26 (.11)**	.36 (.07)***	.42 (.11)***
Constant	6.51 (.16)***	5.70 (.31)***	6.22 (.16)***	6.27 (.30)***
R^2	.03	.11	.06	.07
N	1741	867	1746	870

Note: Unstandardized regression coefficients are followed by standard errors in parentheses. The dependent variables measuring intolerance of irrelevant messages and intolerance of uncivil messages range from 2 (very tolerant) to a high of 8 (very intolerant). Strength of party ranges from 3 (strong) to 1 (independent). Ideology ranges from 1 (extremely liberal) to 7 (extremely conservative). Political interest ranges from 1 (not very interested) to 3 (very interested). Age is an interval measure. Gender is coded 1 = female, 0 = male.

***p < .01.

**p < .05.

*p < .10.

(i.e., interest, strength of partisanship) and their ideological proclivities. Across two election years, we find that women are less tolerant of uncivil negative messages compared to their male counterparts. With regard to the irrelevance of negative messages, we see a less consistent pattern. While women were less tolerant of irrelevant messages in 2016, we fail to find a significant relationship between gender and tolerance of irrelevant messages during the 2014 Senate elections.

Turning to the age of citizens, we find a consistent and strong relationship between people's age and their level of tolerance for negative campaigning. For presidential elections and Senate elections, we find older people are significantly less tolerant of negativity, compared with younger respondents. Furthermore, age is related to intolerance of negativity for both irrelevant negative messages and uncivil negative messages. The impact of age on intolerance for negativity is one of the most powerful findings displayed in Table 3.1.[8]

We find that ideology and strength of partisanship are not consistently related to tolerance for negativity in the CCES data sets. Across the four models, people's attachment to a political party influences their tolerance of negativity in only one instance. We find that strong partisans were more tolerant of irrelevant negative messages during the 2014 campaigns.

The impact of ideology on tolerance of negativity changes between 2014 and 2016. In 2014, we find support for our expectation that conservatives are more tolerant of negativity than are liberals. During the 2014 Senate elections, as people move from left to right on the ideological scale, they were significantly more likely to be tolerant of uncivil and irrelevant negative messages. However, in 2016, the findings in Table 3.1 indicate there is no relationship between ideology and tolerance of uncivil messages. Furthermore, when we look at people's tolerance of irrelevant negative messages in 2016, we find that liberals are more tolerant of irrelevant negative messages than are conservatives. We can speculate that the unconventional presidential campaign between Donald Trump and Hillary Clinton may be responsible for this unexpected relationship. Perhaps messages disseminated during the campaign, including the release of the *Access Hollywood* tape as well as the Clinton campaign's decision to air advertisements focusing almost exclusively on Trump's personal foibles (Fowler, Ridout, and Franz, 2016), may have been interpreted by conservatives as irrelevant, possibly producing lower levels of tolerance for irrelevant negative messages among these voters.[9]

We can also examine the relationship between political and demographic factors on people's tolerance for negativity with our two student samples: the

---

8. We predicted that age and gender would be related to intolerance of irrelevant and uncivil messages, and we find strong support for our expectations. These findings help support the construct validity of our measure of intolerance of irrelevant and uncivil messages. In chapter 5 we will test and find support for the predictive validity of our measures of intolerance to negativity.

9. We replicated the analysis predicting tolerance for irrelevant messages for the 2016 CCES data set, looking only at respondents who completed the preelection survey before the release of the *Access Hollywood* tape on October 7, 2016. In the replication of the OLS regression equation, ideology is not significantly related to tolerance for irrelevant messages, suggesting that the release of the tape may have altered conservative and liberal views of what are relevant and irrelevant messages. We continue to find that people with more interest in politics, men, and younger people are significantly more tolerant of irrelevant messages, when compared to people with less interest in politics, women, and older people.

Table 3.2 OLS Regression Predicting Arizona State University Respondents' Intolerance of Irrelevant and Uncivil Commercials

	Intolerance of Irrelevant Commercials		Intolerance of Uncivil Commercials	
	2015	2016	2015	2016
Political Characteristics				
Strength of Party	−.13 (.06)**	−.20 (.16)	−.04 (.07)	−.21 (.15)
Ideology	−.30 (.04)***	−.20 (.06)***	−.22 (.04)***	.002 (.06)
Political Interest	−.05 (.09)	−.38 (.16)**	−.16 (.10)	−.15 (.15)
Demographics				
Gender	.35 (.13)***	.34 (.20)*	.36 (.24)**	1.04 (.19)***
Constant	6.64 (.30)***	7.28 (.56)***	6.65 (.33)***	5.80 (.53)***
R^2	.08	.10	.07	.13
N	477	241	471	241

Note: Unstandardized regression coefficients are followed by standard errors in parentheses.

The dependent variables measuring intolerance of irrelevant messages and intolerance of uncivil messages range from 2 (very tolerant) to a high of 8 (very intolerant). Strength of party ranges from 3 (strong) to 1 independent). Ideology ranges from 1 (extremely liberal) to 7 (extremely conservative). Political interest ranges from 1 (not very interested) to 3 (very interested). Gender is coded 1 = female, 0 = male.

***$p < .01$.

** $p < .05$.

* $p < .10$.

2015 and 2016 ASU samples.[10] In these models, we do not include the age of the respondent since we have little variation in age. Still, the findings in Table 3.2 indicate the gender of the respondents strongly predicts their level of tolerance for incivility and tolerance for irrelevance. Women are significantly and consistently less tolerant of negative campaign messages than their male counterparts. The most dramatic difference is seen among the 2016

---

10. We looked at the relationship between intolerance for incivility and conflict orientation for a sample of 255 ASU students in 2017. Mutz and Reeves (2005) and Sydnor (2015) have shown that people who are conflict "approachers" find political incivility entertaining, while people who like to avoid conflict dislike incivility in politics. We employ Sydnor's five-item measure of conflict avoidance, drawn from a larger battery developed by Goldstein (1999), and find a strong positive correlation between conflict avoidance and intolerance for incivility (correlation = .23, p<.001). Conflict orientation is not significantly correlated with intolerance for irrelevant messages (correlation = .007).

ASU sample, where women score more than one point lower on the six-point measure of tolerance for incivility compared to men, holding the remaining variables constant.

We also find ideology influences people's tolerance for negative messages. In three of the four models, as people become more conservative, they become more tolerant of uncivil and irrelevant messages.[11] We find evidence for a modest relationship between people's strength of partisanship and political interest and their levels of tolerance for negativity. However, these two factors are not consistently related to tolerance for negativity across the two student samples.

Changes in Tolerance of Negative Campaigning during an Election

We have shown that certain people are more tolerant of irrelevant and uncivil messages. Are people's levels of intolerance to negativity affected by an ongoing campaign? In other words, as the weeks and months of an electoral season unwind, do people become less tolerant of negative campaigning as they are bombarded with negative political commercials on television, more critical commentary in the news, and heated exchanges during debates?

To examine this question, we rely on the 2014 CCES data, where we interviewed the same respondents before and after the election.[12] We expect that people who report witnessing a negative campaign will report lower levels of tolerance during the postelection survey than people who report that the Senate election in their state was more positive.[13] The findings presented in Table 3.3 support our expectations. Looking first at tolerance for incivility, we see that people are more tolerant of incivility when they have just experienced a very positive campaign (i.e., an average of 5.51 on the tolerance to incivility scale), compared to their counterparts who report watching a very negative

---

11. The 2016 ASU student survey was conducted on September 26, 2016, before the release of the *Access Hollywood* tape, and we see our standard pattern that conservatives are more tolerant of irrelevant messages, compared to liberals.

12. The 2014 CCES data set is the only data set where we have preelection and postelection measures of tolerance of negative campaigning.

13. We measure the tone of the campaign during the preelection survey with the following question: "How would you describe the tone of the U.S. Senate campaign between [insert names of Democratic Senate Candidate and Republican Senate Candidate]? Would you characterize the campaign as very positive (4), somewhat positive (3), somewhat negative (2), or very negative (1)?"

Table 3.3 The Relationship between Assessments of the Tone of the Campaign and Postelection Intolerance to Negativity (2014 CCES)

	Intolerance of Irrelevant Commercials (T2)	Intolerance of Uncivil Commercials (T2)
Tone of Campaigns		
Very Positive	4.91 (.29)	5.51 (.31)
Somewhat Positive	5.83 (.13)	6.16 (.13)
Somewhat Negative	5.86 (.09)	6.31 (.09)
Very Negative	6.04 (.13)	6.63 (.11)
F-Statistic	4.37***	5.90***
N	587	599

Note: The tone of the campaign is measured during the preelection survey with the following question: "How would you describe the tone of the U.S. Senate campaign between [insert names of Democratic Senate Candidate and Republican Senate Candidate]? Would you characterize the campaign as very positive, somewhat positive, somewhat negative, or very negative?" The postelection measures of intolerance of irrelevant messages and intolerance of uncivil messages range from 2 (very tolerant) to a high of 8 (very intolerant).

*** $p < .01$.

** $p < .05$.

* $p < .10$.

campaign (i.e., an average of 6.63 on the intolerance to incivility scale). In general, we see a highly significant relationship between people's tolerance for incivility as measured in the postelection survey and respondents' assessment of the negativity of the campaign as reported in the preelection survey.

People's tolerance of irrelevance in negative messages also decreases with the tenor of the campaign. Citizens who rate their Senate campaign as very negative in October are less tolerant of irrelevant negative messages after the election compared to people who rate their campaign as very positive (an average of 6.04 vs. an average of 4.91 on the intolerance to irrelevance scale). As the data in Table 3.3 demonstrate, observing an election where the messages emanating from the rival campaigns are positive leads people to report significantly more tolerance for irrelevant negative messages. These results indicate that negative campaigning depresses people's tolerance for negative messages.

To examine the dynamic nature of people's tolerance for negativity more explicitly, we develop two OLS regressions where we examine how people's assessment of the tone of the campaign in October produces changes in their

Table 3.4 OLS Regression Predicting Changes in CCES Respondents' Intolerance of Irrelevant and Uncivil Commercials

	Intolerance of Irrelevant Commercials (T2)		Intolerance of Uncivil Commercials (T2)	
Intolerance to Commercials (T1)	.59 (.03)***	.57	.57 (.03)***	.57
Tone of Campaign (T1)	−.09 (.06)*	−.05	−.15 (.06)**	−.09
Constant	2.65 (.25)***		3.12 (.26)***	
R^2	.34		.35	
N	587		600	

Note: Unstandardized regression coefficients are followed by standard errors in parentheses; standardized coefficients are reported after levels of statistical significance. Given our directional hypothesis, we utilize one-tailed statistical tests.

The dependent variables measuring intolerance of irrelevant messages and intolerance of uncivil messages range from 2 (very tolerant) to a high of 8 (very intolerant). Intolerance to commercials (T1) is intolerance of irrelevant commercials (T1) in the first model, and intolerance of uncivil commercials (T1) in the second model. T1 measures are assessed during the preelection wave of the survey, while T2 measures are assessed during the postelection wave. Tone of campaign is measured during the preelection wave with the following question: How would you describe the tone of the U.S. Senate campaign between [insert names of Democratic Senate Candidate and Republican Senate Candidate]? Would you characterize the campaign as very positive (4), somewhat positive (3), somewhat negative (2), or very negative (1)?"

***p < .01.

** p < .05.

* p < .10.

tolerance for negative messages, as measured in the postelection survey (see Table 3.4). To render our models dynamic, we include preelection measures of intolerance for negativity as independent variables. In addition, we include the preelection assessment of campaign tone as an independent variable. Therefore, we can explore whether people's views of the tone of the campaign during the election produce *changes* in people's tolerance of negativity. We expect that people who report viewing more negative campaigns will become less tolerant of negativity.[14]

The data in Table 3.4 show preelection measures of intolerance to negative messages strongly predict postelection levels of intolerance to negativity.

14. Given that our hypothesis is directional, we report one-tailed tests of statistical significance.

However, people's views of the tone of their Senate contest, measured during the ongoing electoral campaign, affect changes in intolerance for negativity. In particular, as citizens see their Senate campaign as more negative, they become significantly more intolerant of uncivil negative messages and somewhat more intolerant of irrelevant negative messages. These results show that people's intolerance of negativity is not static but responds to the tenor of the election.

Conclusion

We began this chapter contrasting Mary's and Rita's tolerance for negative campaigning. We presented a series of analyses demonstrating that their divergent attitudes toward attack advertising are more typical than unusual. In fact, we showed that people differ systematically in their attitudes toward negative message. We find women and older people are less likely to tolerate uncivil and irrelevant negative advertisements, while people who are more engaged in politics and people who land on the right side of the ideological scale are more likely to tolerate these same messages. Furthermore, analysis indicates that people's attitudes toward negative campaigning are not static, but rather they change over the length of the campaign. In particular, we show that people's tolerance for negativity decreases when they view their senatorial contest as more negative in tone.

Understanding how people differ in their tolerance of negative messages is the first step in testing the tolerance and tactics theory of negativity. We now know that people's receptiveness to irrelevant and uncivil messages is predictable and varies with stable political and demographic characteristics as well as being responsive to the political environment. According to our theory, these systematic differences in tolerance of negativity should lead to important differences in people's impressions of negative messages as well as their susceptibility to attack advertising. In particular, we expect that the people who are the least tolerant of negativity will be more likely to view negative advertisements as utilizing an uncivil tone and focusing on irrelevant topics. Furthermore, we contend that people who are less tolerant of negativity will be most sensitive to negative messages. That is, negative advertisements are more likely to influence their evaluations of candidates as well as their likelihood of voting on Election Day. We will empirically test these expectations in chapters 6 and 7.

However, before turning to these detailed tests of the tolerance and tactics theory of negativity, we need to explore the actual content and tone of negative advertisements disseminated during campaigns. In chapter 4, we rely on an extensive content analysis of all of the negative advertisements disseminated during the 2014 Senate elections. We examine the topics discussed in negative messages, who sponsors these messages, as well as when these messages are aired during the weeks and months approaching Election Day. Finally, we look at the civility and relevance of the negative messages aimed at the Senate contestants during the 2014 campaigns.

An Examination of the Amount, Substance, and Tone of Negative Commercials in Senate Elections

SENATOR MITCH MCCONNELL, the minority leader in the U.S. Senate, was running for reelection to his sixth term as senator of Kentucky in 2014. The senior senator from Kentucky was viewed as vulnerable. According to a *Herald-Leader*/WKYT Bluegrass poll published in February 2014, only 32% of Kentuckians approved of Senator McConnell's job performance, and he was trailing his likely Democratic rival, Secretary of State Alison Lundergan Grimes, 42% versus 46% in the same poll (Youngman, 2014). Grimes, a lawyer and the youngest female secretary of state in the nation, campaigned on protecting women's rights, veterans' rights, workers' rights, and human rights in her quest to unseat McConnell.[1]

The contest between McConnell and Grimes for Kentucky's Senate seat was one of the most expensive in the nation, with McConnell spending more than $30 million and Grimes spending almost $19 million.[2] Outside groups spent millions more: conservative groups spent more than $16 million running advertisements critical of Grimes, and liberal groups (including over $5 million from the Senate Majority PAC) spent more than $9 million attacking McConnell. Two conservative groups made the largest expenditures by outside groups: The Kentucky Opportunity Coalition and Kentuckians

_____

1. Grimes website, http://alisonforkentucky.com/meet-alison/.

2. Open Secrets, Kentucky Senate Race, 2014, https://www.opensecrets.org/races/indexp.php?cycle=2014&id=KYS1&spec=N.

for Strong Leadership. These two groups spent more than $13 million on advertisements aimed at defeating Grimes.

Negative advertisements were aired more than 40,000 times during the run-up to Election Day. The most frequently aired advertisement was a negative message sponsored by the Grimes campaign called "30 Years Is Long Enough." The negative advertisement features Wayne Chambers, who states that he worked at the Continental Tire Plant for 38 years until the factory closed down and moved all the jobs to Mexico and Brazil. Chambers says more than 1,000 jobs were lost and a lot of families were hurt. The advertisement continues, "We got no help at all from Mitch McConnell. He just sent us a form letter. Mitch voted three times for tax loopholes that made it easy to ship jobs overseas. Why should we lose our jobs and Mitch McConnell keeps his?" This negative commercial aired more than 2,000 times in Kentucky during the campaign.

McConnell aired a number of negative advertisements attacking his challenger, including an advertisement titled "After All That." In the advertisement, Grimes is being tied to President Obama's record. The advertisement begins, "In 2008, Alison Grimes supported Barack Obama and his liberal platform." Then, white words appear on a black background: "Obama's War on Coal," with President Obama saying "If somebody wants to build a coal-powered plant, they can; it's just it will bankrupt them." A sequence of additional phrases is displayed with white words on a black screen, including "2000 Kentucky Coal Miners Lose Jobs in Past Year—Associated Press, 11/12/12"; "Exploding Debt"; "Jobs Report is More Bad News for Obama—Washington Post 9/7/12"; "Vladimir Putin"; "Benghazi"; "Chaos in the Middle East"; "The IRS Scandal"; "The VA Scandal." President Obama is then heard saying "If you like your health care plan, you can keep your health care plan," and the following phrase is displayed with white letters on a black background: "Obama's 'Lie of the Year' on Obamacare—PolitiFact 12/12/13." Then a female narrator says, "And after all this, Alison Grimes still supports Obama. Is there any doubt how she would vote in Washington?" This advertisement linking Democrat Grimes with President Obama in conservative Kentucky was aired more than 1,000 times during the campaign.

The Kentucky campaign illustrates the amount and tone of negativity possible in highly competitive contemporary senatorial campaigns. Approximately 40% of U.S. Senate races reach this level of intensity every two years, about 10 to 14 races per election cycle. The goal of this chapter is to examine and characterize the prevalence, tone, amount, and timing of negative advertisements during campaigns. Ultimately we need to know the

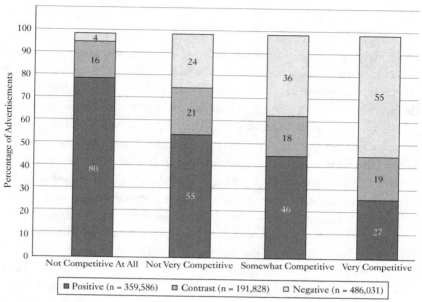

Note: The data were made available from the Wesleyan Media Project.
We rely on the WMP's coding of the tone of the advertisements.

FIGURE 4.1 Airing of ads by competition.

exact nature of the campaign messages potential voters experience before we can understand how negative and critical information interacts with citizens' levels of tolerance for negative campaigning. We begin by examining when negative advertisements are aired, during what times, on what television programs, and who is sponsoring the advertisements. Most important, we document how the 2014 negative advertisements vary in terms of their relevance and civility.

The Timing of Negative Advertising

Negative advertisements are pervasive during modern senatorial campaigns. The data from the Wesleyan Media Project indicate 46% of all the advertisements aired during the 2014 Senate races were negative, 19% were contrast advertisements, and 35% were positive.[3] The data in Figure 4.1

---

3. For more details about the content analysis conducted by the WMP, see chapter 2. By relying on the data available via the WMP, we are examining only political advertisements that were aired on television and are not examining other sorts of advertisements, such as online or radio advertisements.

show that the proportion of negative advertisements aired increases with the competitiveness of the race.[4] In the least competitive races, eight out of 10 advertisements aired on television were positive, and only a handful of advertisements (fewer than 5%) were negative. As the competitiveness of the race increases, so does the proportion of negative advertisements.[5] For example, the proportion of negative advertisements airing on television increased six-fold as we move from the least competitive races to campaigns that were a bit more competitive (i.e., "not very competitive"). In contests classified as somewhat competitive, the proportion of negative advertisements accounts for more than one-third of all airing advertisements. In the most competitive races, negative advertisements are the most common advertisement airing on television, making up 55% of all the advertisements. These results indicate people's exposure to negative commercials is related powerfully to the competitive nature of the Senate race being contested in their state.

We turn now to examining the amount, sequencing, and content of negative advertisements. While people living in states with hotly contested races are more likely to be exposed to negative commercials, we also see negative advertisements accelerate as Election Day nears. As Figure 4.2 illustrates, negative advertisements appear on television almost a full year before the November election. However, the airing of these attack advertisements does not surpass 10,000 per week until three months before Election Day; as Election Day nears, the number of commercials with negative messages begins to increase dramatically. Within the last two weeks of the campaign, the number of negative advertisements increases to more than 50,000 airings per week. These results indicate that people living in states with competitive races in late October are likely to be saturated with negative messages about the candidates competing for their state's seat in the U.S. Senate.

The placement of negative televised advertisements is not a random decision. The data in Figure 4.3 demonstrate that campaigns are much more likely to air negative political commercials during news programming. Local news, in particular, is a favored location for the dissemination of negative advertisements during Senate contests. Negative advertisements are much less

---

4. Positive advertisements focus exclusively on highlighting the strengths of one candidate, while negative advertisements emphasize negative qualities of the targeted candidate. In comparison, contrast advertisements compare positive aspects of one candidate with negative characteristics of the opponent.

5. We relied on four-point ratings provided by the Cook Political Report, http://cookpolitical.com/, to categorize the competiveness of campaigns.

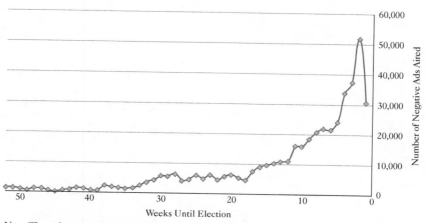

Note: These data were made available from the Wesleyan Media Project. Negative ads were aired 486,031 times in the year leading up to Election Day.

FIGURE 4.2 Number of negative ads aired weekly.

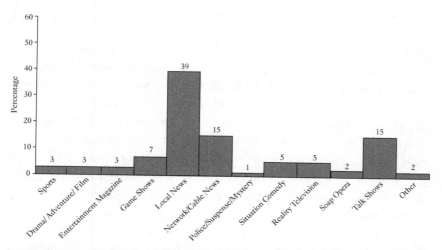

Note: The data were made available from the Wesleyan Media Project Negative ads were aired 486,031 times the campaign.

FIGURE 4.3 Percentage of negative ads aired by type of television program.

likely to appear during entertainment programming. For instance, only 5% of all negative commercials are aired during situation comedies like *Modern Family* or *Big Bang Theory*. Similarly, advertisements attacking the Senate candidates are not likely to appear during a college football game or during an NBA game. The preference for local news and news programs in general reflects the assumption that viewers who are watching news programs are more interested in politics and will be more likely to vote on Election Day.

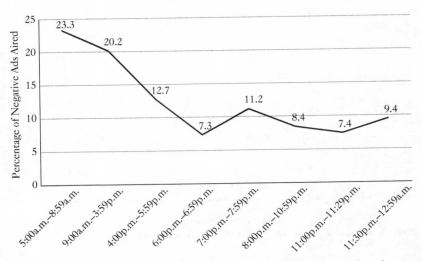

Note: The data were made available from the Wesleyan Media Project. Negative ads were aired 486,031 during the campaign.

FIGURE 4.4 Time of day when negative ads were aired.

Furthermore, the airing of negative commercials is focused on certain times of day. People watching television are likely to encounter commercials offering pointed criticisms of the Senate candidates early in the viewing day. As people are getting up, having their breakfast, and preparing for their day, negative advertisements are being aired at a high rate on the morning television news programs. The data in Figure 4.4 illustrate that almost one-quarter of all negative advertisements air before 9:00 a.m. in the morning. Given the preference for local news programming, it is not surprising that most negative commercials are aired during the morning hours, when news programming dominates the airwaves.

The majority of negative commercials are disseminated before dusk. Evening television programming is relatively free of attack advertisements. In general, people are left alone to enjoy watching their favorite reality television program or their preferred dramatic series without the intrusion of negative campaigning. Fewer than 20% of all negative advertisements are aired between the evening hours of 7:00 and 11:00. Similarly, late night programming is not a favorite choice for negative political commercials.[6]

---

6. When we look at the number of airings, instead of the percentage of advertisements aired, we see the same pattern. For instance, the most negative advertisements (111,602) were aired during the early morning, while the second most negative advertisements (96,869) were aired during the day, 9:00 a.m. to 3:59 p.m. We find the fewest airings of negative advertisements (35,006) during the early evening time slot, 6:00 p.m. to 6:59 p.m.

The data from WMP demonstrate that negative advertisements are most pervasive in competitive races, during the last weeks of the campaign, on local news broadcasts, and during the early morning and afternoon. We turn next to examining the relevance and civility of the negative advertisements.

Civility and Relevance of Negative Advertisements

As we discussed in chapter 1, negative political advertisements vary in their civility (i.e., the harshness of the tone of the commercial) as well as the relevance of the content of the message. We supplemented the content analysis conducted by the WMP by coding the civility and relevance of each advertisement aired during the 2014 U.S. Senate elections. Our coders rated each advertisement on a three-point scale, ranging from low civility to high civility as well as from low relevance to high relevance.[7] The findings, illustrated in Figure 4.5, reveal that most of the negative advertisements aired during the 2014 Senate election were classified as somewhat civil (68%); 23% were rated low in civility, and fewer than 10% were considered highly civil.[8]

An example of a negative advertisement coded as low in civility is one titled "Defer," funded by the End Spending Action Fund and aired during the Georgia open-seat contest between Republican David Perdue and Democrat Michelle Nunn. The advertisement begins with threatening music and an image of dark clouds covering the sky above the White House. A narrator says, "Because of Barack Obama's mismanagement, Georgia veterans died waiting for the care our country promised them," and the visuals change to a photo of graves at Arlington Cemetery. The visuals then change to an image of Michelle Nunn, and the narrator says, "But Michelle Nunn says [a video recording of Nunn appears on the screen] 'I defer to the president's judgment.'" The narrator continues, "Georgia families are losing their coverage, yet Nunn would keep Obamacare. And Nunn even initially refused a travel ban to help stop Ebola. Michelle Nunn's would be Obama's senator, not Georgia's."

This commercial has several elements that we associate with uncivil advertisements. First, the imagery is negative: recall the dark clouds over the White House and the picture of graves at Arlington. Second, the advertisement uses hyperbolic language, such as blaming Obama for the deaths of

---

7. See Appendix E and Table 2.2 for more details about the content analysis coding of the relevance and civility of the negative advertisements.

8. In this analysis, as well as the remaining analysis in this chapter, the political advertisement, rather than the airing of the political advertisement, is the unit of analysis.

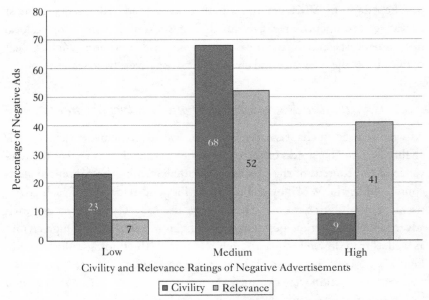

Civility and Relevance Ratings of Negative Advertisements

■ Civility   ■ Relevance

Note: The advertisements were made available from the Wesleyan Media Project. The number of advertisements examined was 656. Civility was scored on a scale from 1 (not very civil) to 3 (very civil). Relevance was scored on a scale from 1 (not very relevant) to 3 (very relevant).

FIGURE 4.5 Civility and relevance ratings of negative advertisements.

Georgia veterans. Third, the advertisement plays to people's fears by saying that Nunn refused a travel ban to help stop the spread of Ebola. Fourth, the advertisement begins with menacing music that becomes louder and more threatening as the advertisement continues. These different characteristics produce a negative advertisement that we consider uncivil in tone.

In contrast, another negative advertisement in the Georgia Senate race, disseminated by Nunn's campaign, was coded as high in civility. The advertisement begins with Roy Richards saying, "My dad founded Southwire in Carrollton more than sixty years ago, and today it is the leading manufacturer of power cable in North America. When I hear David Perdue say that he is proud to have outsourced jobs to other parts of the world, I have to wonder. Every time we invest in Georgia workers, they can compete with anyone in the world. So, I don't know how you can be proud of having sent American jobs overseas."

This advertisement, featuring a Georgian business owner, simply recalls Perdue's statement about being proud of outsourcing jobs overseas. There is no hyperbole, no menacing music, no unflattering pictures of Perdue.

Instead Roy Richards merely expresses disappointment and surprise at Perdue's pride at outsourcing jobs and not keeping those jobs in Georgia, as his company has done.

Just as commercials differ in the civility of their tone, commercials also vary in the relevance of their subject matter. In our content analysis of the 2014 political advertisements, we found that only 7% were rated as low in relevance, 52% as somewhat relevant, and 41% high in relevance.

An example of an advertisement rated low in relevance is an attack advertisement targeting Senator Mary Landrieu of Louisiana. This advertisement, titled "Actress Mary," begins by showing a scene from a recent advertisement created by Landrieu's campaign. The narrator says, "Have you seen this ad? Mary Landrieu created a fake newscast for her TV commercial and got caught." An arrow appears on the screen, pointing to a picture of Landrieu from the advertisement being condemned. The narrator continues, "This is not a U.S. Senate hearing room. This is not Mary talking at a Senate hearing." Then two arrows appear, pointing to two people sitting behind Landrieu, and the narrator says, "And these are actors. Mary's an actress too. On TV, actress Mary pretends to be Louisiana's voice. But real-life Mary supported Obama 97% of the time. Tell Mary Landrieu to stop acting and stand up for Louisiana." This advertisement focuses on the fact that Landrieu's campaign may have staged a commercial to look like she was speaking during a congressional hearing. We believe Louisiana voters are unlikely to think the topic of this advertisement is important.

Many of the advertisements aired during the 2014 senatorial elections emphasized more substantive issues, like the passage and implementation of Obamacare or the qualifications, experience, and record of the candidates. An advertisement rated high in relevance was sponsored by Republican Shelley Moore Capito, criticizing her Democratic opponent, Natalie Tennant, in West Virginia. The advertisement attacks Tennant on personal and policy grounds. The narrator asks, "Does Natalie Tennant ever tell the truth? Tennant says she supports our coal jobs, and then Tennant stood with Obama and defended his war on our coal jobs. Tennant says she supports our Second Amendment rights, and then Tennant joined with Obama to try to kill our rights. Now Tennant is running a TV ad so blatantly false that one newspaper called Tennant downright desperate. The Martinsburg paper said it best: 'Tennant makes it easy to vote for Capito.'" Capito's attack on Tennant likely resonated with many West Virginia voters given the emphasis on the salient issues of coal jobs and gun rights as well as questioning Tennant's integrity.

Given the centrality of relevance and civility for the tolerance and tactics theory of negativity, we investigate how different types of negative advertisements vary in these areas. We begin with an investigation into who is sponsoring the negative advertisements.

Who Sponsors Negative Advertising?

At the start of this chapter, we discussed the two most frequently aired advertisements in the Kentucky Senate race. Both of these advertisements were sponsored by the candidates' campaigns. However, candidates are not the only sponsors of negative advertisements. In fact, in the Kentucky Senate race, 58 distinct negative advertisements were aired and the candidates sponsored fewer than 30% of them. Interest groups sponsored the vast majority (65%) of the negative advertisements in Kentucky. These interest groups included state-level groups like the Kentucky Opportunity Coalition, a 501c organization that spent more than $7.5 million running negative advertisements against Grimes. Kentuckians for Strong Leadership, a Super PAC, spent over $6 million attacking her. These two groups produced and delivered 18 of the 28 negative advertisements (64%) attacking Grimes.[9]

In support of Grimes, two national political action committees affiliated with Senate Democrats, the Democratic Senate Campaign Committee and the Senate Majority PAC, created and aired 11 of the 24 (46%) advertisements attacking McConnell. The Senate Majority PAC alone spent more than $5 million trying to unseat the sitting minority leader.

The Kentucky race is illustrative when we examine who is sponsoring the negative advertisements airing in the 2014 Senate races. The data compiled in Figure 4.6 demonstrate that interest groups sponsor almost 33% of all negative advertisements aired in contests for the U.S. Senate. In contrast, the candidates' campaigns produce and air fewer than 20% of advertisements in a typical Senate race, and the political parties rarely sponsor negative advertisements, instead relying on their affiliated PACS, like the Senate Majority PAC, to deliver critical messages about the opposing candidate. The reliance on interest groups as sponsors of negative

---

9. Super PACs, also known as 527 Independent Expenditure PACs, spend money independently of the candidates. These groups are not subject to contribution limits. However, Super PACS must report their contributors and contributions. The 501(c)(4) groups, in contrast, are classified as social welfare organizations, and they can fund political advertising as long as political campaigning is not their primary purpose. Furthermore, these organizations have no spending limits and do not have to disclose their contributions or contributors.

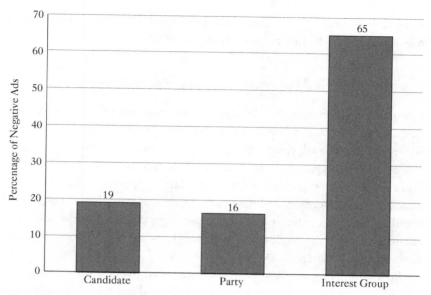

Note: The data were made available from the Wesleyan Media Project. The number of negative advertisements examined was 661.

FIGURE 4.6 The sponsors of negative advertisements.

advertisements makes sense. The candidates and the political parties prefer to steer clear of airing attack advertisements whenever possible since negative advertisements may boomerang on the sponsoring candidate, creating negative impressions of the candidate airing the negative commercial (e.g., Dowling and Wichowsky, 2015; Jasperson and Fan, 2002; Krupnikov and Bauer, 2014).[10]

While interest groups are much more likely than candidates and political parties to sponsor negative advertisements, we do not find that interest groups are more likely to air advertisements that are harsher in tone (i.e., low in civility) or less relevant to potential voters. In fact, the civility ratings and relevance ratings for advertisements sponsored by interest groups (mean civility rating = 1.9; mean relevance rating = 2.3), parties (mean civility rating = 1.9;

---

10. We conducted two-way analyses of variance to see if the sponsor of negative advertisements varies with the status of the candidate (i.e., incumbent, challenger, candidates in open races) or party of the candidate. When looking at the proportion of candidate-sponsored advertisement, we see that Republican candidates are more likely to face candidate-sponsored attack advertisements, compared to Democratic candidates (22% vs. 15%, $p<.10$). For interest group–sponsored advertisements and party-sponsored advertisements, we see no significant differences by party or status.

mean relevance rating = 2.4), and candidates (mean civility rating = 1.8; mean relevance rating = 2.3) are remarkably consistent.[11]

Who Is Narrating Negative Advertisements?

Campaign architects, in developing their political advertisements, can utilize the candidates to deliver the negative messages. However, this is a risky strategy. Voters may develop critical impressions of candidates who air negative commercials against their opponent. This backlash or boomerang effect is likely to be more pronounced if the candidate is appearing in his or her own attack advertisements. Candidates and campaign consultants understand the risk; only 5% of the negative advertisements delivered during the 2014 campaign feature the candidate as narrator (Dowling and Wichowsky, 2015; Krupnikov and Bauer, 2014).

Instead of using the candidates, political operatives need to decide who should narrate the attack advertisements. In making these decisions, the gender of the narrator is likely to be an important strategic consideration. In product advertising, marketers often employ a matching strategy, coordinating the gender of the narrator with the gender of the product (Peirce, 2001). For instance, male announcers dominate in advertisements aimed at a primarily male audience (e.g., shaving products targeting men), while woman narrators are more common in product advertisements directed at a female audience (e.g., hair coloring products aimed at women). The product matching strategy is based on the premise that matching the gender of the target audience with the gender of the spokesperson will produce a more persuasive advertisement.

Given the pervasiveness of the matching strategy in product commercials, we expect political consultants are likely to consider a similar matching strategy in the political realm. In particular, advertisements attacking a male candidate may be considered to be more credible (i.e., more persuasive) when these advertisements feature a male narrator rather than a woman narrator. By the same logic, we expect female announcers to be used more frequently in advertisements attacking female candidates. In addition, male announcers may be less likely to narrate a negative advertisement attacking women candidates because this approach violates gender norms about proper behavior, leading to a backlash against the candidate

---

11. These differences are far from statistically significant, based on the difference in means test.

sponsoring the negative advertisement (Garramone, 1985; Dowling and Wichowsky, 2015).

When we look at the gender of announcers in attack advertisements, we see that men announcers are utilized somewhat more often than women announcers, 46% to 43%.[12] However, we also find support for our "matching" expectation. In particular, women narrators are utilized much more frequently than men narrators for advertisements attacking women candidates (52% vs. 37%), and men are the preferred narrator for advertisements attacking male candidates (50% vs. 39%).[13] These stark differences suggest political consultants developing negative commercials believe attacks on candidates are likely to resonate with voters if the gender of the narrator matches the gender of the targeted candidate.

We also look at whether the presence of male versus female narrators varies with the civility and relevance of the negative advertisements. Given common gender stereotypes about appropriate behavior for women, we expect nastier commercials will be less likely to utilize women as narrators. In particular, since women are supposed to embrace communal traits like being thoughtful, kind, and sensitive to people's feelings (Rudman and Glick, 2001), political consultants may be cautious about featuring women narrators in commercials that are particularly uncivil and irrelevant. Relying on women narrators in the most negative political commercials may be a riskier and less effective strategy since such an approach conflicts with common gender stereotypes.

The data in Table 4.1 show that advertisements employing women narrators are significantly more civil and relevant than advertisements utilizing male narrators. The relationship between the gender of the narrator and the negativity of the advertisement is consistent, even when we control for the gender of the targeted candidate and the party of the candidate. Women narrators are consistently and significantly less likely than male narrators to be featured in negative advertisements rated as low in civility and low in relevance. These findings suggest that campaign architects are likely to be cognizant of pervasive gender stereotypes; therefore, they are less likely to utilize women narrators in their most uncivil and irrelevant negative advertisements.

---

12. Negative advertisements contain voice-overs by the candidates 5% of the time, and 4% of negative advertisements feature a voice-over by both a female and a male narrator.

13. Both of these differences are statistically significant at $p<.01$, according to the difference in proportions test.

Table 4.1 Civility and Relevance of Negative Advertisements by
the Gender of the Narrator

Gender of the Narrator	Female	Male	F-Statistic
All Advertisements (282; 305)[1]			
Civility of Advertisement	1.93 (.03)	1.80 (.03)	8.63***
Relevance of Advertisement	2.44 (.03)	2.22 (.62)	19.40***
Ads Targeting Women Candidates (94; 66)			
Civility of Advertisement	1.87 (.05)	1.68 (.50)	6.05**
Relevance of Advertisement	2.42 (.06)	2.18 (.08)	5.99**
Ads Targeting Men Candidates (188; 239)			
Civility of Advertisement	1.96 (.04)	1.83 (.04)	5.49**
Relevance of Advertisement	2.45 (.04)	2.23 (.04)	13.83***
Ads Targeting Democratic Candidates (166; 105)			
Civility of Advertisement	1.92 (.04)	1.68 (.05)	12.75***
Relevance of Advertisement	2.49 (.05)	2.31 (.07)	5.17**
Ads Targeting Republican Candidates (110; 187)			
Civility of Advertisement	1.95 (.05)	1.86 (.04)	1.73
Relevance of Advertisement	2.35 (.05)	2.17 (.56)	7.50***

Note: In the parentheses we present the number of advertisements coded with female narrators, followed by male narrators for each subset of advertisements examined.

In each cell, means are presented, followed by standard errors. Civility and Relevance ratings range from 1 (low in civility or relevance) to 3 (high in civility or relevance).

*** $p < .01$.

** $p < .05$.

* $p < .10$.

The Substance of Negative Ads

The common characteristic of negative advertisements is the focus on the rival candidate, irrespective of whether the message is coming from the opposing candidate, a political party, or an interest group sponsoring the advertisement. However, in attack advertisements, the sponsor can focus on policy matters, like the candidate's stand on an issue, or criticize the candidate's personal weaknesses, such as the candidate's lack of experience or questionable character. Some advertisements offer a blended critique of the candidate, combining both policy and personal criticisms in the same advertisement.

In the 2014 U.S. Senate campaigns, the most frequently aired negative advertisement was sponsored by the sitting North Carolina senator Kay Hagan attacking Republican Thom Tillis for his stand on women's issues. This advertisement primarily criticizes Tillis's voting record and his policy preferences if elected to the U.S. Senate. The following is the text of the advertisement: "For women and families, Speaker Thom Tillis has a record you should check. In July 2012, Thom Tillis led the fight to defund Planned Parenthood, cutting funding for cancer screenings and birth control. Last April, Thom Tillis killed equal pay for women legislation in North Carolina. And said he would vote against the 'Paycheck Fairness Act' in Congress. It's true. Thom Tillis opposes equal pay for equal work and defunded Planned Parenthood. Not someone our women and families can trust."

Another negative advertisement aired during the North Carolina Senate race was one sponsored by the National Republican Senate Committee. This advertisement focused the brunt of the attack on personal grounds, criticizing Hagan's attendance record as a U.S. senator. The advertisement begins with a narrator saying, "Kay Hagan serves on a committee overseeing terrorist threats but skipped half of public meetings last year. Hagan even missed a classified hearing on ISIS to fundraise in New York City." The advertisement ends with a picture of an empty chair with Hagan's name plate with the following words superimposed on the picture: "KAY HAGAN: Doesn't Deserve Re-Election."

Some negative advertisements combine a critique on policy with a character attack. An advertisement sponsored by Crossroads GPS attacked Hagan's vote on Obamacare as well as her character. The advertisement begins by quoting both Obama and Hagan saying, "If you want to keep your health care plan, you can keep your health care plan." Then the announcer says, "This is not true," and the graphics display the phrase "Washington's Obamacare Deception." The advertisement continues, "When Kay Hagan had the chance to keep her word and protect our health insurance plans, she voted no. Thousands of North Carolinians were told their policies were canceled. Hagan's promise on keeping our doctors was not true. Typical Washington. Deceiving us, pushing their agenda."

These three advertisements represent the three main foci of negative advertisements: (1) policy, (2) personal traits, and (3) a mixture of policy and traits. Figure 4.7 illustrates that the vast majority of negative commercials focus on policy matters, with 74% of all attack advertisements criticizing the candidate's policy stands or legislative votes. Advertisements focusing on personal matters, like the advertisement complaining about Senator Hagan's

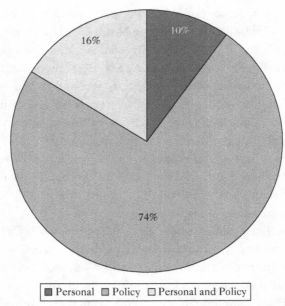

Note: The data were made available from the Wesleyan Media Project.
The number of negative advertisements examined was 661.

FIGURE 4.7 The primary focus of negative ads.

absenteeism, are far less common, making up only 10% of advertisements. The rest of the negative advertisements, like the advertisement on Obamacare questioning Hagan's trustworthiness, emphasize both personal and policy matters.[14]

We find that the major focus of negative advertisements are related to assessments of the advertisement's relevance and civility. Beginning with the civility of the advertisement, the data in Table 4.2 show that advertisements focusing mostly on personality matters are rated, on average, about one-half

14. We conducted two-way analyses of variance to see if the emphasis on policy or personal traits varied with the status of the candidate (i.e., incumbent, challenger, candidates in open races) or party of the candidate. We failed to find a significant additive effect of party or status on emphasis on policy or personal matters in negative commercials. However, we do find a significant interaction effect ($p < .05$) between status and party on emphasis on policy matters. In particular, Republican incumbents are *less* likely to be attacked on policy grounds, compared to Republicans challengers and open-race Republican candidates (59% for Republican incumbents vs. 76% for Republican challengers and 72% for Republicans in open races). We do not see the same pattern for Democrats, where 78% of the advertisements attacking Democratic incumbents emphasize issues, compared to 72% for Democratic challengers and 67% for Democrats in open races.

Table 4.2 Civility and Relevance of Negative Advertisements
by Primary Focus

	Civility Rating	Relevance Rating
Primary Focus		
Mostly about Traits (n=65) [1]	1.46 (.07)	1.85 (.08)
Mix of Traits and Issues (n=103)	1.68 (.05)	2.28 (.06)
Mostly about Issues (n=487)	1.96 (.02)	2.41 (.02)
F-statistic	32.90***	28.10***

Note: In the parentheses we present the number of advertisements coded for each subset of advertisements examined.

In each cell, means are presented, followed by standard errors. Civility and Relevance ratings range from 1 (low in civility or relevance) to 3 (high in civility or relevance).

*** $p<.01$.

** $p<.05$.

* $p<.10$.

of a point less civil than advertisements mostly about policy. Advertising targeting a candidate's personality weaknesses often use pointed language such as "dishonest," "liar," "in the pocket of special interests," and "doesn't care about you" when describing the targeted candidate.

We also find that policy-oriented advertisements are classified as significantly more relevant than trait-oriented messages. We compare two commercials to illustrate the covariation between the primary focus of negative advertisements and the relevance of these advertisements. The first advertisement, coded as mainly about issues and high in relevance, targeted Republican Dan Sullivan in Alaska. In this advertisement, sponsored by the Democratic Senatorial Campaign Committee, the narrator explains, "Dan Sullivan has a plan for social security." The advertisement then displays a video of Sullivan during an Anchorage Chamber of Commerce GOP debate, saying "I do think we need to look at raising the retirement age. I do think we also need to look at means testing." Then the narrator asks, "What does this mean for Alaska? His plan cuts social security by raising the retirement age, forcing us to work longer, retire later. Means testing would reduce or even end benefits for many people who pay into it their entire lives. Dan Sullivan's plan for social security is wrong for Alaska."

The second advertisement, also targeting Sullivan, focused mainly on traits and was classified as low in relevance. This advertisement, titled "Fishy" and sponsored by the Put Alaska First Super PAC, criticized Sullivan for not being a true Alaskan. The narrator begins, "Dan Sullivan's claims for being an Alaskan just got fishier. You already know that as a Maryland resident, he pocketed a tax credit on his million-dollar home there. Now we learn he had a nonresident Alaskan fishing license like every other tourist. But when he decided to run for Senate here instead of there [a graphic shows Alaska and Maryland on a map], he claimed he lived in Alaska for ten years. Next time Sullivan calls himself an Alaskan, don't take the bait." This advertisement's emphasis on Sullivan's integrity by questioning his residency status was rated as less relevant than the advertisement discussing Sullivan's position on social security.

Predicting the Civility and Relevance of Negative Advertisements

We conclude our investigation of the content and tone of the 2014 negative advertisements by developing a multivariate analysis to see if we can predict the civility and relevance of the negative commercials aired during the election.[15] With our bivariate analysis, we have seen that the civility and relevance of negative advertisements varies with the focus of the advertisements (i.e., advertisements emphasizing traits or issues) and with the gender of the narrator, but not with the sponsor of the advertisements. We also want to examine whether the party of the candidate or the status of the candidate being targeted (i.e., incumbent, challenger, open candidate) is associated with differences in relevance and civility ratings. We are agnostic regarding the relationship between the party of the candidate, on the one hand, and the civility and relevance ratings, on the other hand. In other words, we have no reason to expect that the types of advertisements targeting Democrats and Republicans will differ in their civility or relevance. However, with regard to the status of the candidate, we hypothesize that negative advertisements aimed at incumbents are likely to be viewed as more relevant since these advertisements can focus on germane topics such as the sitting senator's policy positions, issue priorities, and voting record in office. In contrast, it may be more difficult to criticize nonincumbents on relevant topics because they do not have an established record in the U.S. Senate to critique.

---

15. If we can predict the classification of advertisements in terms of civility and relevance, we have more confidence in the validity of our coding of these advertisements as well as confirmation of the importance of civility and relevance as significant constructs in negative advertising.

The results of our analysis, presented in Table 4.3, indicate the relationship between the focus of political commercials and civility and relevance ratings persists when we control for a series of additional factors. In particular, advertisements focusing more heavily on issues (relative to traits) are rated as significantly more civil and more relevant. In addition, and consistent with

Table 4.3 Ordinal Regression Explaining Civility and Relevance Ratings in Negative Commercials

	Civility Ratings	Relevance Ratings
Targeted Candidate		
Party	$-.63^{1}$ (.25) **	.22 (.23)
Incumbent	.24 (.28)	.63 (.26) **
Open Race Candidate	−.20 (.26)	.20 (.24)
Sponsor		
Interest Group Sponsor	−.08 (.26)	−.28 (.24)
Candidate Sponsor	.13 (.32)	.06 (.30)
Primary Focus of Advertisement	.94 (.14) ***	.99 (.14) ***
Gender of Narrator	.67 (.19) ***	.61 (.18) ***
Threshold 1	−.82 (.45)	−3.07 (.45) ***
Threshold 2	3.10 (.47) ***	.24 (.42)
Model Chi^2	63.46 ***	83.86 ***
−2 Log Likelihood	296.96	341.29
DF	7	7
Pseudo R-Squared (Cox and Snell)	.11	.14
N	565	564

Note: Unstandardized logit coefficients are followed by standard errors in parentheses.

Civility and Relevance ratings range from 1 (low in civility or relevance) to 3 (high in civility or relevance). Given the ordinal nature of the dependent variable, we use ordinal regression. Party is coded as 1 for Democrats and 0 for Republicans. Incumbent and open-race candidate are dummy variables, and challenger is the excluded category. Interest group sponsor and candidate sponsor are dummy variables, and party sponsor is the excluded category. Issue versus Trait is a variable measuring the main focus of the advertisement (1 = mainly about issues, 0 = mixture of traits and issues, -1 = mainly about traits). Gender of Narrator is coded 1 for female and 0 for male.

*p<.10.

** p<.05.

*** p<.01.

our prior findings, we see that the gender of the narrator is powerfully related to civility and relevance ratings. Advertisements featuring female narrators are coded as significantly more civil and relevant compared to advertisements relying on male narrators.

Turning to the status of the candidates, we find support for our prediction that advertisements targeting senators running for reelection are likely to be rated more relevant compared to advertisements attacking nonincumbents. We find some evidence that the party of the candidates matters: advertisements targeting Democrats are rated as less civil than advertisements criticizing Republicans. These results are consistent with prior work showing that Republicans are more likely to air negative advertisements compared to Democrats (e.g., Fowler and Ridout, 2012). Consistent with our earlier bivariate results, we find no relationship between the sponsor of the advertisement and civility and relevance ratings.

Conclusion

Mitch McConnell was reelected to a sixth term as U.S. senator from Kentucky with 56% of the vote in 2014, after more than $80 million was spent airing more than 88,000 advertisements. Both candidates launched relentless attacks on their opponent. McConnell portrayed Grimes as a rubber stamp for Obama's agenda in a state where the president was extremely unpopular. Grimes, on the other hand, portrayed McConnell as an entrenched Washington insider who has not been taking care of Kentucky.

In many ways, the negative messages in Kentucky are emblematic of the general trends described in this chapter. To review: we find negative advertisements are most pervasive in competitive races, during the last weeks of the campaign, on local news broadcasts, and during the early morning and afternoon. Advertising attacking women candidates often employ women narrators, while male narrators are employed more often in advertisements attacking men, especially Republican men. We find the same pattern in Kentucky, where advertisements attacking Grimes employed a woman narrator 71% of the time, compared to 15% of the advertisements targeting McConnell. Similarly, male narrators are utilized in 80% of advertisements aimed at McConnell and in only about 20% of advertisements criticizing Grimes.

With regard to substance, we find that 74% of all attack advertisements criticize the candidate's policy stands or legislative votes. Advertisements focusing on personal matters make up only 10%. The majority (68%) of the negative advertisements aired during the 2014 Senate elections are classified as somewhat civil; 23% rate low in civility; and 9% are considered highly civil. With regard to the relevance of negative advertisements, we find about 90% of all attack advertisements are considered somewhat or very relevant.

In Kentucky, while most advertisements are classified as (somewhat or very) relevant and (somewhat or very) civil, there are important exceptions. For example, an advertisement sponsored by MoveOn.org is coded as low in civility and relevance. The advertisement begins with an audio tape of McConnell telling the Koch brothers that the worst day of his political life was when the Senate passed a law to get big money out of politics. The narrator asks, "Really, Mitch? Not 9/11? Not the day of the financial collapse? Nope. It was the day a law passed to make Washington a bit less corrupt that McConnell called 'The worst day of my political life.'"

Documenting differences in the relevance and civility of negative commercials is integral to the tolerance and tactics theory of negativity. That is, if candidates do not vary the content and tone of negative messages, then it is highly unlikely voters will make judgments about candidates or decisions on whether to vote or not based on these crucial concepts. Now that we have established systematic patterns in the use of negative advertisements varying in their relevance and civility, we will explore whether voters make distinctions about the relevance and civility of negative critiques. In particular, we examine whether people are able to accurately detect differences in the civility and relevance of negative advertisements. We begin by looking at the correspondence between the relevance and civility coding of the negative messages in the 2014 Senate elections with respondents' assessments of these same advertisements. We also examine whether people discuss matters related to civility and relevance when asked to describe what they like and dislike about negative commercials. Finally, we look at people's emotional reactions to negative messages that vary dramatically in their relevance and civility.

5

Reactions to the Civility and Relevance of Negative Advertisements

SENATOR MARK UDALL was running for his second term as U.S. senator from Colorado in 2014. Udall was being challenged by U.S. Representative Cory Gardner, who had been representing Colorado's U.S. House Fourth District since 2010. The early polls indicated that the contest was going to be a nail-biter. A Quinnipiac Poll showed the race to be a dead heat as early as April 2014, and that result was almost unchanged during the length of the campaign; a poll on October 24, 2014, showed Gardner with a lead of 5% a couple of weeks before Election Day.[1]

The Colorado campaign, like virtually all competitive Senate elections, featured plenty of negative advertising. These advertisements varied in the civility of their tone and the relevance of their content. A negative advertisement titled "Backwards" graced the airways in Colorado nearly 1,000 times during the course of the campaign. This advertisement was sponsored by the Udall campaign and targeted Gardner on the emotional issue of abortion. It featured women describing Gardner's support for harsh anti-abortion laws, including sponsoring a bill to make abortion a felony even in cases of rape and incest. The advertisement argued Gardner had embarked on an "eight-year crusade that would ban birth control." Near the end of the advertisement, a mother with her young daughter says, "I want my daughter to have the same choices as I do." Another woman exclaims, "Seriously. It's 2014." A third woman concludes, "The only place that Cory Gardner will take women's rights is backwards." This advertisement focuses on an issue

---

1. See Quinnipiac University Poll, https://poll.qu.edu/colorado/.

likely to be considered relevant to a large swath of voters. Similarly, while the advertisement is clearly critical of Gardner's position on abortion, it utilizes a measured tone, refraining from employing pejorative words or displaying unflattering pictures of Gardner, and is not accompanied by an ominous soundtrack.

In 2014, the first-term senator Kay Hagan from North Carolina was fighting for her political life against Thom Tillis, the speaker of the North Carolina House of Representatives. As in Colorado, the North Carolina polls found the candidates running neck-and-neck in public support from early spring to the eve of Election Day.[2] Negative advertisements, as we have come to expect, were pervasive. One advertisement, called "The Apartment," sponsored by the Senate Majority PAC, tied Tillis to a sex scandal involving his chief of staff. The following is the text of the advertisement: "Thom Tillis shared an apartment with his chief of staff when North Carolina *News & Observer* reported that the chief of staff was having an extramarital affair with a lobbyist. He was caught on camera and resigned. Then one week later, another Tillis staffer resigned for another sexual relationship with a lobbyist. Thom Tillis's reaction: He claims he was surprised by his roommate's affair but rewarded both aides with taxpayers' paid bonuses. Thom Tillis: Spending our money to clean up his mess."

This advertisement seeks to blame Thom Tillis for the misbehavior of his staff. The main focus of the commercial is probably not relevant or useful for most voters. The claim at the end, that Tillis rewarded the misbehavior of his staff with bonuses, may be viewed with skepticism among viewers. The civility of the message may also be considered low given the use of innuendo to attack Tillis. Furthermore, black-and-white pictures of Tillis and foreboding music were featured in the advertisement, contributing to the incivility of the message.

The commercials from Colorado and North Carolina personify differences described and documented in chapter 4. In this chapter, we begin to explore whether people notice and respond to variations in the tone and content of political advertisements. It is critical for the tolerance and tactics theory to be able to substantiate that citizens see variation in the key concepts of relevance and civility of the actual negative campaign messages.

---

2. https://www.realclearpolitics.com/epolls/2014/senate/nc/north_carolina_senate_tillis_vs_hagan_vs_haugh-5136.html

Discerning Differences in the Civility and Relevance of Negative Messages

In chapter 4 we presented a great deal of evidence about how campaign messages vary in their content (i.e., relevance) as well as in their tone (i.e., civility). But we have yet to explore whether people are able to identify differences in the relevance and civility of negative advertisements. In this chapter, we present two sets of data demonstrating that people are adept at differentiating between negative advertisements differing in their substance and tenor. First, we look at whether people's impressions of the civility and relevance of negative advertisements correspond to our content analysis coding of those advertisements. Second, we examine people's emotional reactions to advertisements that differ in their civility and relevance.

We conducted a focus group study where we presented undergraduate respondents with 14 advertisements aired during the 2014 Senate elections.[3] We asked these participants a series of questions about each advertisement, including evaluations of the relevance and civility of each one.[4] We are interested in comparing respondents' impressions of the civility and relevance of the negative advertisements with the content analysis coding of the same advertisements discussed in chapter 4.[5]

---

3. In Appendix F we present summaries of each of the 14 advertisements examined in the focus group, along with a YouTube link of the actual commercial, and the content analysis coding of the relevance and civility of the advertisement.

4. The respondents were randomly assigned to one of two groups. In each group, respondents watched seven advertisements and answered a series of questions about each one. The advertisements examined in each group were different; therefore, we have assessments of 14 different negative advertisements disseminated during the 2014 campaign. See chapter 2 for more details about the methodology of this study.

5. Respondents were asked to rate the civility and relevance of each advertisement immediately after viewing them. The exact wording for the civility question is "Thinking about the tone of the [number of advertisement], how would you characterize the tone of the advertisement on a scale ranging from (1) Very hostile to (5) Not hostile at all?" The exact wording for the relevance question is "Thinking about the content of the [number of advertisement], how useful do you consider the advertisement on a scale ranging from (1) Not useful at all to (5) Very useful?" We utilized a five-point scale instead of the three-point scale used in the content analysis to examine the precision of people's perceptions of the civility and relevance of the political advertisements. In this chapter, we compare the average respondents' assessments of the advertisements (on the five-point scale) to the content analysis of these same advertisements, classified as low (1), medium (2), or high (3) in relevance and civility. See Appendix G for a copy of the complete questionnaire.

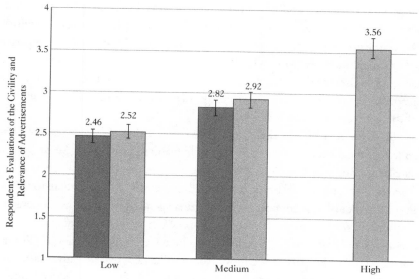

Note: Advertisements are classified as low, medium, or high relevance and low or medium in civility based on the content analysis of the 2014 advertisements. (Respondents are not asked to assess any advertisements rated high in civility since these types of negative advertisements are quite rare.) the respondents evaluations of the relevance and civility of the advertisements are based on the close-ended survey questions. We present the means with 95% confidence intervals.

FIGURE 5.1 Comparison of respondents' perceptions of the relevance and civility of negative advertisements with content analysis ratings.

Figure 5.1 presents negative advertisements from 2014 scored by content coders as low, medium, and high in terms of civility and relevance.[6] The coders' assessments are arrayed on the horizontal axis. The assessments by the focus group of the same negative commercials are presented along the vertical axis. For example, in the first column, respondents in the focus group gave a mean score of 2.46 (the scale ranges from 1 to 5, with 1 representing "very hostile" and 5 capturing "not hostile at all") for the negative ads the content coders had placed in the low civility category. We find a strong correspondence between the respondents' ratings of the commercials and

---

6. In selecting advertisements for this study, we attempted to locate negative advertisements that varied in their civility and relevance. However, we were unable to identify any negative advertisements with a highly civil tone. These types of advertisements, according to our content analysis, are quite rare, occurring only 9% of the time. (This focus group was conducted before the completion of the content analysis of the relevance and civility of the population of 2014 U.S. Senate advertisements.)

the content analysis coding of these same messages. The findings are consistent for each category of low, medium, and high for ratings of civility. We also find that respondents' assessments of the relevance of the negative advertisements correspond with the content analysis categorization of these same advertisements. As the relevance of the political commercials increases, according to our content analysis, respondents' evaluations of the relevance of these advertisements also escalates.

To illustrate a step further, an advertisement titled "Chicken Dance" was coded as low in relevance; this advertisement featured Democratic Senate candidate Bruce Braley of Iowa "doing the chicken dance" for claiming to be a farmer when he is actually a trial lawyer. Another advertisement criticizing Senator Mark Pryor of Arkansas for supporting the Obama agenda was coded as moderately relevant, according to our content analysis. We find that respondents viewed the attack on Braley as less relevant than the advertisement critiquing Pryor's voting record.[7] Similarly, as we move from moderately relevant advertisements to advertisements classified as highly relevant (e.g., the attack advertisement aired by Udall criticizing Gardner for his extreme stand on abortion-related issues), respondents' views of the relevance of the advertisements also increases significantly.[8]

We also asked respondents to write down at least one thing they liked and one thing they disliked about each of the advertisements they viewed. People listed a variety of different types of "likes," including the use of news clips to support assertions and that the advertisement was entertaining, easy to follow, and relied on music to set the tone. Respondents also identified a number of criteria when describing aspects of the advertisement they disliked, including that there was too much repetition, the production value appeared substandard, the music was annoying, and information presented was taken out of context.

We examined the content of the open-ended responses to see whether respondents spontaneously mentioned dimensions associated with the relevance and civility of the advertisements when describing what they liked

7. Respondents gave the Braley advertisement an average score of 1.69 (with a standard error of .08) on the five-point relevance scale, while the Pryor attack received an average score of 2.86 (with a standard error of .10). This difference is statistically significant at p<.01.

8. Respondents gave the Gardner advertisement an average relevance score of 3.78 (with a standard error of .08) on the five-point relevance scale, compared to the 2.86 relevance rating (with a standard error of .10) for the Pryor advertisement. This difference is statistically significant at p<.01.

and disliked about them.[9] For example, when respondents describe liking the tone of the advertisement or when they mention disliking the hostility of the advertisement, we coded these sorts of comments as relating to the civility of the advertisements. Similarly, we categorized responses as related to the relevance of the advertisements when respondents say they like the advertisement because it focuses on an important issue or they find the issue discussed in the advertisement to be relevant for the election or they believe the advertisement is presenting evidence to support an important claim. When respondents point out they dislike the use of unsubstantiated claims because the claims are not useful or a particular criticism is targeting a trivial issue, we consider these mentions to be related to the irrelevance of the advertisements.

Respondents mention the tone as something they like only 4% of the time when assessing negative advertisements. However, they are more than twice as likely to comment on the incivility of the advertisement as something they dislike, mentioning the harsh or overly strident tone of the advertisement 10% of the time. We also find people are more likely to spontaneously mention the relevance or irrelevance of aspects of the advertisements when asked to identify something they like or dislike about the advertisement. In particular, people mention the relevance of the content (e.g., important issue, salient topic) when discussing what they like about the advertisements 22% of the time, on average. And they discuss the irrelevance of the subject matter (e.g., inconsequential issue, topic not germane to the election) when considering what they dislike about the commercial, on average, 20% of the time.[10]

We looked at whether people's discussion of what they like and dislike about the advertisements varies with the civility and relevance of the

---

9. We think it is unlikely that the close-ended questions about relevance and civility primed the open-ended responses assessing what respondents liked and disliked about each advertisement. First, the civility and relevance questions are not asked immediately before the open-ended questions. Second, the relevance question is asked after the civility question in the survey, yet people are more likely to mention likes and dislikes related to relevance than likes and dislikes related to civility. Third, respondents often mention noncivil and nonrelevant aspects of the commercials when answering the open-ended questions.

10. In addition to discussing relevance and civility, respondents mention the graphics and production values as something they like about 26% and as something they dislike about 15% of the time. The next most common like or dislike mentioned by respondents is how the message is presented (e.g., the characteristics of the narrator, getting to the point quickly or slowly), mentioned 10% of the time as something they liked and 9% of the time as something they disliked.

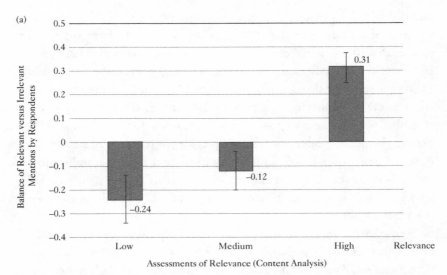

FIGURE 5.2A Differences in relevance mentions (positive-negative mentions) for advertisements varying in relevance.

advertisement.[11] To examine this question, we subtract mentions of dislikes from mentions of likes for both respondents' discussions of civility and relevance. We then examine these difference measures for advertisements against those coded as low, medium, and high in relevance as well as for advertisements coded as low and medium in civility by the coders conducting the content analyses. The results are displayed in Figure 5.2.

The data in the top panel (Figure 5.2A) reveal a strong correspondence between the relevance of the advertisements and whether people are more likely to mention relevant aspects of the commercial as something they like compared to mentioning irrelevant features among the things they dislike about the commercial. In particular, among advertisements scored by content analysis coders as high in relevance, people mention more relevant than irrelevant items when discussing what they like and dislike about the advertisements. In comparison, people are more likely to mention irrelevant aspects of the commercial, compared to relevant dimensions, as the relevance of the advertisement declines.

---

11. As we did earlier (Figure 5.1), we utilize the content analysis coding of the commercials to determine the relevance (low, medium, and high) and civility (low, medium) of the advertisements.

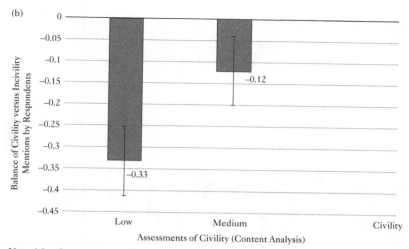

(b)

Note: Advertisements are classified as low, medium, or high in relevance and low or medium in civility based on the content analysis of the 2014 advertisements. (Respondents are not asked to assess any advertisements rated high in civility since these types of negative advertisements are quite rare.) The respondents evaluations of the relevance and civility of the advertisements are based on the open-ended survey questions. We present the means with 95% confidence intervals.

FIGURE 5.2B Differences in civility mentions (positive-negative mentions) for advertisements varying in civility.

In the bottom panel (Figure 5.2B), we look at advertisements scored as low and medium in civility by the coders.[12] We see a similar pattern. While the number of dislikes mentioned about incivility always outnumber the number of likes when discussing the civility of these commercials, the difference between civility likes and dislikes is significantly larger when people are viewing advertisements rated by coders as low in civility compared to advertisements rated as medium in civility (−.33 for low civility advertisements versus −.12 for medium civility advertisements). The results displayed in Figure 5.2, along with the data in Figure 5.1, indicate that (1) the coding of the advertisements in the content analysis has predictive validity (i.e., the coding of advertisements is related to people's evaluations of the commercials) and (2) people's close-ended assessments of the advertisements' civility and relevance as well as their open-ended discussion of what they like and dislike about commercials suggests they are adept at distinguishing between negative messages varying in civility and relevance.

12. As discussed earlier, respondents did not view an advertisement rated high in civility since these types of negative advertisements are rare.

(a)

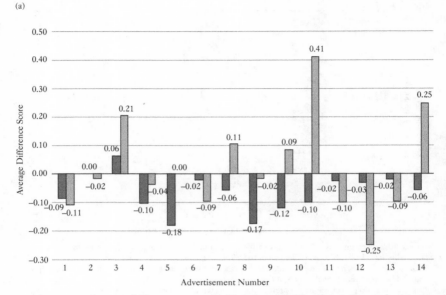

FIGURE 5.3A Average difference scores for likes versus dislikes for civility and relevance mentions in open-ended comments per advertisement.

Furthermore, people's willingness to mention things they like or dislike about negative messages varies in predictable ways when we examine the 14 advertisements individually. We present difference scores (i.e., likes about civility/relevance, dislikes about civility/relevance) for each of the advertisements and display these summary measures in Figure 5.3A. There are some interesting patterns. First, one advertisement (#3) receives a net positive score for relevance and civility mentions. This is the Udall attack on Gardner ("Backwards"), discussed at the beginning of the chapter. Respondents consider this advertisement to focus on a highly relevant topic (i.e., abortion) and they believe the tone of the advertisement to be civil.

Second, several advertisements (e.g., #1, #4, #11) had net scores for relevance less than zero. For these commercials, respondents discuss more irrelevant mentions than relevant mentions. Given the tolerance and tactics theory of negativity, we expect people's evaluations of the candidates targeted in these advertisements are unlikely to be affected by these messages since these advertisements focus on irrelevant topics.

The tolerance and tactics theory of negativity leads us to expect messages delivered in an uncivil manner but targeting an important topic will be most likely to influence people's impressions of the targeted candidate. According

(b)

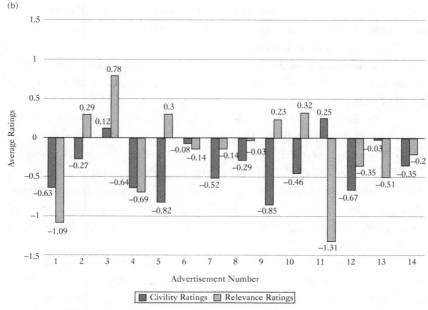

Note: In Figure 5.3A, we present difference scores between open-ended "likes" and "dislikes" about civility and relevance mentions. In Figure 5.3B, we present average relevance and civility ratings, relying on the close-ended survey questions. The advertisements associated with each number are described in Appendix F.

FIGURE 5.3B   Average close-ended civility and relevance ratings per advertisement.

to the data in Figure 5.3A, four advertisements fit these criteria: #7, #9, #10, and #14. For instance, advertisement #10 receives a civility score of -.10 and a relevance score of .41. This advertisement, an attack by the Gardner campaign on Udall, focused on Udall's attendance record in the U.S. Senate.[13]

We can also examine respondents' evaluations of the relevance and civility of each of these 14 advertisements using the close-ended measures of civility and relevance. We present average civility and relevance scores for each of the commercials in Figure 5.3B.[14] As expected, the close-ended civility and relevance averages are highly correlated with the open-ended mentions for the commercials. In particular, the correlation coefficient between the two measures of civility is positive and significantly correlated at .66 ($p<.01$), and the correlation coefficient between the two measures of relevance is positive and significantly correlated at .56 ($p<.05$). The substantial relationship between

13. See Appendix F for the text of the commercial.

14. In Figure 5.3B, we recode the values so they run from -2 to 2 (instead of the original 1 to 5) to increase comparability between the open-ended comments and the close-ended comments.

these disparate measures indicates respondents are making valid judgments regarding the civility and relevance of these political commercials.

When we look at advertisements receiving a positive relevance score and a positive civility score on the close-ended scale, we once again see that advertisement #3 ("Backwards") is the only advertisement rated as civil and relevant. Similarly, we see overlap in the advertisements receiving the most irrelevant ratings via the open-ended and close-ended formats (i.e., advertisements #1, #4, and #11). Relying on the close-ended ratings, the advertisement viewed as most irrelevant was #11, the advertisement attacking Braley for doing the "chicken dance." As described earlier, the advertisement focused largely on Barley's off-handed remark that he is a farmer when responding to a citizen during an Independence Day parade.[15] The advertisement employs cartoonish music as well as video editing intended to make Braley look like he is dancing the "chicken dance."

We examine advertisements receiving a positive relevance score and a negative civility scores via the close-ended survey measures. We find four advertisements fitting these criteria: #2, #5, #9, and #10. We expect these advertisements, likely to capture people's attention because of their uncivil tone, may influence people's evaluations since they focus on important topics. The advertisement receiving the highest relevance rating, as well as a negative civility rating, is Gardner's attack on Udall's absences while serving in the U.S. Senate.

These analyses examining respondents' impressions of the relevance and civility of various advertisements via open-ended comments and close-ended survey questions illustrate that people understand and evaluate negative commercials along these two dimensions. We turn now to assessing people's emotional reactions to advertisements varying in their civility and relevance.

Exploring Emotional Reactions to Negative Messages

A growing amount of research in political science and social psychology reveals that people often have emotional reactions to political stimuli (e.g., Lodge and Taber, 2005; Marcus, 2000). These emotional responses can influence attitudes toward political objects, people's likelihood of taking political

---

15. Bruce Braley's parents and grandparents were farmers and owned a farm in Brooklyn, Iowa (Jacobs, 2014).

action, and their propensity to seek out additional political information (e.g., Sullivan and Masters, 1988, Marcus, 2000). In the remaining pages of this chapter, we explore whether people have distinct emotional responses to negative political commercials. In particular, we look at whether certain types of negative commercials (e.g., commercials varying in their relevance and civility) are more likely to elicit negative emotions. Furthermore, we explore whether people's tolerance for negativity influences their emotional reactions to negative advertisements that differ in their civility and relevance.

We recruited 266 undergraduate students to take part in a study of political communication in order to explore the relationship between emotions and negative political advertisements.[16] Subjects viewed eight commercials from the 2014 Senate elections. The eight advertisements were chosen based on the ratings from the content analysis. We chose two advertisements classified as low in civility and low in relevance, two classified as medium in relevance and civility, two rated high in relevance and civility, and two coded low in civility and high in relevance.[17] When the students arrived at the political science laboratory for the study, they were seated at a laptop computer and given instructions to complete a survey. The survey included general questions about politics as well as our standard measures assessing tolerance for uncivil and irrelevant negative messages.[18] After completing the entire pretest questionnaire, subjects were asked to click on a series of political advertisements, answering questions about each one before proceeding to the next. Subjects were debriefed at the end of the experimental session.

While viewing the commercials on the laptops, the subjects' facial reactions were recorded via the webcams on their laptops.[19] After the conclusion of the study, the videos of the subjects' facial expressions were edited and post processed utilizing Emotient FACET software. This system, utilized by the Emotient software, has been used to study different emotional processes, including expressions of pain in babies (e.g., Grunau and Craig, 1987),

---

16. See chapter 2 for more details about the methodology.

17. For each type of advertisement (e.g., low in civility and low in relevance), we chose an advertisement where a woman candidate was the target and another advertisement where the target of the advertisement was a male candidate. See Appendix H for the order and description of each advertisement included in the focus group, along with a YouTube link of the actual commercial.

18. See Appendix I for a copy of the full questionnaire.

19. During the introduction of the study, subjects were told that their research sessions were being recorded via the webcam on laptop computers.

affective states during learning (e.g., Craig et al., 2008), and grief after the loss of a spouse (e.g., Bonanno and Keltner, 1997). The FACS system enables the measurement and scoring of facial activity in an objective, reliable, and quantitative way and is often used to measure the effectiveness of media content, especially for product advertising (e.g., McDuff et al., 2013).

The Emotient FACET software tracks 20 action units (e.g., inner brow raiser, upper lid raiser, nose wrinkle) in real time, allowing the extraction of seven basic emotions (joy, anger, surprise, fear, contempt, sadness, disgust) and two complex emotions (confusion and frustration).[20] We focus on five negative emotions here (anger, contempt, disgust, sadness, frustration).[21] In addition, Emotient FACET allows us to identify both micro expressions (brief expression of an emotion lasting 250 milliseconds or less) and macro expressions (normal expressions usually lasting between a half second and 4 seconds).[22] We look at the percentage of frames displaying a particular emotion for each of the eight advertisements.[23]

We begin by simply presenting people's emotional reactions to the eight Senate commercials from 2014. The pattern of data in Figure 5.4 shows people's expression of negative emotions varies across the negative advertisements. Certain emotions, like contempt, diverge more dramatically across the messages, compared to other emotions, such as disgust.[24]

In exploring people's responses to specific commercials, we see that advertisement #6 generated the highest levels of frustration and anger among the subjects. Titled "Torn Apart," it was sponsored by the Senate Majority

---

20. Different action units make up different facial expressions. For example, expressions of anger contain a combination of six action units (e.g., Cohn, Ambadar, and Ekman, 2007).

21. The most systematic large-scale investigation of reliability in spontaneous facial behavior was done by Sayette et al. (2001). In their study, the researchers induced changes in facial expression by using emotion inductions (e.g., olfactory stimulation); the researchers found high levels of reliability for all but two of the 30 action units examined. In addition, concurrent validity has been established by comparing manual coding with computer-based approaches (e.g., Cohn, Ambadar, and Ekman, 2007; Pantic and Patras, 2006).

22. We are able to determine the displayed emotion of respondents *while* they are experiencing the stimuli using the Emotient FACET software. Other common measures, such as self-report assessments on questionnaires, must be completed after a stimulus has been presented. This delay may influence the accuracy of the respondents' self-report of their emotional state.

23. The classification of each emotion is done probabilistically, calculating and assessing the chance that the expression is displaying the particular emotion (e.g., eyebrows down and together is a classifier of anger).

24. The standard deviation across the average ratings for the eight commercials displayed in Figure 5.4 is 2.06 for contempt and 1.12 for anger.

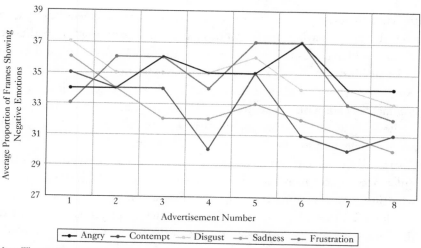

Note: The average proportion of frames showing each emotion are displayed. The advertisements associated with each number are described in Appendix H.

FIGURE 5.4 Negative emotions displayed for Senate advertisements.

PAC, aired in Colorado, and discussed Republican Cory Gardner's extreme positions on abortion. A female narrator says, "Your whole world is torn apart. But Congressman Gardner would make it harder, pushing to outlaw a woman's right to choose. Even in cases of rape and incest. Worse. Gardner tried to redefine rape to mean only forcible rape. In Gardner's bill, victims who were drugged or minors who were victims of statutory rape would not be considered rape victims. Cory Gardner is just too extreme."

This commercial may have been especially salient to our young respondents, particularly the young women. When we compare the level of anger and frustration between men and women watching this commercial, we find women expressed significantly more anger and frustration than men. In particular, women expressed anger in 43% of the frames and frustration in 42% of the frames, on average, while men expressed anger and frustration in 31% and 32% of the frames, respectively.[25]

We see a similar pattern when we examine gender differences in emotional reactions to the only other commercial about abortion in our series. Advertisement #8, titled "Personhood," sponsored by the Democratic Senatorial Campaign Committee and attacking Joni Ernst of Iowa, echoed

---

25. These differences are statistically significant at $p<.01$ for anger and $p<.05$ for frustration, based on the F-statistic.

the same themes as the Gardner commercial. The advertisement begins with a female narrator saying "Joni Ernst pushed for the Personhood Amendment. What would that mean? It would ban many forms of birth control and would make all abortions illegal. Ernst would outlaw abortions even for victims of rape or incest. And would actually impose criminal penalties on doctors." The commercial ends with the tagline "Joni Ernst: Too Extreme for Iowa."

Looking at the averages presented in Figure 5.4, anger and frustration are not as elevated for the "Personhood" advertisement (#8) as for the "Torn Apart" advertisement (#6). However, these averages obscure important differences in how men and women respond to the final advertisement. As with the Gardner commercial, women display significantly more anger when viewing the Ernst advertisement. That is, women displayed anger in 38% of the frames, on average, compared to 29% of the frames for men.[26] Similarly, women are much more likely than men to express frustration when viewing the "Personhood" advertisement; women display frustration, on average, 41% of the time compared to 32% for men.[27]

The greater expression of anger and frustration by women, compared to men, is not something that occurs for each of the advertisements. That is, women do not always express more anger and frustration than men across all of the advertisements. For example, when we look at the advertisement attacking Mark Pryor of Arkansas for his position on Obamacare, we find no differences in men's and women's expression of anger or frustration.[28] These findings suggest women are more angered and frustrated than men by commercials attacking candidates for their extreme positions on abortion, a particularly relevant topic for women.

We turn to a more general discussion of the relevance of the commercial. The tolerance and tactics theory of negativity contends that people's evaluations of candidates will be more influenced by attack advertisements that focus on relevant topics. Once again, we use the content analysis coding of the advertisements to distinguish between advertisements classified as high and those classified as low in relevance.[29] We expect highly

---

26. This difference is statistically significant at p<.05, based on the F-statistic.

27. This difference is statistically significant at p<.05, based on the F-statistic.

28. Women express anger, on average, in 36% of the frames and frustration in 39%. Men, in contrast, show anger in 34% of the frames and display frustration in 35%. These differences are not statistically significant, based on the F-statistic.

29. We limit the remaining analysis in this chapter to negative advertisements rated high (3) or low (1) in relevance and civility since the predictions derived from the tolerance and tactics theory of negativity are more straightforward for these types of commercials.

relevant advertisements will generate more negative affect than less relevant advertisements as these commercials are more likely to engage citizens. We develop an aggregate measure of negative emotion by summing people's expressions of disgust, anger, contempt, frustration, and sadness. We then compare average displays of negative emotions for advertisements classified as low and high in relevance.

As hypothesized, we find relevant advertisements generate more expressions of negative emotions (an average of 34.8% of the frames show negative emotions) than irrelevant advertisements (an average of 32.9% of the frames show negative emotions).[30] When we look at each negative emotion, we continue to find that relevant negative advertisements elicit more negative emotional reactions than advertisements classified as low in relevance (see Figure 5.5).[31] These results suggest people are less moved by the irrelevant attacks on candidates and are less likely to generate negative affect among respondents.

According to our theory, it is important to consider both the relevance and the civility of negative messages. While we expect irrelevant advertisements, whether delivered in a civil or uncivil fashion, to be largely ineffective, the tolerance and tactics theory of negativity contends that the tone of the advertisement (i.e., the level of civility) will modify the impact of relevant negative messages. In particular, we expect uncivil relevant advertisements to be more likely to depress evaluations of the targeted candidate compared to civil relevant advertisements. We theorize that incivility will capture people's attention, encouraging them to pay attention to relevant messages. Civil messages on a relevant topic will be less effective because the courteous tone will be less likely to draw people's attention. If uncivil relevant messages are more likely to be noticed by citizens, then we might expect people to express more negative emotions when watching relevant advertisements delivered in an uncivil manner compared to relevant but civil attacks.

When we examine people's average displays of negative emotions for advertisements varying in their relevance *and* civility, we find negative emotions are relatively stable between relevant and civil advertisements, on the one hand, and relevant and uncivil advertisements, on the other.[32]

---

30. This difference, although in the expected direction, does not reach statistical significance.

31. These differences, while consistent across all five emotions, do not reach statistical significance.

32. Relevant and civil advertisements generate, on average, displays of negative emotions in 35.2% of the frames, while relevant and uncivil advertisements produce, on average, displays of negative emotions in 34.8%.

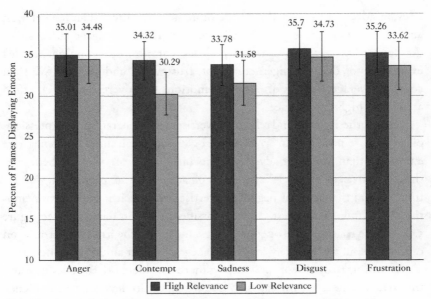

Note: We rely on the content analysis coding to classify advertisements as low or high in relevance and civility. We present the means with 95% confidence intervals.

FIGURE 5.5 Displays of specific negative emotions for advertisements varying in relevance.

Furthermore, we fail to find consistent differences when we look at specific negative emotions. For example, people express more anger while watching uncivil relevant advertisements compared to civil ones. However, they express less disgust with uncivil relevant advertisements compared to the civil messages.[33] These findings fail to support our expectations; we had hypothesized that people would express more negative emotions (e.g., disgust, anger) when exposed to relevant advertisements employing an uncivil tone compared to civil messages focusing on relevant topics.

While differences in the civility of relevant advertisements did not produce systematic alterations in people's emotional responses to these advertisements, we look at whether people's sensitivity to incivility leads to variations in emotional responses to relevant advertisements. In particular, the tolerance and tactics theory of negativity contends that people who do

---

33. Uncivil relevant ads generate an average of 35.4% of frames displaying anger, 34.2% of frames displaying contempt, 33.2% of frames displaying sadness, 35.3% of frames displaying disgust, and 35.6% of frames displaying frustration. Civil relevant ads generate an average 34.9% of frames displaying anger, 34.8% of frames displaying contempt, 34.6% of frames displaying sadness, 36.5% of frames displaying disgust, and 35.1% of frames displaying frustration.

Table 5.1   Percentage of Frames Displaying Negative Emotions for Different Types of Advertisements by Respondents' Tolerance for Incivility

	Tolerant of Incivility	Intolerant of Incivility	F-Statistic	p Value
Type of Commercial				
Relevant and Uncivil (n=180)	31.95 (2.21)[1]	37.39 (1.53)	4.07	**
Relevant and Civil (n=183)	33.92 (2.16)	35.27 (1.21)	0.59	n.s.
Irrelevant (n=184)	31.22 (2.25)	34.87 (1.56)	1.78	n.s.

[1]Each cell presents the average percentage of frames displaying negative emotions, along with the standard error.

Note: People who score above the mean on the intolerance to incivility index are categorized as intolerant of incivility, while people who score below the mean are classified as tolerant of incivility. We rely on the content analysis to classify commercials as high or low in relevance and high or low in civility. See text for more details.

not tolerate incivility easily will be more sensitive to negative advertisements employing a discourteous tone when compared to people with higher levels of tolerance for incivility. If this is the case, we should see that people who are less tolerant of incivility would show more negative emotions when confronted with relevant advertisements employing an uncivil tone.

The data in Table 5.1 support our expectation. People who are intolerant of incivility (i.e., score above the mean on the incivility index) demonstrate more negative emotions than people who are tolerant of incivility when viewing uncivil commercials focusing on an important topic. Furthermore, while the data in Table 5.1 reveal that people who are sensitive to incivility display more negative emotions, regardless of the type of advertisement, the differences are most striking for relevant and uncivil commercials, as we expected.[34]

We have shown that different negative advertisements produce different emotional reactions by young citizens. For instance, negative advertisements focusing on a pertinent topic generate a greater emotional response than commercials emphasizing less germane matters. Also, men and women differ in their affective reactions to negative advertisements detailing a candidate's position on abortion. Finally, people's level of tolerance for negativity influences their emotional displays. Individuals who are less tolerant of

---

34. We do not find that people who are intolerant of irrelevant negative commercials exhibit more negative emotions than people who are more tolerant of these types of commercials.

incivility are more likely to show negative emotions when confronted with attack advertisements.

Conclusion

The tolerance and tactics theory of negativity argues that the interplay between people's tolerance for negativity and the type of negative advertisements disseminated during campaigns shapes the attitudes and actions of citizens. In chapter 3, we demonstrated that citizens differ systematically in their tolerance of uncivil and irrelevant negative messages. In chapter 4, we showed that campaign messages delivered during the 2014 Senate elections varied considerably in terms of their relevance and civility. In this chapter, we demonstrated that people can recognize and make distinctions about the relevance and civility of negative advertisements.

In summary, respondents are able to rate advertisements produced and aired in the 2014 senatorial campaigns in ways consistent with the assessments made by the content analysis coders. We showed that respondents view advertisements coded as highly uncivil as more hostile than messages coded as more civil. Similarly, respondents are able to distinguish between negative advertisements coded as high and low in relevance that are consistent with the content analysis findings. We demonstrated a strong relationship between the respondents' impressions of the advertisements and the results of the content analysis when we examined respondents' answers to close-ended survey questions about the advertisements. This same pattern of consistency is seen when we examine respondents' open-ended descriptions of what they like and dislike about each advertisement. This set of findings is important because we needed to demonstrate that trained coders' assessments of negative commercials can be validated by people witnessing the same messages. This analysis shows that not only do candidates' messages vary in terms of relevance and civility, but people notice and discern these differences.

In addition, we utilized state-of-the-art software to measure people's real-time emotional reactions to different negative advertisements aired during the 2014 Senate elections. We were able to demonstrate that people vary in their emotional reactions to different types of negative messages. Consistent with our theory, we found that people have strong negative reactions to attack advertisements that focus on relevant topics compared to messages emphasizing less useful topics. We also showed that people's varying levels of tolerance for incivility influence their emotional responses to negativity. Specifically, we revealed that people who are intolerant of incivility are more likely to exhibit negative emotions when watching relevant and uncivil advertisements compared to respondents with higher levels of tolerance for rough and tumble negative messages.

We next assess whether the tolerance and tactics theory of negativity explains and predicts voters' attitudes and actions in the midst of campaigns for the U.S. Senate. Does the relevance and civility of campaign messages (i.e., tactics) have differential effects on voters, depending on their tolerance for negative campaigning during actual negative campaigns? In other words, does the interplay between tolerance and tactics shape how citizens respond to negative messages? We answer these questions in chapter 6 in order to assess the veracity of the tolerance and tactics theory of negativity in the context of the 2014 senatorial elections. It is time to take the theory out of the laboratory and focus group settings and determine its generalizability during actual campaigns.

6

Examining Citizens' Impressions of Negativity During U.S. Senate Campaigns

WE BEGAN OUR exploration in America's heartland with the story of Mary and Rita and Iowa's hotly contested senatorial campaign in 2014 to understand how negative campaigning shapes citizens' beliefs and behaviors. We believed Mary and Rita vary significantly in their tolerance of negative messages, and we speculated that these differences were typical across a wide swath of U.S. citizens. To be sure, we know now that Mary and Rita are not unique. In fact, people's levels of tolerance toward negativity not only vary, but they do so in predictable ways (see chapter 3). We also noted that the political advertisements disseminated during the Iowa Senate campaign differed dramatically in terms of the relevance and civility of the messages. Again, we had a strong suspicion the variance in these messages was not unique to Iowa, and sure enough, the Iowa campaign is not unusual; in states where negative advertisements are prevalent, differences in the relevance and civility of negative messages are relatively predictable (see chapter 4).

While we know people like Mary and Rita vary in their tolerance of negative messages, and we have shown that campaign messages differ dramatically in their relevance and civility, we have yet to explore whether people's tolerance for negativity influences their assessments of negative messages. In this chapter, we explore a central question of the tolerance and tactics theory of negativity: Does citizens' levels of tolerance for negativity shape their views of political messages during an ongoing campaign? We have theorized that people with less tolerance for negativity will be more sensitive to variation in the civility and relevance of negative appeals: people with lower levels of tolerance for negativity will view negative advertisements as less civil and less relevant than people who are more tolerant of negativity.

Furthermore, we expect people's level of tolerance for negativity is different from traditional political factors, like partisanship, ideology, and views about policy. For example, even though Rita and Mary hold similar partisan and ideological proclivities and share (mostly) the same views about the pressing issues of the day, we expect they will view the same negative commercials quite differently. According to our theory, Mary will view the advertisement titled "Slick," linking Bruce Braley to Michael Bloomberg (discussed in chapter 1), as less relevant than Rita because Mary has lower levels of tolerance for irrelevant messages. The difference in relevance ratings for this commercial cannot be explained by differences in political perspectives. Instead, we expect the difference is caused by varying levels of tolerance for negativity.

In this chapter, we examine citizens' reactions to negativity during actual campaigns. During an electoral contest, voters are evaluating actual candidates with unique histories (e.g., specific voting records, a record of service in the state) during a time when certain issues are especially salient (e.g., Obamacare during 2014). Therefore, voters' partisan proclivities, their policy views, and their feelings about competing candidates (e.g., well-known incumbents) will be activated (e.g., Vavreck, 2009) and will certainly influence their impressions of the negative messages disseminated during the campaign. We believe it is essential to examine people's impressions of negative messages during the height of the campaign, not when negative advertisements are replayed in isolation after the conclusion of the election (e.g., Gimple, Green, and Shaw, 2011; Hill et al., 2013). We turn now to a discussion of the 2014 CCES national survey experiment where we continue to test the tolerance and tactics theory of negativity.

National Survey Experiment

We conducted a survey experiment as part of the 2014 CCES in states holding senatorial campaigns.[1] Respondents were exposed to the storyboards of four actual negative advertisements depending on their Senate race.[2] Respondents

---

1. See chapter 2 for more information about the survey experiment. See Appendix A for a copy of the 2014 CCES questionnaire.

2. In open races, people were shown the Democratic challenger advertisement for the Democratic open candidate and the Republican challenger advertisement for the Republican open candidate.

were randomly assigned to one of two versions of each advertisement: one version of the advertisement relied on a civil tone, and the second version of same advertisement utilized an uncivil tone (see Appendix B for the text of the different advertisements). The differences in tone represented actual variability in the tenor of advertisements aired during the 2014 senatorial campaigns.

We selected for inclusion the most common negative advertisements disseminated in the 2014 Senate races. For Democratic incumbents, the most common negative advertisement attacked Democratic senators for their support of Obamacare. Democratic incumbents were also frequently criticized for "going Washington" by supporting higher taxes and government spending. The most frequent topics used to criticize Republican incumbents were Republican incumbents' ties to Wall Street and blaming Republican incumbents for the shutdown of the federal government.

Turning to advertisements attacking challengers, Democrats running for the U.S. Senate were mainly criticized on two fronts: that the Democratic challenger would be a rubber stamp for President Obama's agenda and that the Democratic challenger was too liberal and out of step with the state's citizens. Republican challengers were attacked for their extreme positions on abortion as well as because of their ties to the conservative and wealthy Koch brothers.

Our research design allows us to see if people respond differently to actual advertisements varying in their civility during an ongoing election. Respondents are randomly assigned to read the civil and uncivil versions of these advertisements. After respondents are given each script, they are asked to assess the civility and relevance of the advertisements. This design provides analytical leverage to determine how people evaluate commercials varying in tone during an actual campaign.

As a manipulation check, we conducted an online survey experiment with Arizona State University students in 2015.[3] In this survey experiment, students were randomly exposed to civil or uncivil versions of the political advertisements utilized in the CCES study; however, respondents were exposed to the actual advertisement instead of the script of the advertisement. In other words, the 2015 ASU student respondents watched actual television advertisements that were run during the 2014 Senate elections.

---

3. See chapter 2 for more details about the 2015 ASU survey experiment. See Appendix C for a copy of the questionnaire used in this study.

Respondents in the 2015 ASU survey experiment were exposed to the following four commercials: (1) an Obamacare commercial, (2) a government shutdown commercial, (3) a rubber stamp advertisement, and (4) an advertisement tying the Republican candidate to the Koch brothers.[4] As in the 2014 CCES study, respondents were randomly assigned to uncivil or civil versions of each advertisement. After watching each commercial, as in the 2014 CCES survey, respondents were asked to assess the civility and the relevance of each commercial.[5] We turn to the results of the 2014 CCES and 2015 ASU survey experiment.

Responses to Alterations in the Civility of Negative Commercials

We begin by exploring whether respondents to the 2014 CCES survey rate commercials differently depending on whether they receive the civil or the uncivil version of the political commercial. In particular, we ask people to rate the civility of a series of advertisements with the following question: "Thinking about the tone of the advertisement, would you characterize the tone of the advertisement as overly hostile (1), somewhat hostile (2), or not hostile at all (3)?" The findings are presented in Table 6.1. The first column presents data from the 2014 CCES survey experiment, and the second column presents data from the ASU 2015 study.

The findings indicate people in the 2014 CCES study are able to differentiate between the civil and uncivil versions of the advertisements. The findings from the analysis of variance show that people view the uncivil versions of the advertisements as less civil than the civil version of the advertisement for seven of the eight commercials, with differences reaching statistical significance in four of the eight cases. For example, people who view the civil version of the negative advertisement tying the Republican incumbent to Wall Street

---

4. See Appendix D for the script of each advertisement used in the 2015 ASU study as well as a YouTube link to the actual advertisement. We looked for differences in people's ratings of the commercials attacking men and women candidates, but we detected no significant differences, so we combined assessments of advertisements aimed at men and women candidates. For instance, we combined people's assessments of the relevance and civility of the uncivil Obamacare advertisement targeting Begich and Landrieu.

5. While the 2015 ASU online study enables us to see how people react to actual advertisements varying in their civility, we realize that study has limitations. First, subjects were asked to respond to negative advertisements aired about a year after the election. Second, they were asked to rate advertisements about candidates running for Senate elections in races outside of their states. Third, the respondents are students and are not representative of the nation's electorate.

Table 6.1 Differences in Assessments of Negative Advertising Based on the
Experimental Manipulation of Civility

	2014 CCES	2015 ASU
Democratic Candidates		
Ad #1: Obamacare (Incumbent)		
Civility	1.97 (.05)	3.08 (.08)
Incivility	1.81 (.05)	2.57 (.06)
	F=5.03 ** (n=393)	F=25.49*** (n=529)
Ad #2: Went Washington (Incumbent)		
Civility	2.05 (.05)	
Incivility	1.78 (.05)	
	F=13.20 *** (n=363)	
Ad #1: Rubber Stamp on Obama (Nonincumbent)		
Civility	1.99 (.05)	3.06 (.08)
Incivility	1.92 (.05)	2.76 (.06)
	F=1.18 (n=419)	F=9.49*** (n=530)
Ad #2: Liberal Agenda (Nonincumbent)		
Civility	1.92 (.05)	
Incivility	1.93 (.05)	
	F=0.01 (n=412)	
Republican Candidates		
Ad #1: Wall Street Ties (Incumbent)		
Civility	2.02 (.05)	
Incivility	1.70 (.04)	
	F=24.13***(n=423)	
Ad #2: Shut Down Government (Incumbent)		
Civility	1.86 (.05)	3.25 (.10)
Incivility	1.78 (.05)	3.16 (.10)
	F=1.49 (n=428)	F=0.43 (n=264)
Ad #1 Koch Brothers (Nonincumbent)		
Civility	1.90 (.05)	3.51 (.06)
Incivility	1.69 (.04)	2.77 (.06)
	F=9.53*** (n=407)	F=66.52 *** (n=530)

Table 6.1 Continued

	2014 CCES	2015 ASU
<u>Ad #2: Abortion</u> (Nonincumbent)		
Civility	1.88 (.06)	
Incivility	1.87 (.06)	
	F=.003 (n=401)	

Note: The results are based on one-way ANOVA. For the CCES survey, civility is measured with the following question: "Thinking about the tone of the advertisement, would you characterize the tone of the advertisement as overly hostile (1), somewhat hostile (2), or not hostile at all (3)?" For the ASU survey, civility is measured with the following question: "Thinking about the tone of the first advertisement, how would you characterize the tone of the advertisement on a scale ranging from (1) Very hostile to (5) Not hostile at all?"

* p<.10.

** p<.05.

*** p<.01.

rate the advertisement somewhat hostile (i.e., 2.02). In comparison, people exposed to the uncivil version of the advertisement view the advertisement as significantly more negative (i.e., 1.70).

In addition, we look at whether people in the 2015 ASU survey experiment rate the uncivil advertisement as less civil than the civil version of the same advertisement. In the 2015 ASU survey, we measure civility on a five-point scale, ranging from very hostile (1) to not hostile at all (5).[6] The findings presented in the second column in Table 6.1 show that respondents, similar to respondents in the 2014 CCES survey, distinguish between advertisements varying in civility. In three of the four commercials, people view the uncivil version of the advertisements as significantly less civil than the civil version. The biggest difference is seen in the advertisements linking Republican nonincumbents to the Koch brothers. People viewing the civil version of the Koch brothers' advertisement give an average civility rating of 3.51, while people viewing the uncivil version rate the advertisement almost one point lower (i.e., 2.77) on the five-point scale.

In summary, our first test reveals that people discriminate between civil and uncivil negative messages across a number of campaigns, across several

---

6. "Thinking about the tone of the first advertisement, how would you characterize the tone of the advertisement on a scale ranging from (1) Very hostile to (5) Not hostile at all?"

different topics, across two modalities (text and video), and across two types of subject pools (one of citizens in real time and one with student subjects a year later). The results are clear: respondents viewed the civil and uncivil messages differently and scored them accordingly. The 2014 CCES data, in particular, show us that people have the ability to sort out differences related to the civility of political advertisements in the midst of competitive campaigns. We now examine whether people's tolerance of negativity affects their assessments of negative advertisements during an ongoing campaign, controlling for important political predispositions.

Understanding People's Views of the Civility of Negative Advertisements

Can we explain people's impressions of the civility of attack advertisements with levels of tolerance while controlling for rival explanations and in real time? We develop models incorporating a set of variables we expect will influence people's assessments of the civility of negative commercials. First, we expect people who tolerate incivility poorly to be less likely to view negative commercials as civil. In particular, people with a low tolerance for uncivil negative messages will rate negative commercials as less civil compared to people with higher tolerance levels.

Second, we expect people's assessments of the civility of negative messages will be affected by their political proclivities. For example, a strong Democrat viewing a negative commercial attacking a Democratic senator running for reelection is likely to view the commercial as less civil than a strong Republican viewing the exact same commercial. Differences in people's political inclinations can lead potential voters to view the same advertisement in very different ways (e.g., Gervais, 2014, 2016).

Consider the following advertisement, which aired against Democrat Jeanne Shaheen in her bid for reelection to the U.S. Senate in New Hampshire: "Senator Jeanne Shaheen told the lie of the year. She told you that if you liked your insurance plan, you could keep your insurance. But President Obama and Senator Shaheen knew it was impossible for the government to keep their promise. Health care costs are up and so is the cost of Medicare. Senator Shaheen, you looked us in the eyes and lied." We expect Democrats and Republicans will react very differently to this advertisement. Democrats are more likely to view the advertisement as crossing the bounds of good taste, while Republicans are more likely to see the advertisement as "fair game." In the language of motivated reasoning, Democrats will be more motivated to reject the negative commercial attacking the Democratic senator compared to Republicans (e.g., Redlawsk, 2002; Redlawsk, Civettini, and Emmerson, 2010; Taber and Lodge, 2006).

Furthermore, we expect people's views about the content of the negative advertisement will influence their views regarding the tone of the advertisement. In particular, certain messages are more aligned with people's specific policy positions, thereby influencing how these individuals view the civility of these messages. For example, Democratic incumbents were criticized for casting the deciding vote on Obamacare. People who are most opposed to Obamacare will be more receptive to this message, leading these individuals to view the Obamacare advertisements as civil. Similarly, Republican nonincumbents were attacked for their extreme position on abortion. Pro-life respondents are unlikely to consider these criticisms as important since they conflict with their policy views. Therefore, we expect people with strong pro-life attitudes to view these anti-abortion advertisements as uncivil. It is important, then, for us to measure the attitudes of voters on the issues represented in the ads.[7]

We identify specific measures available in 2014 CCES common content to assess people's attitudes toward the issues discussed in each of the eight commercials. We begin with the negative advertisement attacking Democratic incumbents for their stand on Obamacare. We utilize the following series of questions to assess people's attitudes toward Obamacare: "Would you have voted for the Affordable Care Act if you were in Congress in 2010?"; "Would you vote to repeal the Affordable Care Act if you were in Congress today?"; "Should your state refuse to implement the expansion of health care for poor people, even if it costs the state federal Medicaid funds?"[8] The second commercial attacks Democratic incumbents for "going Washington." We employ a measure capturing attitudes toward the Washington establishment with the following question: "How much of the time can you trust your district's representative in Congress to do what is right—just about always, most of the time, or only some of the time?"

Turning to the advertisements attacking Democratic nonincumbents for being a rubber stamp of Obama's policies and for endorsing the liberal

---

7. Scholars have developed measures of voters' positions on issues utilizing the CCES over the past decade (e.g., Ansolabahere and Jones, 2010).

8. Respondents who said yes to the first question and no to the remaining two questions are most supportive of Obamacare, while people who said no to the first question and yes to the remaining two questions are least supportive of Obamacare.

agenda of Washington elites, we measure people's general attitudes to-ward Obama. In particular, we rely on people's responses to the following item: "Do you approve of the way President Obama is doing his job?" Respondents are categorized as strongly disapproving, somewhat disap-proving, somewhat approving, or strongly approving of President Obama's job performance.

Republican incumbents were criticized for their Wall Street ties. We in-clude a measure of the respondent's family income because we expect people with lower levels of income would be more open to critiques of candidates for their Wall Street ties. In addition, Republican incumbents are chastised for shutting down the federal government. We expect the government shutdown message will resonate more with people who dislike the federal government (e.g., people with lower levels of trust in government). Hence, we measure attitudes toward the Washington establishment with the "trust in your repre-sentative" question presented above.

Finally, Republican nonincumbents are attacked for their extreme positions on abortion. Since we expect pro-choice respondents to be more receptive to this advertisement, we measure attitudes toward abortion with the following question: "Do you support or oppose the following proposals: Always allow a woman to obtain an abortion as a matter of choice; Permit abortion only in case of rape, incest or when the woman's life is in danger; Prohibit abortions after the 20th week of pregnancy; Allow employers to decline coverage of abortions in insurance plans; Prohibit the expenditure of funds authorized or appropriated by federal law for any abortion."[9] In the last advertisement attacking Republican nonincumbents, the candidates were criticized for their ties to the Koch brothers. We expect people's openness to this message may depend on their income level, assuming people with less income will be more receptive to the commercial's message, so we include a measure of the respondent's family income when predicting people's assessments of this advertisement.

When developing models to predict people's assessments of the civility of negative commercials, we include a variable measuring the experimental treatment (i.e., civil or uncivil version of the negative advertisement). We ex-pect that people will rate the uncivil version of the advertisement as lower in civility, compared to the civil version of the advertisement, all else being

---

9. People who agree with the first proposal and disagree with the remaining proposals are coded as pro-choice, while people who agree with the limits on abortion and disagree with the first proposal are coded as pro-life.

equal. In summary, we estimate a model where we take into account people's partisanship, their tolerance of negativity, their views of the issue discussed in the advertisements, as well as the experimental manipulation of civility, in order to explore how people, evaluate the tone of negative commercials.

The results of our analysis examining people's assessments of the civility of the advertisements are presented in Table 6.2. The top panel presents analyses of two advertisements attacking Democratic incumbents and two criticizing Republican incumbents. The bottom panel presents results of two advertisements targeting Democratic nonincumbents and the two focusing on Republican nonincumbents. The explanatory variables are arrayed in the first column of Table 6.2.[10]

We see some evidence that people rate advertisements differently based on the experimental manipulation across the eight advertisements (i.e., the first explanatory variable in both panels). We find the experimental treatment leads to statistically significant differences in civility ratings in three of the eight cases (one for Democratic and Republican incumbents, respectively, and one for the GOP nonincumbents). Controlling for intolerance to negativity, partisanship, and views about issues, the experimental manipulation of civility continues to matter for three of the advertisements.

As an illustration, respondents rate the uncivil version of the advertisement attacking Republican incumbents for their Wall Street ties as significantly more hostile than the alternative version of the same advertisement. A few changes in the text of the advertisement produce important differences in people's assessment of the civility of the message. In the civil version, the advertisement refers to "big banks," while the uncivil versions refer to "corrupt banks." In addition, the final lines of the advertisement differ. In the civil version, the final line reads (inserting Lindsey Graham of South Carolina for illustrative purposes): "That's good for Wall Street, but bad for the people of South Carolina." In the uncivil version, the last line reads, "But Senator Lindsey Graham could care less about middle-class families in South Carolina. Senator Graham is looking out for himself and big banks."

---

10. We combine challengers and candidates in open races into one category. In our analysis, we included a dummy variable for open races, but the variable never reached statistical significance in any of the models, so we dropped the variable from the models presented here. In addition, we looked at whether the gender of the targeted candidate affected people's assessments of the civility and relevance of political advertisements. However, the gender variable did not consistently or significantly influence assessments of the advertisements; the gender variable reached statistical significance in only two of the 16 models presented in Table 6.2 and Table 6.3.

Table 6.2 Logistic Ordinal Regression Predicting Civility Ratings of Negative Ads

Target of Advertisement	Democratic Incumbents		Republican Incumbents	
	Ad #1 (Obamacare)	Ad#2 (Went Washington)	Ad #1 (Wall Street Ties)	Ad#2 (Shutdown)
Civil/Uncivil Advertisements	−.24 (.21)[1]	−.67 (.23) ***	−1.52 (.22) ***	−.39 (.26)
Party Identification	.21 (.06) ***	.37 (.06) ***	−.17 (.06) **	−.25 (.06) ***
Ad-Specific Attitude	−.39 (.10) ***	−.47 (.15) ***	−.06 (.04)	−.47 (.17) ***
Intolerance of Incivility	−.34 (.07) ***	−.31 (.08) ***	−.11 (.10)	−.30 (.09) ***
Threshold 1	−2.88 (.59) ***	−2.28 (.66) ***	−1.81 (.77) ***	−4.54 (.85) ***
Threshold 2	−.36 (.56)	.32 (.65)	.67 (.77)	−2.23 (.80) ***
Model Chi^2	104.81 ***	94.06 ***	47.59 ***	38.99 ***
−2 Log Likelihood	483.92	441.19	391.84	361.16
DF	4	4	4	4
Pseudo R-Squared (Cox and Snell).	.25	.26	.19	.15
N	361	308	220	238

Target of Advertisement	Democratic Incumbents		Republican Incumbents	
	Ad #1 (Obamacare)	Ad #2 (Went Washington)	Ad #1 (Wall Street Ties)	Ad #2 (Shutdown)
Civil/Uncivil Advertisements	−.26 (.20)	−.23 (.20)	−.48 (.18) ***	−.11 (.17)
Party Identification	.24 (.07) ***	.09 (.07)	−.33 (.05) ***	−.20 (.05) ***
Ad-Specific Attitude	.01 (.12)	−.39 (.13) ***	−.01 (.03)	.29 (.06) ***
Intolerance of Incivility	−.43 (.07) ***	−.30 (.07) ***	−.02 (.06)	−.03 (.05)
Threshold 1	−2.65 (.71) ***	−3.08 (.71) ***	−1.85 (.47) ***	−.78 (.44) *
Threshold 2	.23 (.69)	−.72 (.69)	.83 (.47) *	1.20 (.45) ***
Model Chi²	66.20 ***	55.31 ***	44.89 ***	91.07 ***
−2 Log Likelihood	418.40	499.90	580.30	774.60
DF	4	4	4	4
Pseudo R-Squared (Cox and Snell)	.16	.13	.13	.16
N	386	386	486	535

[1] Unstandardized logit coefficients are followed by standard errors in parentheses.

Note: Given the ordinal nature of the dependent variable, we use ordinal regression. We measure the dependent variable with the following question: "Thinking about the tone of the advertisement, would you characterize the tone of the advertisement as overly hostile (1), somewhat hostile (2), or not hostile at all (3)?" Civil/Uncivil Advertisements is the experimental treatment, where o is the civil version of the advertisement and 1 is the uncivil version. Party Identification is measured on a seven-point scale from 1 (strong Democrat) to 7 (strong Republican). Intolerance of Incivility is measured on a scale ranging from 2 (low intolerance) to 8 (high intolerance). For Democratic incumbents, the Ad-Specific Attitude is Obamacare Attitudes for Ad#1 and Trust House Member for Ad#2; for Republican incumbents, the Ad-Specific Attitude is Family Income Level of Respondent for Ad#1 and Trust House Member for Ad#2. For Democratic challengers, the Ad-Specific Attitude is Obama approval for Ad#1 and Ad#2; for Republican challengers, the Ad-Specific Attitude is Family Income Level of Respondent for Ad#1 and Attitudes toward Abortion for Ad#2. See text for more details.

* p<.10.

** p<.05.

*** p<.01.

Next we examine the impact of people's political partisanship on their ratings of the civility of the advertisements. As hypothesized, we find that people's partisanship affects their reactions to the negative commercials. More specifically, when a Democratic candidate is being attacked, Republican voters are more likely to see the attack advertisements as more civil than do Democratic voters exposed to the same commercial. Conversely, when people see an advertisement criticizing a Republican candidate, Democrats are significantly more likely than Republicans to rate the advertisement as less hostile on the three-point civility measure. Party identification powerfully influences civility scores in seven of the eight equations shown in Table 6.2. Simply put, people's perceptions of a negative advertisement depend on who is being attacked because people view attacks through a partisan lens. For example, Democrats view a negative advertisement criticizing Democrat Mark Begich of Alaska for his Washington ties as more uncivil than a similar attack on Republican Mitch McConnell for his connections to Wall Street.

Also, we look at whether people's views on the issue discussed in the negative advertisement affect their assessments of the civility of the message. In five of the eight cases, people's views about the issue discussed in the advertisement significantly influence their impressions of the tone of the commercial. For example, citizens' positions on abortion affected strongly their assessments of the civility of the message attacking Republican nonincumbents. In particular, people who are more supportive of abortion rights are more open to the critique of the Republican as too extreme on abortion and are significantly more likely to view this advertisement as civil compared to people with pro-life beliefs.

Most important for the tolerance and tactics theory of negativity, we expect that people's tolerance for incivility will influence how people view the civility of negative commercials. The findings in Table 6.2 demonstrate people's tolerance levels consistently influence their assessments of the tone of the advertisements. Specifically, as people's intolerance of incivility increases, they are more likely to view the negative commercial as less civil. We find a significant and negative relationship between intolerance toward incivility and civility ratings in five of the eight equations presented in Table 6.2, controlling for partisanship, policy views, and our experimental manipulation of civility.

Overall, the results presented in Table 6.2 demonstrate that people are quite sophisticated in how they judge the tone of attack advertisements and are sensitive to relatively modest changes in tone. In addition, people judge commercials differently depending on whether the advertisements are attacking candidates who share the voters own partisan profiles. When judging the civility of an attack advertisement, people view the advertisement as harsher in tone when aimed at a candidate they like. Furthermore, people's views about the topic of the attack advertisement affect how they view the tone of the advertisement. And their tolerance for civility consistently alters their impressions of specific negative commercials.

Understanding People's Views of the Relevance of Negative Advertisements

We turn next to predicting people's ratings of the relevance of the eight advertisements presented during the survey experiment. The dependent variable is measured with the following question: "Thinking about this advertisement, do you find the advertisement very useful (3); somewhat useful (2); not useful at all (1)?" We include the same independent variables: (1) the experimental manipulation of the civility of the commercial, (2) party identification, (3) attitudes related to the topic of the advertisement, and (4) tolerance toward irrelevance of negative messages.

Beginning with the experimental treatment, we do not expect changes in the tone of the advertisement will consistently influence people's views of the advertisement's usefulness. However, people may view overly harsh attacks as less useful than more restrained criticisms of candidates, even when the relevance of the message is constant. Consider the advertisement attacking the Republican nonincumbent for ties to the Koch brothers. The civil version of the advertisement ends with this sentence (inserting Thom Tillis of North Carolina for illustrative purposes): "Thom Tillis might be a good investment for the Koch brothers, but he's the wrong choice for North Carolina." The uncivil version ends with a tougher tone: "Thom Tillis might be a good investment for the Koch brothers, but he's the wrong choice for North Carolina. Just another politician bought and paid for by out-of-state billionaires. Shame on you, Thom Tillis." We hypothesize that people may view the uncivil advertisement as less useful than advertisements employing a more measured tone.

In addition, we expect people who are less tolerant of irrelevant messages will view advertisements as less useful, compared to people with more tolerance for messages of questionable utility. Furthermore, we hypothesize that a person's political views will color assessments of the utility of negative messages. For instance, Republicans and people with unfavorable views of Obama may view a negative advertisement attacking a Democratic candidate for their support for Obama's agenda as highly relevant. In comparison, Democrats and people with very positive attitudes toward Obama are much less likely to see the relevance of criticizing a candidate for supporting Obama's agenda.

We present these results in Table 6.3. The experimental manipulation of the tone of the advertisement significantly affects relevance scores in two of the eight models. As expected, in these two cases, the uncivil advertisements are rated as significantly less useful than the civil advertisements. While the civility manipulation does not consistently influence relevance assessment, party identification powerfully affects people's views of the advertisement's utility. In particular, party identification significantly shapes people's relevance ratings in seven of the eight models. Republicans are more likely to view attacks on Democrats as relevant, while Democrats are significantly more likely to consider criticisms of Republicans to be useful. For example, Republicans are more likely than Democrats to view as relevant advertisements attacking Democratic nonincumbents as rubber stamps of Obama's policies, while Democrats are more likely than Republicans to consider advertisements tying Republican incumbents to Wall Street banks as a legitimate criticism.

Just as people's partisanship influences their impressions of an advertisement's relevance, we find attitudes related to the issues discussed in the advertisements alter people's views about the advertisement's usefulness. In five of the eight equations in Table 6.3, attitudes related to the issues discussed in the advertisements significantly influence people's impressions of the relevance of the advertisements. For example, people who are less trusting of politicians are more likely to view criticisms of Democratic incumbents as "going Washington" as a relevant critique, compared to people with higher levels of trust in politicians.

We once again find people's level of tolerance for negativity influences their assessments of negative commercials. In this case, we find that people who are more tolerant of irrelevant negative messages are significantly more likely to view negative advertisements as more relevant. We find a significant relationship between tolerance for irrelevant messages and relevance ratings in five of the eight equations presented in Table 6.3. These findings provide support for key elements of the tolerance and tactics theory of negativity; the theory holds up in the face of important rival explanations.

Table 6.3 Logistic Ordinal Regression Predicting Relevance Ratings of Negative Ads

Target of Advertisement	Democratic Incumbents		Republican Incumbents	
	Ad #1 (Obamacare)	Ad #2 (Went Washington)	Ad #1 (Wall Street Ties)	Ad #2 (Shutdown)
Civil/Uncivil Advertisements	-.03 (.21)[1]	-.04 (.22)	-.03 (.27)	-.64 (.26)**
Party Identification	.55 (.06)***	.43 (.06)***	-.32 (.07)***	-.30 (.06)***
Ad-Specific Attitude	-.07 (.06)	-.36 (.15)**	-.18 (.05)***	-.25 (.17)
Intolerance of Irrelevance	-.27 (.08)***	-.05 (.08)	-.10 (.09)	-.03 (.09)
Threshold 1	-.01 (.51)	.12 (.59)	-3.36 (.72)***	-2.64 (.74)***
Threshold 2	1.80 (.53)***	2.16 (.61)***	-1.48 (.69)***	-1.49 (.72)**
Model Chi²	140.53***	81.31***	51.09***	32.37***
-2 Log Likelihood	496.69	467.21	398.89	396.79
DF	4	4	4	4
Pseudo R-Squared (Cox and Snell)	.32	.23	.21	.13
N	366	312	219	235

(continued)

Table 6.3 Continued

Target of Advertisement	Democratic Incumbents		Republican Incumbents	
	Ad #1 (Rubber Stamp)	Ad #2 (Liberal Agenda)	Ad #1 (Koch Brothers)	Ad #2 (Liberal Agenda)
Civil/Uncivil Advertisements	−.03 (.20)	.04 (.20)	−.35 (.18) **	−.21 (.16)
Party Identification	.20 (.07) ***	.10 (.07)	−.38 (.04) ***	−.16 (.04) ***
Ad-Specific Attitude	−.16 (.12)	−.49 (.13) ***	−.11 (.03) ***	.34 (.06) ***
Intolerance of Irrelevance	−.21 (.07) ***	−.27 (.07) ***	−.17 (.06) ***	−.10 (.06) *
Threshold 1	−1.02 (.64)	−2.77 (.65) ***	−3.43 (.47) ***	−1.37 (.44) ***
Threshold 2	.59 (.64) **	−.84 (.64)	−1.51 (.45) ***	−.27 (.43)
Model Chi2	46.46***	78.68***	99.66***	95.69***
−2 Log Likelihood	521.19	524.39	870.468	843.26
DF	4	4	4	4
Pseudo R-Squared (Cox and Snell)	.11	.18	.18	.16
N	384	312	493	541

[1] Unstandardized logit coefficients are followed by standard errors in parentheses.

Note: Given the ordinal nature of the dependent variable, we use ordinal regression. We measure the dependent variable with the following question: "Thinking about this advertisement, do you find the advertisement very useful (3), somewhat useful (2), not useful at all? (1)." Civil/Uncivil Advertisements is the experimental treatment, where o is the civil version of the advertisement and i is the uncivil version of the advertisement. Party Identification is measured on a seven-point scale from 1 (strong Democrat) to 7 (strong Republican). Intolerance of Irrelevance is measured on a scale ranging from 2 (low intolerance) to 8 (high intolerance). For Democratic incumbents, the Ad-Specific Attitude is Obamacare Attitudes for Ad#1 and Trust House Member for Ad#2; for Republican incumbents, the Ad-Specific Attitude is Family Income Level of Respondent for Ad#1 and Trust House Member for Ad#2; for Democratic challengers, the Ad-Specific Attitude is Obama Approval for Ad#1 and Ad#2; for Republican challengers, the Ad-Specific Attitude is Family Income Level of Respondent for Ad#1 and Attitudes toward Abortion for Ad#2. See text for more details.

* p<.10.

** p<.05.

*** p<.01.

Postelection Assessments of the Usefulness of Campaign Strategies

After the 2014 election, the 2014 CCES respondents were contacted and asked a series of questions about the candidates and the campaigns. While we asked a variety of questions about their views of the candidates as well as their own level of political activity, we also asked respondents to assess the usefulness of the campaign advertisement strategies employed by the Democratic and Republican candidates. In particular, respondents were asked whether they felt that the Democratic and Republican candidates chose relevant themes to emphasize during the campaign.[11] We asked about each of the advertisements examined during the preelection questionnaire (e.g., blaming Republicans for the shutdown of government, linking Republicans to the Koch brothers).[12] For example, we asked the following question: "During the 2014 election, Republicans ran negative ads criticizing Democratic incumbents for their support of Obamacare. How useful did you think it was to criticize Democratic incumbents for supporting Obamacare?"

We begin by looking at whether people differed in their assessments of the campaign strategies employed by the Democratic and Republican candidates. Beginning with the attack advertisements aimed at incumbents, the data in Figure 6.1 indicate that advertisements aimed at Democratic incumbents were considered to be significantly more useful than commercials targeting Republican incumbents. In particular, the Republican strategy of criticizing Democrat incumbents for their support of Obamacare as well as for "going Washington" by supporting higher taxes and wasteful spending were considered more relevant messages than commercials blaming Republican incumbents for the shutdown of the federal government or for their ties to Wall Street.

When we look at the advertisements aimed at nonincumbents, the partisan disparity is less consistent (see Figure 6.2). The Republican advertisements do not always produce the highest relevance ratings. However, the attack on Democratic nonincumbents for being a rubber stamp of Obama's "liberal agenda and values" is viewed by respondents as being the most relevant of the four advertising themes. And the Democratic attack on Republican

---

11. See Appendix A for a complete listing of the questions included in the postelection CCES survey.

12. Respondents were asked to rate each advertisement on a four-point scale ranging from "very useful" to "not useful at all."

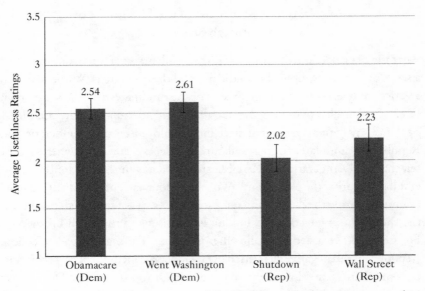

FIGURE 6.1 Postelection assessments of the usefulness of advertisements attacking incumbents.

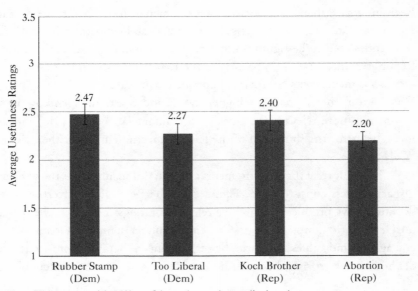

Note: The means, with 95% confidence intervals, are displayed.

FIGURE 6.2 Postelection assessments of the usefulness of advertisements attacking nonincumbents.

nonincumbents for the candidates' extreme stands on abortion is viewed as least relevant. Overall, differences in the relevance ratings for commercials attacking nonincumbents is modest.

The data gathered during the postelection survey suggest that Republicans were somewhat more successful than Democrats at crafting messages that people considered useful. Attacking Democrats for their votes on Obamacare and for supporting a tax-and-spend agenda resonated with voters more than attacking candidates on their ties to Wall Street. Nevertheless, we expect that the partisanship of respondents is likely to influence people's views of the utility of the various advertising strategies. We look at how partisanship colors people's assessments of the candidates' messages in Figure 6.3.

Turning first to incumbents, the data in Figure 6.3 suggest Republican respondents view the attacks on Democratic incumbents for their support for Obamacare and for "going Washington" with their tax-and-spend policies as significantly more relevant than either Democrats or independents. For

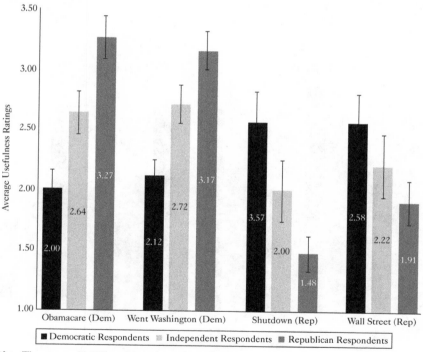

Note: The means, with 95% confidence intervals, are displayed.

FIGURE 6.3 Postelection assessments of the usefulness of advertisements attacking incumbents by the respondent's party.

instance, Republicans rate the Obamacare advertisement as more than one point higher than Democrats do on the four-point relevance scale. Similarly, Democrats are much more likely than Republicans to view as useful an advertisement blaming the Republican incumbent for shutting down the government. Democrats give the advertisement an average relevance rating of 2.57 on the four-point scale, while Republicans, on average, rate the advertisement at 1.48. The partisan difference in relevance ratings is less dramatic for the advertisement criticizing Republican incumbents for their ties to Wall Street.

We see the same partisan differences when we look at people's assessments of the relevance of the commercials attacking nonincumbents (see Figure 6.4). In each case, when the advertisement is attacking the Democratic candidate, Republicans view the advertisement as significantly more relevant than do Democrats. And conversely, when Republican candidates are being criticized, Democratic respondents consider the content of the attacks as more useful than do Republicans. For example, the Democratic attack on Republican challengers for accepting money from the billionaire Koch brothers is rated

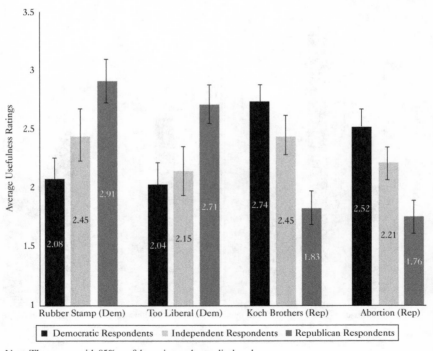

Note: The means, with 95% confidence intervals, are displayed.

FIGURE 6.4 Postelection assessments of the usefulness of advertisements attacking nonincumbents by the respondent's party.

as somewhat useful (average rating of 2.74) by Democrats and not very useful (average rating of 1.83) by Republican respondents.

We look more systematically at the factors driving people's postelection assessments of the relevance of the advertisements criticizing the Democratic and Republican candidates by replicating our earlier analysis presented in Table 6.3, where we predict people's relevance ratings after being exposed to the advertisement script during the preelection period. As we did earlier, we predict relevance ratings by including respondents' partisanship as well as their position on the issue discussed in the advertisement. As before, we also include the measure of tolerance to irrelevant messages since we expect people with low tolerance for irrelevant messages will rate all advertisements as less relevant, compared to people who are more tolerant.[13]

We present our results in Table 6.4. The findings are remarkably similar to the preelection results. As predicted, party identification significantly affects people's views of the advertisements' utility. In seven of the eight models, party identification shapes people's relevance ratings. We continue to see that people's positions on issues influence their views about the usefulness of particular messages. For instance, as people's approval of Obama increases, they are significantly less likely to view the attack on Democrats for being a rubber stamp of Obama's policies as a useful message.

Even after the election is over, people's tolerance for irrelevant messages continues to influence their assessments of the utility of different messages. In four of the eight models, people who are less tolerant of irrelevant advertisements are significantly more likely to view the various campaign messages as less useful compared to people who are more tolerant of irrelevant messages. And this finding appears in the face of stiff controls for partisan attachment and feelings about the issues discussed in the commercials.

Conclusion

The findings in this chapter indicate that the tolerance and tactics theory of negativity helps explain how people react to negative campaign messages. Where do we go from here? We believe we have identified several important findings.

---

13. We do not include the experimental treatment in the postelection models since people are unlikely to be affected by the script presented in the preelection survey when they are reinterviewed several weeks later. We did run an analysis where we included a measure of the civility/incivility treatment in the models in Table 6.4, and the treatment variable significantly influenced relevance scores in only one of the eight models.

Table 6.4 Logistic Ordinal Regression Predicting Postelection Relevance Ratings for Negative Advertising Strategy

Target of Advertisement	Democratic Incumbents		Republican Incumbents	
	Ad #1 (Obamacare)	Ad #2 (Went Washington)	Ad #1 (Wall Street Ties)	Ad#2 (Shutdown)
Party Identification	.38 (.05)[1] ***	.39 (.05) ***	−.31 (.06) ***	−.39 (.07) ***
Ad-Specific Attitude	−.07 (.05)	−.26 (.12) **	−.03 (.17)	−.08 (.04) *
Intolerance of Irrelevance	−.14 (.07) **	−.10 (.07)	−.05 (.09)	.01 (.10)
Threshold 1	−.83 (.45) *	−1.61 (.52) ***	−2.53 (.72) ***	−2.42 (.69) ***
Threshold 2	.33 (.45)	−0.01 (.51)	1.36 (.70) *	−1.27 (.68) *
Threshold 3	1.51 (.45) ***	1.62 (.52) ***	.30 (.70)	.11 (67)
Model Chi^2	90.54***	85.13***	28.92***	45.76***
−2 Log Likelihood	611.80	601.47	370.57	411.14
DF	3	3	3	3
Pseudo R-Squared (Cox and Snell).	.20	.20	.13	.21
N	404	396	200	197

Target of Advertisement	Democratic Nonincumbents		Republican Nonincumbents	
	Ad #1 (Rubber Stamp)	Ad#2 (Liberal Agenda)	Ad #1 (Koch Brothers)	Ad#2 (Abortion)
Party Identification	.08 (.07)	.18 (.07)**	−.35 (.04)***	−.24 (.05)***
Ad-Specific Attitude	−.50 (.14)***	−.25 (.13)*	−.01 (.03)	.21 (.05)***
Intolerance of Irrelevance	−.34 (.07)***	−.42 (.07)***	−.07 (.06)	−.16 (.06)***
Threshold 1	−4.23 (.70)***	−3.38 (.67)***	−2.95 (.44)***	−2.33 (.42)***
Threshold 2	−2.73 (.68)***	−1.89 (.65)***	−1.65 (.43)***	−0.68 (.41)*
Threshold 3	−1.21 (.67)***	−.14 (.65)	−0.32 (.42)	0.76 (.41)*
Model Chi2	74.94***	75.85***	79.90***	87.11***
−2 Log Likelihood	466.46	481.58	1053.54	885.30
DF	3	3	3	3
Pseudo R-Squared (Cox and Snell)	.21	.20	.16	.15
N	323	336	470	515

[1] Unstandardized logit coefficients are followed by standard errors in parentheses.

Note: Given the ordinal nature of the dependent variable, we use ordinal regression. The dependent variable was measured on a four-point scale ranging from very useful (4) to not useful at all (1). Party Identification is measured on a seven-point scale from 1 (strong Democrat) to 7 (strong Republican). Intolerance of Irrelevance is measured on a scale ranging from 2 (low intolerance) to 8 (high intolerance). For Democratic incumbents, the Ad-Specific Attitude is Obamacare Attitudes for Ad#1 and Trust House Member for Ad#2; for Republican incumbents, the Ad-Specific Attitude is Family Income Level of Respondent for Ad#1 and Trust House Member for Ad#2; for Democratic challengers, the Ad-Specific Attitude is Obama Approval for Ad#1 and Ad#2; for Republican challengers, the Ad-Specific Attitude is Family Income Level of Respondent for Ad#1 and Attitudes toward Abortion for Ad#2. See text for more details.

* p<.10.

** p<.05.

*** p<.01.

First, people's level of tolerance consistently and powerfully influences how they perceive and interpret negative campaign rhetoric: those with a low level of tolerance readily see more incivility in negative messages and view negative messages as less useful when compared to citizens who tolerate negative campaigning more easily. We find that tolerance for incivility and tolerance for irrelevant messages are both important and significantly alter how people evaluate negative commercials.

Second, the importance of tolerance for negativity holds up when we take into account important political predispositions, such as party attachment and attitudes about the issues highlighted in the commercials. These findings demonstrate that tolerance for negativity is different from people's partisan and policy profiles. Even in the face of powerful controls long known to shape people's attitudes about political messages and politicians, we find people's tolerance for uncivil and irrelevant discourse shapes their views of negative advertisements.

Third, the importance of tolerance for negativity is critical during the throes of the campaign as well as after the campaign has ended and all votes are tallied. This finding provides some evidence about the stability and resilience of the concept. It is good to know citizens' tolerance for negativity is not transitory and is visible only at certain times during political campaigns, such as in the heat of the campaign.

All told, these findings point us toward a culminating examination of whether the tolerance and tactics theory of negativity helps us to understand the impact of negative advertising during campaigns. We turn to the final test of our theory in chapter 7. There we examine whether tolerance of negativity, combined with the relevance and civility of the negative advertisements peppering the electoral landscape, shape people's beliefs and behaviors during the campaign. We explore how people's tolerance for negativity influences the impact of negative messages. We predict this key interplay will produce differences in citizens' evaluations of the candidates as well as altering their likelihood of voting in Senate elections.

How Negative Campaigning Influences Citizens' Evaluations of Candidates and Likelihood of Voting

CITIZENS IN REPRESENTATIVE democracies must make two key decisions during political campaigns: Should I go to the polls? and Whom should I support? These decisions are important for understanding how effectively campaigns fulfill the legitimacy and accountability aspects of elections where citizens decide who will govern their lives. We are poised to test whether the tolerance and tactics theory of negativity helps predict and explain these two decisions made by citizens every other fall during federal elections in the United States. Negative campaign appeals do provide, if nothing else, an extensive amount of information about politicians and the policies and programs they promote (Geer, 2006). In this chapter we demonstrate how the interplay among people's level of tolerance for negative campaigning and the relevance and civility of negative messages influences their evaluations of the competing candidates as well as their eventual decisions to vote on Election Day. We combine the 2014 CCES survey data with information about the airing and content of negative advertisements in order to connect people's attitudes and actions about the senatorial contestants with their campaign environment.

The tolerance and tactics theory of negativity contends that citizens will consider the relevance of negative campaign messages when developing impressions of candidates. We have shown that people are quite adept at distinguishing between relevant (e.g., Senator Pryor's of Arkansas support for Obamacare) and irrelevant messages (e.g., Senator Hagan's missing one subcommittee vote on the Armed Services Committee). We argue that citizens pay the most attention to criticisms of candidates if these criticisms are focused on topics people consider relevant to governing. However, we also believe the civility of the message will alter the impact of relevant messages. We theorize that the most influential negative appeal is one whose uncivil message is focused on a relevant topic. The incivility heightens people's attention to relevant messages, producing the most powerful negative impressions of the targeted candidates. Relevant and civil messages will influence assessments of targeted candidates too, but the impact will be less consequential since civil messages are less likely to capture the attention of voters. Finally, as we discussed earlier, we do not expect irrelevant messages, delivered in a civil or uncivil manner, to influence people's evaluations of targeted candidates.

Knowing the relevance and civility of negative messages, although important for understanding the impact of negative advertising, is insufficient for developing a more comprehensive explanation of how negative criticisms influence voters' decisions about candidates. As we have theorized throughout this book, it is necessary to consider an individual's tolerance for negativity. Negative information will be far less influential for people with a high tolerance for negativity (i.e., individuals who think irrelevant and uncivil messages are fair game). In contrast, people who are more sensitive to negativity (i.e., citizens with a low tolerance for uncivil and irrelevant messages) will be *more* affected by the relevance and civility of negative messages.

We have shown in chapters 3 and 6 that people's tolerance for negative messages is orthogonal to standard political variables, like partisanship and political interest. Instead people vary predictably in their receptivity to negative political rhetoric. Some people have an easier time tolerating all types of negative messages, while others find uncivil and irrelevant negative messages to be unhelpful and bothersome. For example, we have shown that men and younger people tend to be more tolerant of negativity compared to women and older individuals.

In this chapter, we utilize the 2014 CCES survey data to test specific predictions of the tolerance and tactics theory of negativity. We begin by examining how people's evaluations of Senate candidates are influenced by the civility and relevance of the negative messages disseminated during the campaign. For each survey respondent living in a state with a Senate campaign, we create a measure capturing the relevance and civility of the negative messages aimed at each of the Senate rivals.[1] We can then estimate how

---

1. We employ several steps to create the variable assessing the negativity of messages aimed at a candidate. First, for each candidate, we calculate the average relevance and civility scores of all the negative advertisements targeting the candidate during the 2014 campaign. These scores

these negative messages influence people's evaluations of the Democratic and Republican senatorial candidates.

We begin by exploring whether negative advertisements lower evaluations of a targeted candidate. We focus on two aspects of candidate evaluation: (1) citizens' impressions of the candidates' personality traits (i.e., competence and integrity) and (2) citizens' overall favorability ratings for each candidate. Our analyses take place in two steps. First, we examine how negative campaign messages shape people's evaluations of the candidates. With this initial analysis, we examine how the interplay between the tone (civility) and the content (relevance) of the messages shapes citizens' views of the competing candidates. Second, we examine whether citizens' tolerance of negative campaigning affects how the civility and relevance of negative messages influences people's impressions of candidates.

We need to control for several rival variables in order to estimate properly the impact of the relevance and civility of negative advertisements on people's assessments of the candidates. First, it is important to measure the ideological and political characteristics of the respondents. We know from decades of research that people are much more likely to develop favorable impressions of candidates who share their partisan and ideological profile (e.g., Bafumi and Shapiro, 2009; Campbell et al., 1960; Jacobson and Carson, 2015).

In addition, we control for the candidate's status as an incumbent, since people often develop more positive views of their incumbent senators (e.g., Ansolabehere and Snyder, 2002).[2] Senators running for reelection are advantaged at the polls partly because sitting senators tend to get more press attention and more positive press treatment than nonincumbents. This incumbency advantage in news coverage produces more positive impressions of incumbent senators (e.g., Ansolabehere, Snowberg, and Snyder, 2006;

---

are based on our content analysis findings (see chapter 4). Second, we divide the relevance and civility scores at their means to categorize the negative advertisements for each candidate as relevant or irrelevant and as civil or uncivil. Third, guided by our theory, we combine these two binary measures to develop the relevance/incivility measure: negative advertisements that are relevant and uncivil receive a score of 3, negative advertisements that are relevant and civil receive a score of 2, and negative advertisements that are irrelevant receive a score of 1. Fourth, we multiply the three-point scale by the number of negative advertisements aired in the state to capture the intensity of the negative message. Fifth, we divide the resulting score by 10,000 to make the estimated coefficients more interpretable since the mean and variance of the relevance/incivility measure are quite large (the mean is 6,472 with a range of 59,109 for the relevance/incivility measure targeting Republicans; the mean is 4,861 with a range of 43,936 for the relevance/incivility measure targeting Democrats).

2. We originally included a measure identifying the gender of the candidate, but this measure failed to reach statistical significance in the models presented in this chapter.

Prior, 2006). Also, incumbent senators provide goods and services to their constituents, generating positive feelings among voters (e.g., Johannes and McAdams, 1981; Westlye, 1991). In addition, we include a binary measure assessing whether the candidate is running in an open race (i.e., no incumbent on the ballot) since candidates contesting open seats tend to be high-quality candidates (e.g., Squire, 1989) and respondents may develop more positive impressions of these candidates compared to challengers facing incumbents.

In addition, we include a question assessing whether respondents say they regularly watch television news. We showed in chapter 4 that the bulk of negative advertisements aired during news programs, making it crucial to control for people's likelihood of watching television news when predicting evaluations of the candidates. We include a measure assessing differences in campaign spending by the Democratic and Republican candidates to measure the relative strength of the rival campaigns.[3] With our control measures in place, we examine how negative messages influence impressions of Senate candidates.

Understanding People's Assessments of the Personal Traits of Senatorial Candidates

We begin our analysis by examining how the relevance and incivility of negative messages influence people's assessments of the personal traits of the Senate candidates. Respondents were asked to rate the Democratic and Republican candidates on two trait dimensions: competence and trustworthiness. These two trait dimensions have been shown to influence overall impressions of candidates as well as eventual vote choice in presidential and senatorial campaigns (e.g., Bartels, 2002; Funk, 1996; Hayes, 2010; Markus, 1982). During the October preelection survey, respondents were asked to evaluate how well the word "competent" and the word "trustworthy" described each candidate on a scale from "extremely well" (4) to "not well at all" (1).[4] The average score across these two traits for the Democratic and Republican

3. We develop a proportional measure of campaign spending where we divide the natural log of Democratic candidate spending per eligible voter by the natural log of total spending per eligible voter (Democratic plus Republican candidate). We use the natural log of spending to estimate the diminishing returns of spending (Jackson and Carsey, 2007). We reestimated the models with different specifications of spending (e.g., logging to base 10, spending without logging), but these different specifications did not change the substantive results of the models.

4. See full survey in Appendix A.

candidates hovers around 2.33, suggesting people thought the words "competent" and "trustworthy" described the candidates "not too well."

We are interested in seeing whether the civility and relevance of the negative messages delivered during the campaign affects how people view the competence and integrity of the candidates running for the U.S. Senate in their state. We develop four models to predict assessments of the personality characteristics of the candidates. Our main variable of interest is the measure of negative advertising capturing the relevance of the topic and the civility of the tone of the advertisements.[5] We present the results of our analysis in Table 7.1.[6]

The findings in Table 7.1 show that the relevance and civility of the negative messages consistently influence people's trait assessments of the Democratic and Republican candidates running for the U.S. Senate. As the relevance and incivility of the advertisements increase, people's evaluations of the targeted candidates decline significantly. This finding occurs for Democratic candidates and Republican candidates and for citizens' evaluations of the candidates' competence as well as evaluations of the candidates' trustworthiness. For example, we find that as the relevance and incivility of the attacks on Democratic candidates increase, people become significantly more critical in their evaluations of the competence of these candidates. The measure of negative campaigning consistently and powerfully influences trait assessments, even in the face of stiff controls.

In addition, we find that the ideology and partisanship of the respondent influence assessments of the candidates' competence and integrity. For example, as people move from the liberal to the conservative end of the ideological scale, they develop significantly more favorable views of the Republican candidates' possession of positive traits, and they are significantly more negative in their assessments of the trait characteristics of Democratic candidates. We find the same pattern for partisanship: Democrats are much more positive in their evaluations of the competence and integrity of Democratic

5. In the models in this chapter, we look only at Senate races where at least one negative advertisement was aired.

6. Given the ordinal nature of the dependent variables (i.e., the dependent variable ranged from 1 to 4), we utilize ordinal regression. For the measures of negative advertising, respondents in each state are given the same negative advertising score. Therefore, the data are clustered by states. We calculated the intracluster correlation (ICC) to see whether multilevel analysis was warranted. We found the ICC never exceeded 2%, meaning that being in the different states contributes to about 2% of the variation in the dependent variables. Given the small ICC, we do not believe that multilevel modeling is necessary for the analysis in this chapter.

Table 7.1 Logistic Ordinal Regression Predicting Trait Assessment of Democratic and Republican Senate Candidates

Target of Advertisement	Democratic Candidates		Republican Candidates	
	Competent	Trustworthy	Competent	Trustworthy
Relevance/ Incivility of Negative Ads	−.21 (.06) ***	−.18 (.06) ***	−.10 (.05) **	−.09 (.05) *
Proportional Spending	.01 (.01)	.02 (.01) **	.001 (.006)	.002 (.006)
Incumbency Status	.80 (.21) ***	.41 (.21) *	.47 (.17) ***	.27 (.17)
Open Race Candidate	.49 (.25) **	.23 (.25)	−.01 (.19)	.01 (.19)
Ideology	−.38 (.06) ***	−.43 (.06) ***	.37 (.05) ***	.39 (.05) ***
Party Identification	−.47 (.05) ***	−.44 (.05) ***	.35 (.05) ***	.38 (.05) ***
Watch TV News	.06 (.17)	.49 (.17) ***	.31 (.17) *	.37 (.17) **
Threshold 1	−5.79 (.41) ***	−5.41 (.40) ***	1.06 (.30) ***	1.71 (.30) ***
Threshold 2	−4.43 (.39) ***	−4.04 (.38) ***	2.55 (.31) ***	3.23 (.32) ***
Threshold 3	−1.79 (.35) ***	−1.49 (.35) ***	5.10 (.36) ***	5.74 (.37) ***
Model Chi2	372.48 ***	370.15***	307.67 ***	321.78 ***
−2 Log Likelihood	1242.35	1235.80	1401.32	1347.02
DF	7	7	7	7
Pseudo R-Squared (Cox and Snell)	.42	.42	.35	.36
N	675	672	715	710

Note: Unstandardized logit coefficients are followed by standard errors in parentheses. To measure competence and trustworthy assessments, respondents are asked how well the word "competent" and the word "trustworthy" described each candidate on a scale ranging from 1 ("not well at all") to 4 ("extremely well"). Given the ordinal nature of the dependent variable, we use ordinal regression. The relevance/incivility measure is created by giving negative advertisements that are relevant and uncivil a score of 3; negative advertisements that are relevant and civil receive a score of 2; and negative advertisements that are irrelevant receive a score of 1. The three-point scale is then multiplied by the number of negative advertisements aired in each state, and the resulting measure is divided by 10,000 for ease of interpretation. The proportional spending measure is created by dividing the natural log of Democratic candidate spending per eligible voter by the natural log of total spending per eligible voter (Democratic plus Republican candidate). Incumbency status measures whether the candidate is an incumbent (1) or not (0). Open race candidate indicates whether the candidate is running in an open race (1 = yes, 0 = no). Ideology is measured on a seven-point scale from 1 (very liberal) to 7 (very conservative). Party identification is measured on a seven-point scale from 1 (strong Democrat) to 7 (strong Republican). Watch TV is a binary variable measuring whether the respondent indicated watching television news in the past 24 hours. See text for more details.

*p<.10.

** p<.05.

*** p<.01.

candidates, while Republican respondents are much more likely to view Republican candidates as being competent and trustworthy.

Turning to the remaining variables in the models, we find some evidence for an incumbency effect in trait evaluations. For instance, both Democratic and Republican incumbents, on average, are rated as more competent than nonincumbents. Also, watching television often increases impressions of the candidates' personality characteristics. In contrast, campaign spending does not have a consistent impact on people's evaluations of the candidates' traits. The results in Table 7.1 show that the proportion of campaign spending is only significantly related to assessments of the candidates' traits in one of the four models.

Understanding People's Ratings of Senatorial Candidates on Feeling Thermometers

We turn next to explaining people's overall impressions of candidates. In particular, we examine people's ratings of the Democratic and Republican Senate candidates on a feeling thermometer ranging from 0 (feeling very unfavorable toward the candidate) to 10 (feeling very favorable). Feeling thermometer ratings have been used extensively by political scientists to assess citizens' impressions of the candidates (e.g., Markus and Converse, 1979) since feeling thermometers are intuitive and easy to use. Furthermore, we know that feeling thermometer ratings powerfully predict vote choice in presidential and Senate elections (e.g., Abramowitz, 1980; Franklin, 1991; Markus and Converse, 1979).

We examine whether the relevance and civility of the negative commercials produce more critical impressions of the Senate candidates. As before, we expect that as the relevance and incivility of negative messages targeting a candidate increase, people will develop significantly more negative views of the candidate being attacked. The incivility of the attacks will capture people's attention, and people will be persuaded by messages that focus on legitimate topics. We continue to control for party, ideology, and television watching of the respondents, the incumbency and open race status of the candidates, as well as relative campaign spending.

We present our results predicting people's feeling thermometer ratings in Table 7.2. The relevance and civility of the negative commercials achieve statistical significance in the model explaining feelings for Democratic candidates: as the incivility and relevance of the attack commercials increase,

Table 7.2 OLS Regression Predicting Feeling Thermometer Ratings
of Democratic and Republican Senate Candidates

Target of Advertisement	Democratic Candidates Feeling Thermometer		Republican Candidates Feeling Thermometer	
Relevance/Incivility of Negative Ads	−.18 (.07) **	−.07	.03 (.05)	.02
Proportional Spending	.03 (.01) ***	.11	−.01 (.01)	−.04
Incumbency Status	.13 (.20)	.02	.57 (.19) ***	.09
Open Race Candidate	.02 (.24)	.003	−.19 (.21)	−.03
Party Identification	−.64 (.05) ***	−.46	.39 (.05) ***	.28
Ideology	−.35 (.06) ***	−.20	.59 (.06) ***	.34
Watch TV News	.38 (.18) **	.06	.35 (.17) **	.05
Constant	8.98 (.29) ***		.39 (.26)	
R^2	.37		.34	
N	851		919	

Note: Unstandardized regression coefficients, with standard errors in parentheses, are followed by standardized coefficients.

The dependent variable is measured from 0 (from very unfavorable) to 10 (very favorable). The relevance/incivility measure is created by giving negative advertisements that are relevant and uncivil a score of 3; negative advertisements that are relevant and civil receive a score of 2; and negative advertisements that are irrelevant receive a score of 1. The three-point scale is then multiplied by the number of negative advertisements aired in each state, and the resulting measure is divided by 10,000 for ease of interpretation. The proportional spending measure is created by dividing the natural log of Democratic candidate spending per eligible voter by the natural log of total spending per eligible voter (Democratic plus Republican candidate).). Incumbency status measures whether the candidate is an incumbent (1) or not (0). Open race candidate indicates whether the candidate is running in an open race (1 = yes; 0 = no). Ideology is measured on a seven-point scale from 1 (very liberal) to 7 (very conservative). Party identification is measured on a seven-point scale from 1 (strong Democrat) to 7 (strong Republican). Watch TV is a binary variable measuring whether the respondent indicated watching television news in the past 24 hours. See text for more details.

* p<.10.

** p<.05.

*** p<.01.

people's impressions of the candidates become more negative. In the model predicting overall impressions of the Republican candidates, the parameter estimate for the relevance and civility of negative commercials is far from statistically significant.

The remaining variables in the models perform as expected. We find Republicans are more favorable to Republican candidates compared to Democratic candidates and vice versa. We detect a similarly strong relationship between people's ideological positions and their views of the candidates. We find an incumbency effect, but only for Republican candidates who are evaluated significantly more positively than nonincumbents. We also find that relative campaign spending matters, but only for Democratic candidates: as Democratic spending increases, compared to Republicans, people's impressions of Democratic candidates becomes more positive. As before, we find that people who watch television news are more likely to have favorable views of the Republican and Democratic candidates.

Overall, across the six models examining evaluations of Senate candidates, we find that as the relevance and incivility of negative commercials increase, people's evaluations of the Senate candidates decline significantly in five of the six cases.[7] But, as we have argued, these findings are incomplete because people are not affected by negative campaigning equally. In particular, the tolerance and tactics theory of negativity predicts that people who are the least tolerant of negativity will be most influenced by attack advertising during campaigns. The impact of these messages will be greater because these individuals are more sensitive to the content and tone of the negative advertisements. We now take a closer look at the interplay between citizens' tolerance of negativity and the candidates' tactics.

To test whether tolerance for uncivil and irrelevant messages influences the impact of negative campaigning, we combine the measures of citizens' intolerance for uncivil messages and intolerance for irrelevant messages into a single index, ranging from 4 (high tolerance) to 16 (low tolerance).[8] We then divide our sample at the mean and reestimate the equations presented in Tables 7.1 and 7.2 for people with a low tolerance for

---

7. We replicated the analysis in Tables 7.1 and 7.2 with a traditional measure of negativity that simply assesses the proportion of negative commercials disseminated during the campaign (see Stevens, 2009). In particular, we divide the number of negative advertisements aired attacking a candidate by the total number of advertisements aired about the candidate. We include this traditional measure of negativity because we want to be certain our measure of relevance and civility is not simply picking up overall levels of negativity. We included the traditional variable of negativity in each model and replicated the analyses. When we include the traditional negativity measure, the relevance/incivility measure continues to be significant in four of the six models in Tables 7.1 and 7.2. The traditional measure of negativity achieves statistical significance in only two of the six models.

8. The mean tolerance level for the 2014 CCES sample is 12.11 with a standard deviation of 2.54.

negative messages and for individuals with a high tolerance for negative messages. We begin by looking at whether people's tolerance for negativity influences the impact of negative messages on people's assessments of the candidates' personal characteristics. These analyses are presented in Table 7.3.

The findings in Table 7.3 illustrate that people's level of tolerance for negativity alters their responsiveness to negative advertising. The models in the top panel of Table 7.3 examine people who are tolerant of negativity. These results show that the relevance and civility measure of negative campaigning fails to influence people's trait assessments in any of the four models. In contrast, when we examine people who are less tolerant of negativity, the bottom panel of Table 7.3, we find negative messages are more influential. Specifically, as the uncivil and relevant content of negative messages increases, people's views of the Democratic and Republican candidates become significantly more negative in three of the four equations. We believe the findings in Table 7.3 provide evidence that people's tolerance for negativity shapes the impact of negative advertising on people's assessments of the candidates. People who are the least tolerant of negative messages are most influenced by attack advertising during Senate campaigns, whereas people with high levels of tolerance are far less affected.[9]

When we look at people's overall impressions of the Senate candidates, relying on feeling thermometer scores, we find some support for our expectation that negative messages will be more influential for people with low tolerance for negativity (see Table 7.4). First, looking at the models for people who are tolerant of negativity, we find that changes in the relevance and incivility of negative messages fail to significantly alter impressions of the Democratic and Republican candidates. In addition, and as expected, when we examine people who are less tolerant of negativity, we find the coefficient capturing the civility and relevance of the negative messages is correctly signed in both models and reaches statistical significance in the model predicting evaluations of Democratic candidates.

---

9. By comparing the size of the unstandardized coefficients for the "relevance/incivility" measures across low- and high-tolerance respondents, we see additional evidence that people with less tolerance for negativity are more affected by relevant and uncivil negative messages. The size of the coefficients is always larger in the models for low-tolerance respondents, and sometimes the difference in the magnitude of the coefficients is quite dramatic (e.g., the relevance/incivility coefficient is nine times larger for assessments of the Republican candidate's competence for respondents with low tolerance for negativity, compared to respondents with more tolerance).

Table 7.3 Logistic Ordinal Regression Predicting Trait Assessments of Democratic and Republican Senate Candidates by Tolerance toward Negativity

Target of Advertisement	Democratic Candidates		Republican Candidates	
	Competent	Trustworthy	Competent	Trustworthy
	Tolerant of Negativity			
Relevance/Incivility of Negative Ads	−.13 (.10)	−.16 (.10)	.02 (.07)	−.06 (.07)
Proportional Spending	.01 (.01)	.008 (.01)	−.002 (.008)	−.002 (.008)
Incumbency Status	.68 (.30)**	.22 (.30)	.97 (.25)***	.61 (.24)**
Open Race Candidate	.39 (.37)	−.09 (.37)	.25 (.28)	.43 (.27)
Ideology	−.46 (.08)***	−.52 (.08)***	.39 (.07)***	.36 (.07)***
Party Identification	−.38 (.07)***	−.41 (.07)***	−.35 (.06)***	−.37 (.06)***
Watch TV News	−.29 (.27)	.33 (.28)	.45 (.26)	.64 (.26)**
Threshold 1	−5.75 (.63)***	−5.35 (.62)***	.18 (.44)	0.69 (.42)
Threshold 2	−4.33 (.59)***	−3.87 (.58)***	2.07 (.46)***	2.45 (.44)***
Threshold 3	−1.24 (.53)**	−.74 (.53)**	4.66 (.51)***	5.03 (.50)***
Model Chi^2	163.29***	184.51***	159.01***	152.48***
−2 Log Likelihood	589.35	581.05	677.87	703.39
DF	7	7	7	7
Pseudo R-Squared (Cox and Snell)	.41	.44	.37	.35
N	313	317	322	352

(continued)

Table 7.3 Continued

Target of Advertisement	Democratic Candidates		Republican Candidates	
	Competent	Trustworthy	Competent	Trustworthy
	Intolerant of Negativity			
Relevance/Incivility of Negative Ads	-.28 (.09) ***	-.21 (.09) **	-.18 (.07) **	-.10 (.07)
Proportional Spending	.01 (.01)	.02 (.01) *	-.01 (.01)	-.002 (.01)
Incumbency Status	1.05 (.32) ***	.92 (.32) ***	.12 (.27)	.17 (.29)
Open Race Candidate	.87 (.38) **	-.66 (.38) *	.16 (.29)	.41 (.31)
Ideology	-.30 (.09) ***	-.25 (.10) **	.34 (.09) ***	.39 (.10) ***
Party Identification	-.63 (.08) ***	-.65 (.09) ***	.44 (.08) ***	.50 (.08) ***
Watch TV News	.35 (.27)	.19 (.27)	.27 (.26)	.20 (.28)
Threshold 1	-6.93 (.66) ***	-6.43 (.64) ***	1.78 (.47) ***	2.86 (.51) ***
Threshold 2	-5.28 (.60) ***	-4.69 (.58) ***	3.15 (.50) ***	4.39 (.55) ***
Threshold 3	-2.68 (.53) ***	-2.30 (.52) ***	5.93 (.58) ***	7.00 (.64) ***
Model Chi^2	203.90***	187.99***	154.75***	172.20***
-2 Log Likelihood	519.08	526.76	593.30	541.67
DF	7	7	7	7
Pseudo R-Squared (Cox and Snell)	.50	.48	.40	.45
N	294	286	304	292

Note: Unstandardized logit coefficients are followed by standard errors in parentheses.
See Table 7.1 and text for information on the coding of the independent and dependent variables.

* p<.10.

** p<.05.

*** p<.01.

Table 7.4 OLS Regression Predicting Feeling Thermometer Ratings of Democratic and Republican Senate Candidates by Tolerance of Negativity

Target of Advertisement	Democratic Candidates Feeling Thermometer		Republican Candidates Feeling Thermometer	
	Tolerant of Negativity			
Relevance/Incivility of Negative Ads	−.11 (.10)	−.04	.13 (.08)	.07
Proportional Spending	.03 (.01) ***	.12	−.02 (.01)**	−.07
Incumbency Status	.10 (.30)	.02	1.07 (.27) ***	.17
Open Race Candidate	−.46 (.37)	−.06	.27 (.32)	.04
Ideology	−.43 (.09) ***	−.25	.61 (.09) ***	.37
Party Identification	−.71 (.07) ***	−.50	.37 (.07) ***	.27
Watch TV News	.43 (.29)	.06	.24 (28)	.03
Constant	9.29 (.42) ***		0.24 (.39)	
R²	.46		.38	
N	354		410	
	Intolerant of Negativity			
Relevance/Incivility of Negative Ads	−.22 (.12) *	−.08	−.06 (.08)	−.03
Proportional Spending	.005(.01)	.01	−.01 (.01)	−.04
Incumbency Status	.26 (.33)	.04	.46 (.32)	.07
Open Race Candidate	.47 (.39)	.07	−.60(.34) *	−.08
Ideology	−.12 (.11)	−.07	.56 (.11) ***	.31
Party Identification	−.80 (.09) ***	−.55	.51 (.09) ***	.34
Watch TV News	.31 (.29)	.05	.60 (.28) **	.09
Constant	8.87 (.45) ***		−.002 (.39)	
R²	.37		.42	
N	361		356	

Note: Unstandardized regression coefficients, with standard errors in parentheses, are followed by standardized coefficients.

See Table 7.2 and text for information on the coding of the independent and dependent variables.

* $p<.10$.

** $p<.05$.

*** $p<.01$.

Overall, the analyses in this chapter have demonstrated that the relevance and civility of negative messages consistently influence people's assessments of Democratic and Republican candidates running for the U.S. Senate. The impact of the relevance and civility measure is impressive given the models predicting evaluations of the candidates include powerful predictors, such as the partisanship and ideology of the respondent. Across the full sample, we find people are responsive to the civility and relevance of negative messages. Furthermore, we find people's tolerance of negativity influences their susceptibility to negative campaigning. Among people who are more tolerant of negative advertisements, negative campaigning fails to depress assessments of the competing candidates in any of the six models. On the other hand, for people who are less accepting of attack advertisements, relevant and uncivil negative messages are more influential. Impressions of the candidates are altered in four of the six models presented in Table 7.3 and Table 7.4 for people with low levels of tolerance for negativity. We now turn to an examination of whether negativity shapes people's likelihood of voting in Senate elections.

The Impact of Negative Messages on Turnout

Thus far we have shown that negative advertisements focusing on relevant topics and delivered in an uncivil fashion are powerful and produce more critical impressions of the candidates targeted in these advertisements. We expect the relevance and civility of campaign messages will significantly influence people's likelihood of participating in political campaigns. As we discussed in chapter 1, the tolerance and tactics theory of negativity contends that when negative messages are viewed as relevant and utilizing a civil tone, voters will be mobilized since these kinds of negative messages point out the potential risks associated with specific electoral choices and do so in an appropriate manner (e.g., Lau, 1985). For example, commercials criticizing Democratic senators for their support of Obamacare may have motivated opponents of Obamacare to go to the polls in 2014. In contrast, when negative messages center on questionable topics and are delivered in an overly strident matter, we expect voters will become alienated with the electoral process and will be less likely to participate in the election.

To summarize, we expect "legitimate" (i.e., civil and relevant negative information) criticisms will stimulate participation in elections since these types of messages will be viewed as helpful and may heighten interest in campaigns. On the other hand, "mudslinging" messages focusing on inappropriate topics and presented in an overly harsh manner (i.e., uncivil and irrelevant negative information) will depress political engagement.[10]

We create a "mudslinging" measure for each respondent living in a state with a Senate campaign in order to examine whether irrelevant and uncivil messages produce less engagement in political campaigns. Negative advertisements that are irrelevant and uncivil receive the highest score (3) on the mudslinging measure; negative advertisements that are relevant and civil receive the lowest score (1), and negative advertisements that are either relevant and uncivil or irrelevant and civil receive a middle score (2). We expect people's participation in elections will decline as scores on the mudslinging measure increase.[11]

We utilize the 2014 CCES postelection survey to assess whether mudslinging demobilizes citizens during campaigns. In particular, we develop binary measure assessing whether people said they voted in the 2014 Senate election or otherwise.[12] To predict turnout in the Senate election, we need to control for measures long known to influence people's likelihood of voting. For instance, *The American Voter* (Campbell et al., 1960) demonstrated that people who are more educated are more likely to participate in politics because they have more skills.[13] Similarly, we know that participation increases with age, even controlling for rival demographic forces (e.g., Wolfinger and Rosenstone, 1980).[14] As in the earlier models, we also include a measure assessing whether respondents report watching television news.[15]

---

10. Krupnikov (2011) demonstrates the importance of timing for understanding how negativity influences engagement in presidential elections.

11. We employ several steps to create the mudslinging measure. As before, we calculate the average relevance and civility score (based on the content analysis reported in chapter 4) of all the negative advertisements targeting candidates during the 2014 senatorial campaigns. Second, we divide the relevance and civility scores at their means to categorize the negative advertisements for each candidate as relevant or irrelevant and as civil or uncivil. Third, we combine these two binary measures to develop the mudslinging measure: negative advertisements that are irrelevant and uncivil receive a score of 3; negative advertisements that are relevant and civil receive a score of 1, and negative advertisements that are either relevant and uncivil or irrelevant and civil receive a score of 2. We add the mudslinging measures for the rival candidates and multiply the sum by the number of negative advertisements aired in the state to capture the intensity of the mudslinging message. Finally, we divide the resulting score by 10,000 to make the estimated coefficients more interpretable.

12. Eighty-three percent of respondents reported voting in the Senate election; 17% did not vote.

13. Education is measured on an ordinal scale ranging from no high school to postgraduate education.

14. Age ranges from 18 to 93 with a mean of 47.08 and a standard deviation of 17.33.

15. Seventy-three percent of respondents indicated that they watched television news within the past 24 hours; 27% said they had not seen any television news.

In addition to demographic factors, political predispositions, such as political interest, political knowledge, strength of partisanship, and civic duty, have long been known to influence political participation (Delli Carpini and Keeter, 1993; Rosenstone and Hansen, 1993; Verba, Schlozman, and Brady, 1995).[16] People are more likely to become politically active when they are more interested in politics, when they have a higher sense of civic duty, when they have stronger ties to a political party, and when they are better informed about politics and government. We also know that habitual voters are more likely to vote, so we include a measure of whether the respondent voted in the 2012 election (Gerber, Green, and Sacher, 2003).[17] Similarly, we include a measure of reported campaign contact since people who are contacted by campaigns or political parties are more likely to vote (Gerber and Green, 2000).[18] Finally, we include a variable assessing the amount of money spent by the two candidates during the Senate election.[19] We expect that as spending on political advertisements, campaign events, and campaign canvassing increases, people will be more likely to vote (Jackson, 2002). In the end,

---

16. Political interest ranges from 1 (not very interested) to 3 (very interested), with a mean of 2.04 and a standard deviation of .77. Civic duty is measured with respondents' answer to the following question: "If people don't care how an election comes out, then they shouldn't vote in it." People who strongly disagree receive a score of 4, people who somewhat disagree receive a 3, people who somewhat agree receive a score of 2, people who strongly agree receive a score of 1. The average response is 2.37 with a standard deviation of 1.13. This measure is the traditional measure of civic duty employed by the American National Election Study (see, e.g., Rosenstone and Hansen, 1993). Political knowledge is measured by whether people correctly place Barack Obama, Hillary Clinton, Ted Cruz, and Rand Paul on the ideology scale. A correct response for the Democratic politicians was placing Clinton and Obama to the left of middle (i.e., 1, 2, 3) on the ideological scale, while a correct response for the Republican politicians was placing Cruz and Paul to the right on the ideological scale (i.e., 5, 6, 7). The knowledge index has a mean of 2.53 and a standard deviation of 1.44. Strength of partisanship is based on the standard party identification measure and ranges from 3 (strong partisans) to 1 (independents), with a mean of 2.80 with a standard deviation of 1.16.

17. Respondents who remembered voting in 2012 received a score of 1, and respondents who did not vote or did not remember voting received a score of 0. Seventy-four percent of respondents indicated they voted in 2012, while 26% of the respondents did not.

18. Campaign contact is measured with the following question: "Did a candidate or political campaign organization contact you during the 2014 election?" Fifty-two percent of the respondents recalled being contacted, while 48% did not.

19. Campaign spending is the amount of spending by both candidates per eligible voter. The average spending per voter is $4.62 with a standard deviation of $4.46. We take the natural log of spending to account for diminishing returns of spending on turnout. As before, when we explore different ways of estimating the impact of spending (e.g., logging spending to base 10, not logging spending), we find the results of the model do not change in a substantive way.

we were able to construct a robust model of turnout with the key concepts identified in the literature as important to explaining turnout included.

To reiterate, we hypothesize that as mudslinging increases, the probability of voting will decline. The results of the turnout model are presented in Table 7.5. We find support for our expectation: as the presence of irrelevant and uncivil messages disseminated during campaigns increases, people are significantly less likely to vote on Election Day. The mudslinging coefficient is negative and reaches statistical significance.[20] Furthermore, an examination of the standardized coefficients shows mudslinging is more important than several standard political variables, such as civic duty and strength of partisanship. Mudslinging also has a more influential impact on turnout than some of the campaign-related factors, like campaign contact and campaign spending.

The remaining variables in the turnout models perform as expected. For instance, we find a positive and statistically significant relationship between people's level of political knowledge and their likelihood of voting. We find age is positively associated with turnout in the 2014 senatorial campaigns. And the habitual nature of voting is effectively captured by the strength of the variable "voting in 2012."

We convert the unstandardized coefficients from the logistic regression into probabilities in order to better assess how changes in the amount of mudslinging influence the probability of voting in Senate campaigns.[21] The data in Figure 7.1 demonstrate that when there is no mudslinging in a campaign, the model predicts people have a 95% probability of voting in the off-year election.[22] However, when mudslinging is pervasive, the probability of voting falls precipitously, to an 85% probability of voting.

---

20. We looked at whether our original measure of relevance/civility influences the probability of voting. We sum the relevance/civility measure for Democrats and Republicans. We reestimate the model in Table 7.5 (omitting the mudslinging variable). The original relevance and civility measure does not significantly influence turnout. The unstandardized coefficient (with the standard error in parentheses) is -.09 (.06). We also looked at whether the traditional measure of negativity (total negative advertisements aired/total number of advertisements aired) influences turnout. Again, we reestimate the model in Table 7.5 with the traditional measure of negativity (omitting the mudslinging variable), and we find that the traditional measure of negativity does not significantly influence turnout. The unstandardized coefficient (with the standard error in parentheses) is -.09 (.07).

21. We hold all remaining variables in the model at their means (or mode for binary variables).

22. We vary mudslinging from the minimum of 0 to the average mudslinging score of 15 to the maximum mudslinging score of 30.

Table 7.5 Logistic Regression Predicting Turnout

	Unstandardized Coefficient (Standard Error)	Standardized Coefficient
Negativity of Commercials		
Mudslinging Measure	−.04 (.02) **	−.27
Campaign Characteristics		
Campaign Contact	.35 (.35)	.18
Civic Duty	.11 (.16)	.12
Political Interest	.42 (.26)	.33
Political Knowledge	.43 (.14) ***	.62
Strength of Partisanship	.12 (.14)	.14
Total Campaign Spending	.13 (.16)	.11
Voted in 2012	1.18 (.37) ***	.51
Demographic Characteristics		
Age	.03 (.01) ***	.57
Education	−.18 (.13)	−.27
Watch TV News	.61 (.35) *	.27
Constant	−2.48 (.84) ***	
Percentage Correctly Predicted	90	
Pseudo R-Squared (Cox and Snell)	.16	
N	489	

Note: Each cell contains the unstandardized coefficients (standard errors), followed by standardized coefficient.

Since the dependent variable (from the postelection survey) is a binary variable (1 = voted; 0 = didn't vote), we use logistic regression. For the mudslinging measure, we first calculate the average relevance and civility scores (based on the content analysis reported in chapter 4) of all the negative advertisements targeting candidates during the 2014 campaign. Second, we divide the relevance and civility scores at their means to categorize the negative advertisements for each candidate as relevant or irrelevant and as civil or uncivil. Third, we combine these two binary measures to develop the mudslinging measure: negative advertisements that are irrelevant and uncivil receive a score of 3; negative advertisements that are relevant and civil receive a score of 1; and negative advertisements that are either relevant and uncivil or irrelevant and civil receive a score of 2. We add the mudslinging measures for the rival candidates and multiply the sum by the number of negative advertisements aired in the state to capture the intensity of the mudslinging message. We divide the resulting score by 10,000 to make the estimated coefficients more interpretable. Campaign contact is measure with the following question: "Did a candidate or political campaign organization contact you during the 2014 election?" (yes = 1, no = 0). Civic duty is measured from 1 (low in civic duty) to 4 (high in civic duty). Political interest ranges from 1 (not very interested) to 3 (very interested). Political knowledge ranges from 0 (low) to 4 (high). Strength of partisanship is measured on a three-point scale from 1 (independents) to 3 (strong partisans). Total campaign spending is the natural log of spending (per voter) by both candidates. Voted in 2012 is whether the respondent remembered voting in 2012 (1) or did not vote or did not remember voting (0). Age is an interval measure ranging from 18 to 93. Education is measured on an ordinal scale ranging from no high school to postgraduate education. Watch TV is a binary variable measuring whether the respondent indicated watching television news in the past 24 hours. See the text for more information about the measurement of the independent and dependent variables.

* p<.10.

** p<.05.

*** p<.01.

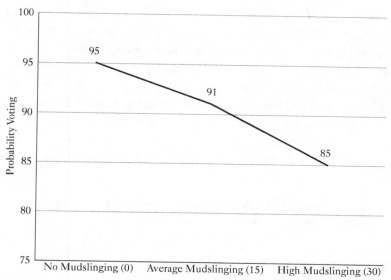

Note: The probabilities in this figure are based on the logistic regression results presented in Table 7.5. See text for more details.

FIGURE 7.1 Probability of voting by mudslinging.

The model presented in Table 7.5 demonstrates the importance of considering the relevance and civility of negative messages in tandem. We find attack advertisements focusing on an important topic and delivered in a respectful manner can heighten engagement in campaigns. In contrast, negative commercials utilizing an overly strident tone and emphasizing irrelevant topics can demobilize the electorate.

We examined whether the impact of mudslinging is more powerful for people who are less tolerant of negativity. Since we are examining participation rates based on responses to the CCES postelection survey, we rely on the postelection measure of intolerance to negativity.[23] We combine the measures of intolerance for uncivil messages and intolerance for irrelevant messages into a single index, ranging from 4 (high tolerance) to 16 (low tolerance).[24] We then divide our sample at the mean and reestimate the equations presented in Table 7.5 for people with a low tolerance for negative messages and for individuals with a high tolerance for negative messages.

---

23. We know from our analysis in chapter 3 that people's intolerance of negative campaigning is dynamic and responsive to the tenor of the campaign.

24. The mean postelection tolerance level for the 2014 CCES sample is 12.30 with a standard deviation of 2.59.

The results of our analysis are presented in Table 7.6. The results are clear: people who are less tolerant of negativity are more influenced by the negativity of the campaign. We see that the mudslinging coefficient is statistically significant only in the model predicting the probability of voting for people intolerant to negativity. Furthermore, the size of the unstandardized coefficient is twice as large in the model predicting turnout for people with low levels of tolerance compared to people with higher levels of tolerance for negativity. An examination of the standardized coefficients shows mudslinging is less powerful for people with higher levels of tolerance compared

Table 7.6 Logistic Regression Predicting Turnout

	Tolerant of Negativity		Intolerant of Negativity	
Negativity of Commercials				
Mudslinging Measure	−.03 (.03)	−.21	−.06 (.03) **	.48
Campaign Characteristics				
Campaign Contact	.25 (.59)	.13	.25 (.53)	.12
Civic Duty	.39 (.31)	.41	−.10 (.22)	−.12
Political Interest	.49 (.41)	.37	.21 (.41)	.16
Political Knowledge	.35 (.27)	.45	.34 (.22)	.44
Strength of Partisanship	.42 (.24) *	.47	−.12 (.22)	−.14
Total Campaign Spending	−.10 (.42)	.09	.99 (.44) **	.81
Voted in 2012	.50 (.66)	.20	1.31 (.58) **	.48
Demographic Characteristics				
Age	.04 (.02) **	.65	.03 (.02)	.47
Education	−.24 (.22)	−.35	.02 (.20)	.03
Watch TV News	−.54 (.60)	−.24	1.31 (.54)**	.57
Constant	−2.30 (1.61)		−2.57 (1.17) **	
Pseudo R-Squared (Cox and Snell)		.12		.18
N		489		217

Note: Each cell contains the unstandardized coefficients (standard errors), followed by the standardized coefficients.

See Table 7.5 and text for information on the coding of the independent and dependent variables.

* p<.10.

** p<.05.

*** p<.01.

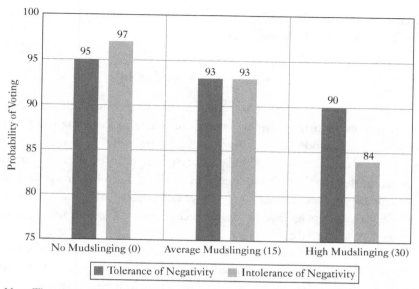

Note: The probabilities in this figure are based on the logistic regression results presented in Table 7.6. See text for more details.

FIGURE 7.2 Impact of mudslinging on probability of voting by tolerance of negativity.

to many of the individual measures of political predispositions (e.g., strength of partisanship). In contrast, though, for people with less tolerance for negativity, mudslinging is among the most influential variables in the turnout model, surpassing the impact of nearly all political predispositions, with the exception of voting in 2012.

We graphically represent the impact of mudslinging for people with high and low levels of tolerance toward negativity in Figure 7.2. As we did earlier, we convert the coefficients from the logistic regression models from Table 7.6 into probabilities.[25] The presentation in Figure 7.2 demonstrates mudslinging matters for people with low tolerance of negativity. Among these individuals, differences in levels of mudslinging changes the probability of voting more than 10 percentage points, from 97% probability of voting in races with no mudslinging to 84% probability of voting in races with a maximum level of mudslinging. In direct contrast, for people with higher levels of tolerance for negativity, changes in levels of mudslinging matter far less, producing small

---

25. We hold all remaining variables in the model at their means (or modes for binary variables). We vary mudslinging from the minimum of 0 to the average mudslinging score of 15 to the maximum mudslinging score of 30.

changes in the probability of voting (95% vs. 90% probability of voting across the range of the mudslinging scale).

Summary and Conclusion

Campaigns have many roles in representative democracies, but none are more important than providing crucial information about the competing candidates and motivating people to go to the polls on Election Day. After all, political campaigns, an integral part of contemporary democracies, are essential for shaping the political agenda of candidates and holding politicians accountable for their actions. This chapter is the culminating exploration for how negative campaign information influences citizens' actions and attitudes during U.S. senatorial campaigns.

We have provided a wealth of findings demonstrating there is a consistent interplay between campaigns, specifically negative campaigns, and people's level of tolerance for critical information that ultimately shapes electoral outcomes in American elections.

People's underlying tolerance toward negative information is the lens through which citizens assess campaign messages delivered by the candidates and their surrogates. Candidates attack their opponents with a compilation of messages falling along a continuum of relevance and civility. Citizens are well equipped to recognize these tactics as they search for information centered on topics they view as related to governing. But they are busy with their daily lives, and political campaigns are rarely a top priority. Uncivil messages, often pervasive during electoral contests and disseminated via different mediums, break through the noise of people's busy lives, grabbing their attention when accompanied with relevant critiques of the candidates.

The impact of relevant and uncivil messages on people's views of the political rivals depends on how well individuals tolerate negative messages. For people who tolerate critical communications and consider negativity to be part and parcel of contemporary political campaigns, negative messages will have little impact on their views of the candidates. But people with a low tolerance for negativity who find uncivil and irrelevant messages to be annoying are far more likely to be persuaded by these types of attacks. This key finding moves the literature forward, demonstrating under what circumstances negative information will shape voters' attitudes during campaigns. People's tolerance for negativity has a strong and consistent impact on how negativity influences their views of the competing candidates.

In addition, the tolerance and tactics theory increases our understanding of when people will participate in elections. The theory predicts that negative critiques will heighten turnout when messages are highly relevant and produced in a civil manner. But when negativity becomes nothing more than mudslinging—irrelevant messages embracing hostile and shrill tones—citizens are more likely to turn off the campaign and stay home on Election Day. We find strong empirical support for our theory. Civil critiques filled with useful information about candidates' policy positions and personal traits mobilize citizens. However, when information veers into mudslinging, citizens lose interest in the candidates and the campaign.

Finally, we find the relationship between mudslinging and turnout is conditioned by people's level of tolerance for negativity. Consistent with our theory, people's tolerance for negativity conditions the impact of mudslinging on their likelihood of voting. People who are not bothered by negativity do not alter their decision to vote based on the amount of uncivil and irrelevant attacks delivered during the campaign. However, among people who are less tolerant of negativity, the level of mudslinging significantly conditions their decision to turn out on Election Day. Turnout drops significantly in races with the highest levels of mudslinging. We turn now to our final chapter, where we review our key findings and explain their importance for understanding the nature and health of American's campaigns and elections.

8

The Consequences of Negative Campaigning

IN THIS FINAL chapter, we begin by reviewing our findings regarding the impact of negative campaigning in U.S. Senate races and evaluate the evidence for the veracity of the tolerance and tactics theory of negativity. We believe our theory contributes to scholars' understanding of several debates in American politics. For example, in light of our findings, we reassess the evidence regarding the impact of negative advertisements on people's evaluations of candidates. We also discuss how negative messages enhance or depress turnout in elections. Since the bulk of negative advertisements are sponsored by outside groups, we discuss how the increased role of outside money, especially dark money, shapes political campaigns. We conclude with some thoughts about the role of contemporary campaigns in America.

Evidence for the Tolerance and Tactics Theory of Negativity

The tolerance and tactics theory of negativity contends that knowing how citizens feel about negativity as well as identifying the relevance and civility of negative messages improves our understanding of the impact of negative messages in electoral campaigns. In particular, people vary in their tolerance of negativity; some people are more sensitive to attack advertising, finding these messages inappropriate as well as enervating. Others are more likely to consider negative campaigning an important element of modern campaigns; these individuals do not mind the heated attacks between the candidates. We argue that people with less tolerance for negative campaigning are more influenced by the dissemination of negative messages.

While people's tolerance of negativity determines their susceptibility to negative advertisements, we also contend it is essential to consider the relevance of the negative messages simultaneously with the tone of these messages. Uncivil but relevant negative messages powerfully shape citizens' views about candidates, especially for people with lower levels of tolerance of negativity. Messages with a harsh tone are more likely to be noticed, and critiques on relevant topics provide important information about the risks of supporting certain candidates. In contrast, irrelevant messages, whether delivered in a civil or an uncivil manner, are unlikely to influence voters' impressions of candidates.

The civility and relevance of negative messages also influence the likelihood citizens will turn out at the polls on Election Day. When citizens view negative messages as focusing on a relevant topic and employing a courteous tone, they will be mobilized to vote. On the other hand, when negative messages center on unimportant topics and are presented in an overly strident matter, voters will be less likely to vote. It is difficult to be motivated to take the time to vote when there is little helpful information and when it is presented in a distasteful and annoying manner.

To test the tolerance and tactics theory of negativity, we focus primarily, but not exclusively, on the 2014 U.S. Senate campaigns. We rely on four original data sets to examine the antecedents of citizens' tolerance to negativity: the 2014 CCES, the 2016 CCES, an ASU survey of online students in 2015, and an in-person survey of ASU students conducted in 2016. To examine the relevance and civility of negative messages disseminated during the 2014 Senate elections, we turn to political advertising data collected by the WMP, supplemented with an original content analysis of the relevance and civility of all the negative commercials aired in the 2014 Senate contests.

In addition, we conducted two focus group studies to gain detailed information about how people react to variance in the relevance and civility of the negative advertisements from the 2014 Senate elections. We also rely on a survey experiment embedded in the 2014 CCES to examine how people's tolerance for negativity affects their reactions to negative messages during ongoing senatorial elections. We combine the 2014 CCES survey data with the data from the WMP to connect people's attitudes toward the Senate candidates with the specific advertisements aired during the 2014 senatorial campaigns. These data allow us to examine how people's tolerance for negativity shapes the impact of negative advertisements in the midst of the 2014 U.S. Senate campaigns.

From these diverse data sets, we find strong support for the tolerance and tactics theory of negativity. First, we find people differ systematically in their tolerance for negativity, and these differences do not simply reflect partisan and ideological differences. For instance, women and older people are less likely to tolerate uncivil and irrelevant negative advertisements, while people who are more engaged in politics are more likely to tolerate these same messages. People's tolerance of negativity is dynamic, decreasing over time as they are continually exposed to negative campaigns.

Second, we examine all the negative advertisements disseminated during the 2014 Senate elections and show these messages differ markedly in their civility and relevance. In addition, the focus group results confirm people are able to accurately assess advertisements that differ in their tone and in the usefulness of their message. Also, people's emotional reactions to negative advertisements are affected by their tolerance for negativity as well as by the type of negative message.

Third, our analyses of the 2014 CCES survey experiment demonstrate that people's levels of tolerance consistently and powerfully influence how they assess negative messages. People with a low level of tolerance see more incivility in negative messages and view negative messages as less useful compared to citizens who tolerate negative campaigning more easily. The importance of tolerance persists even when we consider powerful political predispositions long known to shape how people view politics, such as partisan attachments and ideological proclivities.

Finally, we combine the 2014 CCES survey data with information about the airing and content of negative advertisements disseminated during the Senate campaigns. We find the relevance and civility of negative messages consistently influence people's assessments of candidates running for the U.S. Senate. Indeed, we find support for our expectation that negative messages are persuasive when they focus on a useful topic and are delivered in an un-civil manner. In addition, people's tolerance of negativity influences their sus-ceptibility to negative campaigning; relevant and uncivil messages are most influential for people who are least tolerant of negative campaigning.

The relevance and civility of campaign messages also influence people's decisions about going to the polls. When campaign messages are focused on irrelevant topics and delivered in an uncivil manner (i.e., mudslinging), people's willingness to vote in a Senate election declines. Our analysis demonstrates that as mudslinging increases (i.e., the amount of uncivil and irrelevant messages increases, compared to relevant and civil messages), people's probability of voting declines significantly. Furthermore, the impact of uncivil and irrelevant messages on political participation is conditioned by people's level of tolerance for negativity. People who are more bothered by negativity are much more likely to be influenced by changing levels of mudslinging compared to people who are more tolerant of negativity. These findings hold up in the face of stiff controls. The turnout models employed a range of variables related to the likelihood of citizens' decisions to turn out on Election Day.

Does Negative Campaigning Work?

Over the past 40 years, more than 100 studies have been conducted to explore the impact of negative advertising on citizens' evaluation of candidates and political engagement. We examined the studies published in the top political science journals (*American Political Science Review, American Journal of Political Science, Journal of Politics*), focusing on the effectiveness of negative campaigning. We located 65 articles published in these three journals between 1994 and 2017.[1] Many of these studies begin by explaining the conflicting nature of the findings regarding the impact of negative advertising. For instance, Krupnikov (2011: 797) examines whether negative campaigning increases or decreases political engagement and begins her study by saying, "The relationship between negativity and turnout has proven difficult to specify. Over the last decade, the relationship between negativity and turnout has emerged as one of the most enduring debates in political science." Similarly, in their extensive review of the impact of negative advertising on people's evaluations of candidates, Lau et al. (1999: 859) conclude, "We did not uncover consistent, let alone strong, evidence that negative ads work to the advantage of their sponsors and/or the disadvantage of their targets. In this respect, it appears that, a la Newton's third law, for every research finding there is an equal and opposite research finding."

We believe that the tolerance and tactics theory of negativity helps clarify the impact of negative messages during electoral campaigns. The theory advances the literature in several important ways. First, our single theoretical framework provides guidance regarding two key questions motivating the literature on negative campaigning: how negative messages shape citizens' assessments of candidates and when negative campaigning demobilizes the electorate. We are not aware of another theory that makes contributions to explaining, via empirical testing, both of these central questions. Second, the theory builds on the existing literature showing that the impact of negativity

---

1. We could not find any studies on negative advertising published in these journals before 1994.

is not straightforward and requires the exploration of important forces that condition the influence of negative campaigning on voters' beliefs and behavior. We identify two critical components that alter the impact of negative campaigning: characteristics of citizens (tolerance) and the tactics of candidates (relevance and civility of their negative messages). We believe our theoretical framework can be generalized across different types of elections as well as over time. To be sure, it needs further rigorous testing, but the elements in the theory are found in every negative campaign and can be replicated and expanded in a straightforward manner.

We see the utility of the tolerance and tactics theory for understanding citizens' assessments of candidates in the most recent political contests. Negative advertisements have focused on a wide range of topics, including "draining the swamp," Confederate monuments, voting rights for ex-felons, and the rise of MS-13. Some of these topics will be germane to potential voters, while others will be viewed as largely irrelevant. Consider the advertisement aired by the Ed Gillespie campaign during the 2017 gubernatorial race in Virginia. The advertisement claims that Democrat Ralph Northam is increasing the threat of MS-13[2] and begins with a montage of newscasts bemoaning the rise of the violent street gang, followed by a narrator stating "MS-13 is a menace, yet Ralph Northam voted in favor of sanctuary cities that let dangerous illegal immigrants back on the street, increasing the threat of MS-13. Ralph Northam's policies are dangerous."

According to exit polls in Virginia, immigration was an important issue for only 14% of voters.[3] For this segment of Virginia citizens, the topic of the advertisement is relevant and we expect those with less tolerance for negativity to be most persuaded by the advertisement. In addition to being relevant to these voters, the advertisement also embraces elements of uncivil messages (e.g., the use of words like "dangerous," employing dark photographs of Northam). This enhances the impact of the message, especially for voters who find the topic salient.

Likewise, the theory has direct applicability in recent contests regarding the likelihood that people will be motivated to go to the polls. The advertisement aired by the Principled Leadership Project PAC in the 2017 Georgia special election was viewed by subjects in our 2017 focus group as low in

---

2. The advertisement can be viewed at https://www.youtube.com/watch?v=ToUiqMDbpAw.

3. See https://www.nbcnews.com/card/early-exit-polls-health-care-most-important-issue-virginia-voters-n818691.

relevance and low in civility.[4] The advertisement began with gun shots firing in rapid succession; then a narrator says, "Now, the unhinged left is endorsing and applauding shooting Republicans. When will it stop? [More gun shots are heard.] It won't if Jon Ossoff wins on Tuesday. Because the same unhinged leftists cheering last week's shooting [of House Majority Whip Steve Scalise at a congressional softball practice] are all backing Jon Ossoff, and if he wins, they win. Stop them. [Picture of Kathy Griffin holding mock-up of bloody Trump head.] Stop Them now. Stop Jon Ossoff. Stop Nancy Pelosi. Vote Karen Handel for Congress."[5]

In advertisements like these, the bounds of incivility are crossed with unsubstantiated claims like "the unhinged left is endorsing and applauding shooting Republicans." Furthermore, when these types of uncivil messages neglect to address issues important to voters, the voters are likely to be turned off by the electoral campaign and will have little motivation to take part in the spectacle. Our research shows that the combination of uncivil and irrelevant messages pervading the political landscape demobilizes citizens, leading to lower levels of political engagement in elections. Furthermore, citizens with the least tolerance for negativity are more likely to be demobilized by mudslinging messages. In summary, we hope future researchers will apply the tolerance and tactics theory to broaden and deepen our understanding of the ever increasing use of negativity in contemporary campaigns.

Who Is to Blame for Attack Advertising?

The role of money in U.S. elections has changed dramatically over the past 50 years, and we believe these changes have contributed to the prevalence of negativity in political campaigns. To understand the shifting role of money in politics, we briefly review significant decisions regarding campaign contributions and expenditures.[6] We begin with the Supreme Court's decision in *Buckley v. Valeo* in 1976. James Buckley argued that the 1971 Federal Election Campaign Act, by limiting campaign contributions and

---

4. Respondents rated this advertisement as uncivil (an average of 1.64 with a standard deviation of 1.03) on a five-point scale ranging from 1 (very hostile) to 5 (not hostile at all) and as irrelevant (an average of 2.11 with a standard deviation of 1.29 on a five-point scale ranging from 1 (not useful at all) to 5 (extremely useful).

5. See the video at https://www.youtube.com/watch?v=aZgKN_HjZL8&feature=youtu.be.

6. See Brown (2017) for a summary of how court cases have influenced campaign finance throughout U.S. history.

expenditures, violated the First and Fifth Amendment rights to freedom of expression and due process. In deciding the case, the Supreme Court ruled that contribution limits were necessary to discourage corruption but that spending limits violated freedom of speech and was especially applicable for House and Senate elections. The Supreme Court also ruled that spending by outside groups was protected by the First Amendment, as long as the outside groups did not coordinate with the candidates.

In the years following the *Buckley v. Valeo* decision, the amount of money raised and spent during campaigns increased, especially spending by outside groups (Brown, 2017). Congress sought to reform the campaign finance system, primarily with the Bipartisan Campaign Reform Act in 2002. The act sought to limit independent expenditures by banning corporations from airing political advertisements mentioning a candidate within 30 days of a primary election and 60 days of a general election.

The Wisconsin Right to Life group challenged the Bipartisan Campaign Reform Act, and the resulting Supreme Court decision (*Federal Election Commission v. Wisconsin Right to Life*, 2007) ruled that advertisements that are focused on issues and not explicitly advocating voting for or against a candidate are free speech and cannot be regulated. This decision produced increases in spending by dark money groups, like political nonprofits, who are not required to report their contributions. During the 2008 presidential election, the first election cycle following the decision, dark money spending increased to $102 million.[7]

In 2010 the Supreme Court ruled in *Citizens United v. FEC* that corporations can make unlimited expenditures on electoral messages (explicitly supporting or opposing a candidate) as long as the group does not coordinate with the candidates or the political parties. The *Citizens United* decision granted legal rights to corporations, associations, and unions to spend unlimited amounts of money advocating for or against candidates during campaigns. A follow-up decision by the Court of Appeals in 2010 (*SpeechNow.org v. FEC*) removed all contribution limits to outside groups, leading to the creation of super PACs. These independent, expenditure-only committees can raise unlimited sums of money from corporations, unions, associations, and individuals, with no spending limits, to explicitly support or oppose political candidates. However, super PACS cannot donate money to political candidates and cannot coordinate with the candidates or political

---

7. See https://www.opensecrets.org/outsidespending/disclosure.php?range=tot. Dark money spending was $312 million in 2012 and $178 million in 2016.

parties. Like traditional PACs, they are required to report their donors to the Federal Election Commission.

Decisions made in *Citizens United, Wisconsin Right to Life,* and *SpeechNow.org* have dramatically increased the amount of outside spending in political campaigns. In a recent report, Vandewalker (2015) found that outside spending in Senate elections more than doubled since 2010, increasing to $486 million in 2014. In highly competitive Senate races in 2014, outside groups accounted for the greatest share of spending (47%); candidate spending made up 41% of total expenditures; and party spending accounted for only 12% of total expenditures. Dark money more than doubled from 2010 to 2014, from $105 million to $226 million. In the most competitive Senate races in 2014, dark money constituted 28% of total spending.

The dramatic increase in spending by outside groups is problematic. The current campaign finance system stacks the deck in favor of a handful of wealthy special interests who can try to gain influence with politicians via their campaign contributions. Oftentimes wealthy donors can conceal their identity by contributing to political nonprofits that are not required to disclose their donors. Super PACs, while legally required to disclose their donors, can accept unlimited contributions from political nonprofits that may not have disclosed their donors.

These outside groups spend most of their money on political advertising. According to the WMP, outside group advertising, as a proportion of all ads on the air, has grown steadily since 2006. By 2016, almost half (49%) of all advertisements aired in Senate contests were sponsored by outside groups.[8]

Outside groups are not only sponsoring roughly half of all advertisements in Senate races; more important, they are much more likely than candidates to air negative commercials. According to our analysis of the 2014 advertising data, eight out of 10 advertisements aired by outside groups were negative. This translates into more than 280,000 airings. In contrast, fewer than one-quarter of all the negative advertisements sponsored by the candidates were negative, producing about 111,000 airings.[9]

When we examine all the positive advertisements aired in the 2014 Senate races, we find that 81% (approximately 290,000 airings) were sponsored by candidates. Yet positive advertisements sponsored by outside groups, such

---

8. Data available at http://mediaproject.wesleyan.edu.

9. The political parties, by themselves or coordinated with candidates, aired fewer than 74,000 negative advertisements in 2014, accounting for 16% of all negative advertisements.

as super PACs and political nonprofits, accounted for fewer than 20% of advertisements (about 65,000 airings).[10] These findings demonstrate that increases in spending by outside groups, primarily allocated to television advertising, dramatically intensify the negativity of political campaigns.

If we look at the most uncivil advertisements aired in 2014 (i.e., advertisements receiving a score of 1 in our content analysis), we see that outside groups are much more likely to sponsor these attacks: more than twice as often as candidates and political parties (62% for outside groups, 23% for candidates, and 15% for political parties). Similarly, the most irrelevant advertisements (i.e., advertisements receiving a score of 1 in our content analysis) are much more likely to be sponsored by outside groups. In fact, interest groups are almost three times as likely to air irrelevant advertisements, compared to advertisements sponsored by candidates and the political parties (69% of the negative advertisements rated as low in relevance were sponsored by interest groups; 24% were sponsored by candidates; 7% were sponsored by the political parties). Looking at negative commercials that were categorized as low in civility and low in relevance, we find that interest groups sponsor these types of advertisements 75% of the time, compared to 20% of the time for candidates and 6% of the time for political parties.[11]

In the 2017 electoral cycle, some of the most negative advertisements were sponsored by outside groups (Hains, 2017). As an illustration, in the 2017 Virginia gubernatorial campaign, the Latino Victory Fund released a commercial titled "American Nightmare."[12] The advertisement shows minority children being chased by a driver in a pickup truck adorned with a Confederate flag, a "Gillespie for Governor" bumper sticker, and a "Don't tread on me" license plate. The driver makes his way toward the scared children, who shout, "Run! Run! Run!" to other minority children, including a Muslim girl and an African American boy. The advertisement concludes with a scene of a Charlottesville-like rally, with a narrator asking, "Is this what Donald Trump and Ed Gillespie mean by the 'American Dream'?"

---

10. The political parties, either by themselves or coordinated with candidates, aired about 2,400 positive advertisements in 2014, accounting for about 1% of all positive advertisements.

11. These are advertisements receiving a score of 1 for civility and a score of 1 for relevance in the content analysis of the negative advertisements.

12. Latino Victory Fund is an outside group, classified as a "Carey committee," a hybrid political action committee that can operate as a traditional PAC, contributing funds to a candidate's committee, and as a super PAC, which makes independent expenditures. See OpenSecrets.org. View the commercial at https://www.youtube.com/watch?v=8cD_rievoSE&feature=youtu.be.

In summary, outside groups have grown sharply in their influence in campaigns over the past few decades. Our analysis and others' (e.g., WMP) show that outside groups engage in negative campaigning more often than do candidates and political parties. Outside groups are more likely than candidates and parties to sponsor advertisements that exhibit an uncivil tone and focus on irrelevant topics. These outside groups do not need to worry about a potential backlash from voters since these groups are largely unknown to the public and dark money groups do not even reveal where they obtain funds for their negative commercials. In fact, it is incumbent on researchers exploring backlash effects to determine, first and foremost, if citizens connect the harshest and most irrelevant advertisements directly to candidates, given that there is no mention of the attacking politician anywhere in these ads. Outside groups are free to make the most outrageous, ad hominem, and inaccurate advertisements because they are not accountable to voters. Yet these negative advertisements, especially messages low in civility and relevance, are precisely the type that produce detrimental effects for the functioning of our democracy, including diminishing turnout.

Taking Stock of the Quality of America's Campaigns

Campaigns play a number of crucial roles in representative democracies. These functions are important for healthy and functioning democratic societies. Chief among these are electing politicians, holding legislators accountable, motivating citizens to participate in the campaign and to go to the polls on Election Day, generating discourse and debates on public policy, and providing symbolic support for the nation's electoral institutions. In efforts to protect and invigorate these goals, America's various legislatures, courts, and executives, along with millions of citizens, have worked for nearly 250 years to create fair, free, and regular campaigns and elections. Progress has come in fits and starts, but the quality and effectiveness of elections have improved steadily over the arc of U.S. history.

Still, improvements are needed in various arenas (e.g., voter turnout), most immediately in the quality of political discourse during campaigns. Democratic theorists have argued that reasoned political discussions among elites and citizens are not only possible but yield great benefits for democratic societies. Theorists, like John Stuart Mill in *Considerations on Representative Government,* believed civic discussions led by elites would encourage citizens to see beyond their self-interests, create positive connections between the representatives and the represented, and provide an arena where citizens could see conflicting views discussed, debated, and ultimately resolved. Tocqueville's ([1835] 1956) concept of "enlightened self- interest" was possible once citizens engaged in discussions with people who joined together in groups, creating a forum among citizens. Dahl (1956) noted that majority views should be "reflective" and can be achieved only after considerable deliberation.

Rawls's (1971) thought experiment—that citizens could aspire to an "original position" where their beliefs about heady concepts of justice and fairness are based on fair and impartial reasoning—is possible because people discover a "veil of ignorance" about their own existing preferences, biases, and attitudes. Habermas's "ideal speech situation" argues that political communications and debates among elites or citizens are possible if orchestrated by a set of rules and norms allowing for positions to be weighed against reason and evidence (Villa, 1992). Even Madison ([1788] 1981), the hardboiled practical theoretician, believed political debate among America's diverse legislators representing distinct regions and localities of the nation could locate the broad "public interest" if debate was confined in a legislative institution guided by some rules of order.

Campaigns, especially given the size of America's democracy, could be a forum to generate regular and sweeping discussions on important topics of the moment. After all, campaigns are precursors to a sacred and central feature of democratic societies whereby citizens cast ballots on Election Day, ideally with some retrospective and prospective views about where the nation has been and where it is headed. The ability of candidates to convince a plurality or even a majority of citizens to nudge or move boldly in a specific direction on key issues such as health care, education, immigration, the environment, national defense, and social programs, or gut-wrenching issues like abortion, the death penalty, or sending young people to war, is a key goal of campaigns and elections.

But there is nearly unanimous agreement that America's campaigns, big and small, do not fulfill the democratic ideal of generating thoughtful, reasoned, balanced, reflective, and prospective debate and discussion by the candidates and their supporters about the issues of the moment. The First Amendment and a host of Supreme Court decisions provide candidates and political parties wide latitude in terms of conducting their campaigns, discussing relevant issues on the minds of citizens, and attacking their opponents. In other words, the hopes and recommendations of democratic theorists for meaningful campaign discussions are in the hands of political and media elites. The tactics used by current campaign strategists are on full display across the pages of this book and often leave little to be admired.

If we accept the notion that future electoral campaigns will emulate the themes and messages of recent contests, then what does the tolerance and tactics theory of negativity say about the future of America's electoral institutions? That is, are campaign architects approaching a tipping point, where they are actually damaging democracy? We do find evidence that uncivil and irrelevant campaign tactics depress voting on Election Day. We also know that citizens vary in their tolerance for negative attacks and that levels of tolerance shape people's attitudes and actions during campaigns. Potential voters become less tolerant of negativity when they witness the back-and-forth of attack advertisements across the months of a campaign. Therefore, the negativity of contemporary campaigns, especially the uncivil and irrelevant attacks, serve to increase people's intolerance for negativity while simultaneously discouraging participation in elections. This is a negative outcome for anyone reflecting on the ability of elections to deliver accountability and responsiveness in representative democracies.

Campaign strategists and candidates have no clear idea, especially during the heat of battle, exactly when their campaign rhetoric becomes too uncivil, too shrill, and too irrelevant for large numbers of potential voters. Recent electoral contests are far from a respectful exchange of ideas on important topics advocated by political philosophers. During the 2016 presidential campaign, candidates hurled insults at each other, including Donald Trump's pervasive use of demeaning nicknames, like "Crooked Hillary" and "Lyin' Ted" (Chavez and Stracqualursi, 2016). Trump was not alone in his use of highly critical language. For instance, Clinton called Trump's opinions "dangerously incoherent" and argued that he was "temperamentally unfit to be president" (Gearan, Phillip, and Tumulty, 2016). During a 2016 GOP debate, Trump called Senator Marco Rubio "Little Marco." Shortly afterward, during a campaign rally, Rubio admitted that Trump was taller but suggested that Trump had small hands for someone of his height. After commenting about Trump's hands, Rubio targeted Trump's tan, saying "[He] doesn't sweat because his pores are clogged from the spray tan. Donald Trump isn't gonna make America great, he's gonna make America orange" (Jaffe, 2016).

The slights, insults, and mean-spirited remarks characterizing much of the 2016 presidential campaign fall far short of the respectful exchange of ideas illustrative of a highly functional democratic system. We believe candidates, political consultants, and interest groups need to take a closer look at the long-term effects of their actions on the body politic. Madison's representative democracy is built for surviving, even embracing the rough and tumble of political debates on pressing policy matters, but the quality of our democratic system may not thrive amid harsh attacks on trivial topics. We are overdue for political elites to take stock of their tactics and strive to locate their own "enlightened self-interest" for the health of America.

Appendices

Pretest/Posttest Questionnaire for 2014 CCES and ASU Module

Pretest Questionnaire

Interest in Campaigns
Some people don't pay much attention to political campaigns. How about you? Would you say that you are very much interested, somewhat interested, or not much interested in political campaigns?

    1 Very Much Interested
    2 Somewhat Interested
    3 Not Much Interested
    9 Don't Know

Feeling Thermometer for Democratic Senate Candidate
Using a scale from 0 to 10, where 10 means you feel very favorable toward the person and 0 means you feel very unfavorable toward the person, please rate [insert name of Democratic candidate for Senate].

Feeling Thermometer for Republican Senate Candidate
Using a scale from 0 to 10, where 10 means you feel very favorable toward the person and 0 means you feel very unfavorable toward the person, please rate [insert name of Republican candidate for Senate].

Competent Democratic Senate Candidate
How well does the word "competent" describe [insert name of Democratic Senate candidate], the Democratic candidate for the U.S. Senate?

    1 Extremely Well
    2 Quite Well

3 Not Too Well
4 Not Well at All
9 Don't Know

Trustworthy Democratic Senate Candidate
How well does the word "trustworthy" describe [insert name of Democratic Senate candidate], the Democratic candidate for the U.S. Senate?

1 Extremely Well
2 Quite Well
3 Not Too Well
4 Not Well at All
9 Don't Know

Competent Republican Senate Candidate
How well does the word "competent" describe [insert name of Republican Senate candidate], Republican candidate for the U.S. Senate?

1 Extremely Well
2 Quite Well
3 Not Too Well
4 Not Well at All
9 Don't Know

Trustworthy Republican Senate Candidate
How well does the word "trustworthy" describe [insert name of Republican Senate candidate], Republican candidate for the U.S. Senate?

1 Extremely Well
2 Quite Well
3 Not Too Well
4 Not Well at All
9 Don't Know

Tone of Senate Campaign
How would you describe the tone of the U.S. Senate campaign between [insert names of Democratic Senate candidate and Republican Senate candidate]? Would you characterize the campaign as very positive, somewhat positive, somewhat negative, or very negative?

1 Very positive
2 Somewhat positive
3 Somewhat negative
4 Very negative
9 Don't Know

Civility 1

The following questions assess your views about negative advertisements, in general. Please indicate the degree to which you agree with the following statement:

Some negative advertisements are so nasty that I stop paying attention to what the candidates are saying.

 1 Agree strongly
 2 Agree somewhat
 3 Disagree somewhat
 4 Disagree strongly
 9 Don't Know

Relevance 1

Please indicate the degree to which you agree with the following statement:

Negative advertisements discussing a candidate's personal misbehavior are fair game.

 1 Agree strongly
 2 Agree somewhat
 3 Disagree somewhat
 4 Disagree strongly
 9 Don't Know

Civility 2

Please indicate the degree to which you agree with the following statement:

Hard-hitting commercials attacking the opponent are not helpful during election campaigns.

 1 Agree strongly
 2 Agree somewhat
 3 Disagree somewhat
 4 Disagree strongly
 9 Don't Know

Relevance 2

Please indicate the degree to which you agree with the following statement:

I find negative political commercials attacking a candidate for conduct occurring long before the candidate entered public life as uninformative.

 1 Agree strongly
 2 Agree somewhat
 3 Disagree somewhat
 4 Disagree strongly
 9 Don't Know

During this year's campaign, many negative advertisements have been aired attacking the candidates running for the U.S. Senate. In this section of the survey, you will read a summary of a negative advertisement and then answer a series of questions about the advertisement. The first advertisement attacked [insert Democratic candidate's Name].[1]

First Attack Ad on Democrat: Useful
Thinking about this advertisement, do you find the advertisement very useful, somewhat useful, not useful at all?

1   Very Useful
2   Somewhat Useful
3   Not Useful at All
9   Don't Know

First Attack Ad on Democrat: Civil
Thinking about the tone of the advertisement, would you characterize the tone of the advertisement as overly hostile, somewhat hostile, or not hostile at all?

1   Very Hostile
2   Somewhat Hostile
3   Not Hostile at All
9   Don't Know

First Attack Ad on Democrat: Support
Does the advertisement make you more or less likely to support (insert name of Democratic candidate for Senate) in this year's race for the U.S. Senate?

1   Much More Likely to Support
2   Somewhat More Likely to Support
3   Somewhat Less Likely to Support
4   Much Less Likely to Support
9   Don't Know

The second advertisement attacked [insert Democratic Candidate's Name].

Second Attack Ad on Democrat: Useful
Thinking about this advertisement, do you find the advertisement very useful, somewhat useful, not useful at all?

1   Very Useful
2   Somewhat Useful
3   Not Useful at All
9   Don't Know

---

1. See Appendix B for the advertisement scripts used in the survey experiment.

Second Attack Ad on Democrat: Civil
Thinking about the tone of the advertisement, would you characterize the tone of the advertisement as overly hostile, somewhat hostile, or not hostile at all?

1 Very Hostile
2 Somewhat Hostile
3 Not Hostile at All
9 Don't Know

Second Attack Ad on Democrat: Support
Does the advertisement make you more or less likely to support (insert name of Democratic candidate for Senate) in this year's race for the U.S. Senate?

1 Much More Likely to Support
2 Somewhat More Likely to Support
3 Somewhat Less Likely to Support
4 Much Less Likely to Support
9 Don't Know

Now you will read summaries of negative advertisements aired during the campaign criticizing [insert Republican Senate candidate's name].

First Attack Ad on Republican: Useful
Thinking about this advertisement, do you find the advertisement very useful, somewhat useful, not useful at all?

1 Very Useful
2 Somewhat Useful
3 Not Useful at All
9 Don't Know

First Attack Ad on Republican: Civil
Thinking about the tone of the advertisement, would you characterize the tone of the advertisement as overly hostile, somewhat hostile, or not hostile at all?

1 Very Hostile
2 Somewhat Hostile
3 Not Hostile at All
9 Don't Know

First Attack Ad on Republican: Support
Does the advertisement make you more or less likely to support (insert name of Republican candidate for Senate) in this year's race for the U.S. Senate?

1 Much More Likely to Support
2 Somewhat More Likely to Support

3 Somewhat Less Likely to Support

4 Much Less Likely to Support

9 Don't Know

Second Attack Ad on Republican: Useful

Thinking about this advertisement, do you find the advertisement very useful, somewhat useful, not useful at all?

1 Very Useful

2 Somewhat Useful

3 Not Useful at All

9 Don't Know

Second Attack Ad on Republican: Civil

Thinking about the tone of the advertisement, would you characterize the tone of the advertisement as overly hostile, somewhat hostile, or not hostile at all?

1 Very Hostile

2 Somewhat Hostile

3 Not Hostile at All

9 Don't Know

Second Attack Ad on Republican: Support

Does the advertisement make you more or less likely to support (insert name of Republican candidate for Senate) in this year's race for the U.S. Senate?

1 Much More Likely to Support

2 Somewhat More Likely to Support

3 Somewhat Less Likely to Support

4 Much Less Likely to Support

9 Don't Know

Posttest Questionnaire for 2014 CCES and ASU Module

Feeling Thermometer for Democratic Senate Candidate
Using the feeling thermometer, where 10 means you feel very favorable toward the person and 0 means you feel very unfavorable toward the person, please rate [insert name of Democratic candidate for Senate]

Using a scale from 1 to 10, where 10 means you feel very favorable toward the person and 1 means you feel very unfavorable toward the person, please rate [insert name of Republican candidate for Senate]

Competent Democratic Senate Candidate

How well does the word "competent" describe [insert name of Democratic Senate candidate], the Democratic candidate for the U.S. Senate?

1 Extremely Well
2 Quite Well
3 Not Too Well
4 Not Well at All
9 Don't Know

Trustworthy Democratic Senate Candidate

How well does the word "trustworthy" describe [insert name of Democratic Senate candidate], the Democratic candidate for the U.S. Senate?

1 Extremely Well
2 Quite Well
3 Not Too Well
4 Not Well at All
9 Don't Know

Competent Republican Senate Candidate

How well does the word "competent" describe [insert name of Republican Senate candidate], Republican candidate for the U.S. Senate?

1 Extremely Well
2 Quite Well
3 Not Too Well
4 Not Well at All
9 Don't Know

Trustworthy Republican Senate Candidate

How well does the word "trustworthy" describe [insert name of Republican Senate candidate], Republican candidate for the U.S. Senate?

1 Extremely Well
2 Quite Well
3 Not Too Well
4 Not Well at All
9 Don't Know

Tone of Senate Campaign

How would you describe the tone of the U.S. Senate campaign between [insert names of Democratic Senate candidate and Republican Senate candidate]? Would you characterize the campaign as very positive, somewhat positive, somewhat negative, or very negative?

1 Very positive.
2 Somewhat positive
3 Somewhat negative
4 Very negative
9 Don't Know

The following questions assess your views about negative advertisements in general. Please indicate the degree to which you agree with the following statement:
Some negative advertisements are so nasty that I stop paying attention to what the candidates are saying.

1 Agree strongly
2 Agree somewhat
3 Disagree somewhat
4 Disagree strongly
9 Don't Know

Please indicate the degree to which you agree with the following statement:
Negative advertisements discussing a candidate's personal misbehavior are fair game.

1 Agree strongly
2 Agree somewhat
3 Disagree somewhat
4 Disagree strongly
9 Don't Know

Please indicate the degree to which you agree with the following statement:
Hard-hitting commercials attacking the opponent are not helpful during election campaigns.

1 Agree strongly
2 Agree somewhat
3 Disagree somewhat
4 Disagree strongly
9 Don't Know

Please indicate the degree to which you agree with the following statement:

I find negative political commercials attacking a candidate for conduct occurring long before the candidate entered public life as uninformative.

1 Agree strongly
2 Agree somewhat
3 Disagree somewhat
4 Disagree strongly
9 Don't Know

For the following statements, please tell me whether you agree strongly, agree somewhat, disagree somewhat, or disagree strongly.

If people don't care how an election comes out, then they shouldn't vote in it.

1 Strongly Agree
2 Somewhat Agree
3 Somewhat Disagree
4 Strongly Disagree
9 Don't Know

I don't think public officials care much about what people like me think.

1 Strongly Agree
2 Somewhat Agree
3 Somewhat Disagree
4 Strongly Disagree
9 Don't Know

During the 2014 election, Republicans ran negative ads criticizing Democratic incumbents for their support of Obamacare. How useful did you think it was to criticize Democratic incumbents for supporting Obamacare?

1 Very Useful
2 Somewhat Useful
3 Not Very Useful
4 Not Useful at All
9 Don't Know

During the 2014 election, Republicans ran negative ads criticizing Democrats incumbents for "going Washington" and supporting higher taxes and wasteful spending. How useful did you think it was to criticize Democratic incumbents for higher taxes and wasteful spending?

   1 Very Useful
   2 Somewhat Useful
   3 Not Very Useful
   4 Not Useful at All
   9 Don't Know

During the 2014 election, Democrats ran negative ads criticizing Republican incumbents for ties to Wall Street and helping big banks make risky investments. How useful did you think it was to criticize Republican incumbents for their Wall Street ties?

   1 Very Useful
   2 Somewhat Useful
   3 Not Very Useful
   4 Not Useful at All
   9 Don't Know

During the 2014 election, Democrats ran negative ads criticizing Republican incumbents for shutting down the federal government. How useful did you think it was to criticize Republican incumbents for shutting down the federal government?

   1 Very Useful
   2 Somewhat Useful
   3 Not Very Useful
   4 Not Useful at All
   9 Don't Know

During the 2014 election, Republicans ran negative ads criticizing Democratic challengers for being a rubber stamp for Obama's liberal agenda and values. How useful did you think it was to criticize Democratic challengers for being a rubber stamp for Obama's liberal agenda and values?

   1 Very Useful
   2 Somewhat Useful
   3 Not Very Useful
   4 Not Useful at All
   9 Don't Know

During the 2014 election, Republicans ran negative ads criticizing Democratic challengers for receiving support from Harry Reid, Nancy Pelosi, and Elizabeth Warren and for supporting their liberal agenda. How useful did you think it was to criticize Democratic challengers for their ties to Washington liberals?

1 Very Useful
2 Somewhat Useful
3 Not Very Useful
4 Not Useful at All
9 Don't Know

During the 2014 election, Democrats ran negative ads criticizing Republican challengers for accepting money from the billionaire Koch brothers. How useful did you think it was to criticize Republican challengers for their ties to the Koch brothers?

1 Very Useful
2 Somewhat Useful
3 Not Very Useful
4 Not Useful at All
9 Don't Know

During the 2014 election, Democrats ran negative ads criticizing Republican challengers for their extreme positions on abortion. How useful did you think it was to criticize Republican challengers for their positions on abortion?

1 Very Useful
2 Somewhat Useful
3 Not Very Useful
4 Not Useful at All
9 Don't Know

Scripts of Negative Political Advertisements in 2014 CCES Survey Experiment

Democratic Incumbent Advertisement #1

Civil Version: Senator [Insert Name] was the deciding vote on Obamacare. Obamacare has led to higher health care costs; millions of people have lost their coverage and Medicare spending has been reduced. The nation can't take any more votes like this. It's time to end Obamacare. We need to send Senator [Insert Name] home.

Uncivil Version: Senator [Insert Name] told the lie of the year. She/he told you that if you liked your insurance plan, you could keep your insurance. But President Obama and Senator [Insert Name] knew it was impossible for the government to keep their promise. Health care costs are up and so is the cost of Medicare. Senator [Insert Name], you looked us in the eyes and lied.

Democratic Incumbent Advertisement #2

Civil Version: Senator [Insert Name] went to Washington and "went Washington." Senator [Insert Name] voted for more spending and higher taxes. She/he voted to increase the debt limit. Senator [Insert Name] can't say no to more spending, more taxes, and more debt. [Insert State] families pay the price. Senator [Insert Name] is wrong for [Insert State]. It's time to bring him/her home.

Uncivil Version: Senator [Insert Name] went to Washington and "went Washington." Senator [Insert Name] voted for more spending and higher taxes. Senator [Insert Name] can't say no to more spending, and [Insert State] families pay the price. The spending has led to an increase in the nation's debt. Senator [Insert Name] is irresponsible and reckless. It's disgraceful how she/he burdened our children with this debt. It's time to bring her/him home.

Democratic Challenger/Open Candidate Advertisement #1

Civil Version: What kind of senator would [Insert Name] be? [Insert Name] is quoted as saying: "I will be proud to work with President Obama." [Insert Name] will be a rubber stamp for Obama's liberal agenda and values. Obama's liberal friends are pouring money into [Insert State] hoping she/he will be Obama's senator, not yours.

Uncivil Version: What kind of senator would [Insert Name] be? [Insert Name] is quoted as saying: "I will be proud to work with President Obama." [Insert Name] will be a rubber stamp for Obama's liberal agenda and values. Obama's liberal friends like Harry Reid and Nancy Pelosi are pouring money into [Insert State] hoping she/he will be Obama's senator, not yours. The last thing the people of [Insert State] need is a liberal blindly rubber-stamping Obama's bad ideas.

Democratic Challenger/Open Candidate Advertisement #2

Civil Version: Just look at who is supporting [Insert Name] in her/his campaign for [Insert State]'s Senate seat: Harry Reid, Nancy Pelosi, and Elizabeth Warren. Why are Washington liberals interested in our Senate race? Because [Insert Name] supports their liberal agenda, including higher taxes, Medicare cuts, wasteful spending. [Insert Name] is too liberal for [Insert State].

Uncivil Version: Just look at who is supporting [Insert Name] in her/his campaign for [Insert State] Senate seat: Harry Reid, Nancy Pelosi, and Elizabeth Warren. Why are Washington liberals interested in our Senate race? Because [Insert Name] supports their extreme agenda, including higher taxes, Medicare cuts, wasteful spending. [Insert Name] doesn't share our values. Just look at her/his extreme friends. [Insert Name] is just too extreme for [Insert State].

Republican Incumbent Advertisement #1

Civil Version: Senator [Insert Name] delivered for Wall Street, saving big banks billions in taxes. Senator [Insert Name] supported legislation helping big banks make risky investments. Senator [Insert Name] has also been working hard supporting special tax cuts for corporations and multimillionaires. That's good for Wall Street, but bad for the people of [Insert State].

Uncivil Version: Senator [Insert Name] delivered for Wall Street, saving corrupt banks billions in taxes. Senator [Insert Name] supported legislation helping corrupt banks make risky investments. Senator [Insert Name] has also been working hard supporting special tax cuts for corporations and multimillionaires. But Senator [Insert Name] could care less about middle-class families in [Insert State]. Senator [Insert Name] is looking out for herself/himself and big banks.

Republican Incumbent Advertisement #2

Civil Version: Senator [Insert Name] cost us $24 billion by shutting down the government. Her/his actions damaged our economy, hurt middle-class families, and took our government to the brink of default. Instead of working for families, Senator [Insert Name] is playing Washington politics.

Uncivil Version: Senator [Insert Name] cost us $24 billion by shutting down the government. Her/his reckless and irresponsible actions damaged our economy, hurt middle-class families, and took our government to the brink of default. It's just sad that [Insert Name] is playing Washington politics instead of protecting [Insert State] families.

Republican Challenger/Open Candidate Advertisement #1

Civil Version: The out-of-state billionaire Koch brothers are spending millions on attack ads to help elect [Insert Name] because the Koch brothers and [Insert Name] share the same agenda: gutting the Clean Air Act, giving big tax breaks to millionaires, rewarding corporations for shipping American jobs overseas. [Insert Name] might be a good investment for the Koch brothers, but she's/he's the wrong choice for [Insert State].

Uncivil Version: The out-of-state billionaire Koch brothers are spending millions on attack ads to help elect [Insert Name] because [Insert Name] has sold herself/himself to the highest bidder. She/he is willing to give big tax breaks to millionaires and reward corporations for shipping American jobs overseas, while hurting [Insert State] voters. [Insert Name] might be a good investment for the Koch brothers, but she's/he's the wrong choice for [Insert State]. Just another politician bought and paid for by out-of-state billionaires. Shame on you, [Insert Name].

Republican Challenger/Open Candidate Advertisement #2

Civil Version: [Insert Name] would make it a crime to use common forms of birth control, would outlaw abortions for victims of rape or incest, would even allow insurance companies to charge women more than men. [Insert Name] has even supported a policy that would interfere with a woman's decision regarding her own birth control. [Insert Name] is wrong for [Insert State].

Uncivil Version: [Insert State] would make it a crime to use common forms of birth control, would outlaw abortions for victims of rape or incest, would even allow insurance companies to charge women more than men. [Insert State] wants to take medical decisions away from women and their doctors. The only direction that [Insert State] will take women's rights is backwards. Radically wrong ideas for [Insert State].

Questionnaire for ASU 2015 Online Survey Experiment

1. Some people don't pay much attention to political campaigns. How about you? Would you say that you are very much interested, somewhat interested, or not much interested in political campaigns?
   1 Very Much Interested
   2 Somewhat Interested
   3 Not Much Interested
   9 Don't Know

2. Where are you most likely to get news or current events?
   1. Television/local news
   2. Television/national news
   3. Television/cable news (Fox, CNN, MSNBC)
   4. Internet/news sites
   5. Internet/social media
   9. None of the above

3. How often do you pay attention to news about politics and government affairs in a typical week?
   1. Every day
   2. A few times a week
   3. About once a week
   4. A few times a month
   5. Less than once a month
   9 None of the above

The following questions assess your views about negative advertisements, in general.

4. Please indicate how much you agree with the following statement:

Some negative advertisements are so nasty that I stop paying attention to what the candidates are saying.

    1 Agree strongly
    2 Agree somewhat
    3 Disagree somewhat
    4 Disagree strongly
    9 Don't Know

5. Please indicate how much you agree with the following statement:

Negative advertisements discussing a candidate's personal misbehavior are fair game.

    1 Agree strongly
    2 Agree somewhat
    3 Disagree somewhat
    4 Disagree strongly
    9 Don't Know

6. Please indicate how much you agree with the following statement:

Hard-hitting commercials attacking the opponent are not helpful during election campaigns.

    1 Agree strongly
    2 Agree somewhat
    3 Disagree somewhat
    4 Disagree strongly
    9 Don't Know

7. Please indicate how much you agree with the following statement:

I find negative political commercials attacking a candidate for conduct occurring long before the candidate entered public life as uninformative.

    1 Agree strongly
    2 Agree somewhat
    3 Disagree somewhat
    4 Disagree strongly
    9 Don't Know

The following is the first of several political advertisements. Please watch the entire advertisement, and then answer the questions following the advertisement.[2]

8. Thinking about the first advertisement, how useful do you consider the advertisement on a scale ranging from (1) Not useful at all to (5) Very useful?

   1 Not Useful at All

   2

   3

   4

   5 Very Useful

   9 Don't Know

9. Thinking about the tone of the first advertisement, how would you characterize the tone of the advertisement on a scale ranging from (1) Not hostile at all to (5) Very hostile

   1 Not Hostile at All

   2

   3

   4

   5 Very Hostile

   9 Don't Know

10. Thinking about the effectiveness of the first advertisement, how would you rate the advertisement's effectiveness on a scale ranging from (1) Not effective at all to (5) Very effective

   1 Not Effective at All

   2

   3

   4

   5 Very Effective

   9 Don't Know

The following is the second political advertisement. Please watch the entire advertisement, and then answer the questions following the advertisement.

---

2. The links to each of the advertisements, along with the text of advertisements, are provided in Appendix D.

11. Thinking about the second advertisement, how useful do you consider the advertisement on a scale ranging from (1) Not useful at all to (5) Very useful?

    1 Not Useful at All
    2
    3
    4
    5 Very Useful
    9 Don't Know

12. Thinking about the tone of the second advertisement, how would you characterize the tone of the advertisement on a scale ranging from (1) Not hostile at all to (5) Very hostile

    1 Not Hostile at All
    2
    3
    4
    5 Very Hostile
    9 Don't Know

13. Thinking about the effectiveness of the second advertisement, how would you rate the advertisement's effectiveness on a scale ranging from (1) Not effective at all to (5) Very effective

    1 Not Effective at All
    2
    3
    4
    5 Very Effective
    9 Don't Know

The following is the third political advertisement. Please watch the entire advertisement, and then answer the questions following the advertisement.

14. Thinking about the third advertisement, how useful do you consider the advertisement on a scale ranging from (1) Not useful at all to (5) Very useful?

    1 Not Useful at All
    2
    3
    4
    5 Very Useful
    9 Don't Know

15. Thinking about the tone of the third advertisement, how would you characterize the tone of the advertisement on a scale ranging from (1) Not hostile at all to (5) Very hostile

    1 Not Hostile at All

    2

    3

    4

    5 Very Hostile

    9 Don't Know

16. Thinking about the effectiveness of the third advertisement, how would you rate the advertisement's effectiveness on a scale ranging from (1) Not effective at all to (5) Very effective

    1 Not Effective at All

    2

    3

    4

    5 Very Effective

    9 Don't Know

The following is the fourth political advertisement. Please watch the entire advertisement, and then answer the questions following the advertisement.

17. Thinking about the fourth advertisement, how useful do you consider the advertisement on a scale ranging from (1) Not useful at all to (5) Very useful?

    1 Not Useful at All

    2

    3

    4

    5 Very Useful

    9 Don't Know

18. Thinking about the tone of the fourth advertisement, how would you characterize the tone of the advertisement on a scale ranging from (1) Not hostile at all to (5) Very hostile

    1 Not Hostile at All

    2

    3

    4

    5 Very Hostile

    9 Don't Know

19. Thinking about the effectiveness of the fourth advertisement, how would you rate the advertisement's effectiveness on a scale ranging from (1) Not effective at all to (5) Very effective

    1　Not Effective at All

    2

    3

    4

    5　Very Effective

    9　Don't Know

Now, we would to ask you some more general questions.

20. Generally speaking, do you usually think of yourself as a Republican, a Democrat, an independent, or what? Where would you place yourself on the following scale?

    1. Strong Democrat
    2. Weak Democrat
    3. Independent, Leaning toward the Democratic Party
    4. Independent
    5. Independent, Leaning toward the Republican Party
    6. Weak Republican
    7. Strong Republican
    8. Don't Know

Please indicate your level of agreement with the following statements.

21. Most men are better suited emotionally for politics than most women.

    1. Strongly Agree
    2. Agree
    3. Neither Agree nor Disagree
    4. Disagree
    5. Strongly Disagree

22. Women should run for public office and take part in the government just as men do.

    1. Strongly Agree
    2. Agree
    3. Neither Agree nor Disagree
    4. Disagree
    5. Strongly Disagree

23. Men are better qualified to be political leaders than women.
    1. Strongly Agree
    2. Agree
    3. Neither Agree nor Disagree
    4. Disagree
    5. Strongly Disagree

We would like to ask you a few questions about the government in Washington. Many people are too busy to keep up with these topics, so if you don't know the answer, just skip the question.

24. What position or office does Elena Kagan hold today?

25. How much of a majority is required for the U.S. Senate and U.S. House to override a presidential veto?

26. Do you happen to know which party has the most members in the House of Representatives in Washington, D.C., today?

27. Whose responsibility is it to determine if a law is constitutional or not—is it the president's, the Congress's, or the Supreme Court's?

28. Who is currently the U.S. secretary of defense?

29. How long is the term of a U.S. senator?

30. One way that people talk about politics in the United States is in terms of liberal, conservative, and moderate ideology. The political views people might hold are often arranged from extremely liberal (1) to extremely conservative (7). Where would you place yourself on this scale?
    1. Extremely Liberal
    2. Liberal
    3. Somewhat Liberal
    4. Moderate
    5. Somewhat Conservative
    6. Conservative
    7. Very Conservative
    8. Don't Know

31. Finally, we would like to ask you some questions about yourself.

32. What year are you in school?
     1. Freshman
     2. Sophomore
     3. Junior
     4. Senior
     5. Graduate Student

33. What is your major?
     1. Political science
     2. Global studies
     3. Social science major, other than political science and global studies
     4. Humanities major
     5. Natural science major
     6. Engineering major
     7. Business major
     8. Other major

34. In what year were you born?

35. Is your primary residence in the United States?
     1. Yes (go to next question)
     2. No (go to question 37)

36. What state do you consider your primary residence?

37. What country do you consider your primary residence?

38. Please indicate your gender (1 = Male; 2 = Female, 3 = Other)

Text of Advertisements from 2015 ASU Online Survey Experiment

Obamacare Uncivil (Male Candidate)
Title: "Begich Lied"; **State**: Alaska; **Candidate Attacked**: Democrat Mark Begich; **Script of the Commercial**: "OBAMA PROMISED." Video of Obama saying, "No matter what you've heard, if you like your doctor or health care plan, you can keep it." Four Pinocchio's, *Washington Post*, 10/30/13. Another video of Obama saying, "If you like your health care plan, you will be able to keep your health care plan." Obama Administration knew millions would be forced to change insurance, *Yahoo News*, 10/28/13. A third video of Obama saying, "If you like your current insurance, you can keep that insurance. Period." Impossible for the President to keep that pledge, *Washington Post*, 10/30/13. A fourth video of Obama saying, "If you like your doctor, if you like your plan, you can keep your doctor, you can keep your plan. Nobody is talking about taking that away from you." White House knew millions could not keep plans under Obamacare, CNBC, 10/29/13. "Obama Lied. Begich Lied." Video of Mark Begich, "You got an insurance policy you like, that's yours." YOUR HEALTHCARE DIED. https://www.youtube.com/watch?v=LU2gcWfhzgY.

Obamacare Civil (Male Candidate)
Title: "Holding Begich Accountable"; **State**: Alaska; **Candidate Attacked**: Democrat Mark Begich; **Script of the Commercial**: "I trusted the President and Senator Begich. Lots of promises were made to pass Obamacare. They knew the real truth. Now millions are losing their health care, some are even losing their doctor. For too many of us, costs are going way up. Senator Begich didn't listen. How can I ever trust him again? It just isn't fair. Alaska deserves better."
https://www.youtube.com/watch?v=F-HyVYtxBlg.

Obamacare Uncivil (Female Candidate)

Title: "Landrieu Lied"; **State**: Louisiana; **Candidate Attacked**: Democrat Mary Landrieu; **Script of the Commercial**: "OBAMA PROMISED." Video of Obama saying, "No matter what you've heard, if you like your doctor or health care plan, can keep it." Four Pinocchio's, *Washington Post*, 10/30/13. Another video of Obama saying, "If you like your health care plan, you will be able to keep your health care plan." Obama Administration knew millions would be forced to change insurance, *Yahoo News*, 10/28/13. A third video of Obama saying, "If you like your current insurance, you can keep that insurance. Period." Impossible for the President to keep that pledge, *Washington Post*, 10/30/13. A fourth video of Obama saying, "If you like your doctor, if you like your plan, you can keep your doctor, you can keep your plan. Nobody is talking about taking that away from you." White House knew millions could not keep plans under Obamacare, CNBC, 10/29/13. "Obama Lied. Landrieu Lied." Video of Mary Landrieu saying, "Those individuals who like the coverage they already have will be able to keep their current plan." YOUR HEALTHCARE DIED.

https://www.youtube.com/watch?v=Y4qs5sE0b4s.

Obamacare Civil (Female Candidate)

Title: "Obamacare Doesn't Work"; **State**: Louisiana; **Candidate Attacked**: Democrat Mary Landrieu; **Script of the Commercial**: "People don't like political ads. I don't like them either. But healthcare isn't about politics. It's about people. It's not about a website that doesn't work. It's not about poll numbers or approval ratings. It's about people. And millions of people have lost their health insurance. Millions of people can't see their own doctors. And millions are paying more. And getting less. Obamacare doesn't work. It just doesn't work. Tell Senator Landrieu to stop thinking about politics and start thinking about people."

https://www.youtube.com/watch?v=MNRQMqmTmLM.

Abortion Uncivil (Male Candidate)

Title: "Torn Apart"; **State**: Colorado; **Candidate Attacked**: Republican Cory Gardner; **Script of the Commercial**: "Your whole world is torn apart. But Congressman Gardner would make it harder, pushing to outlaw a woman's right to choose. Even in cases of rape and incest. Worse. Gardner tried to redefine rape to mean only forcible rape. In Gardner's bill, victims who were drugged or minors who were victims of statutory rape would not be considered rape victims. Cory Gardner is just too extreme."

https://www.youtube.com/watch?v=9bjx2EJtl3A&feature=youtu.be.

Abortion Civil (Male Candidate)

Title: "Backwards"; **State**: Colorado; **Candidate Attacked**: Republican Cory Gardner; **Script of the Commercial**: "Congressman Gardner just doesn't get it. For some, it's Gardner's support for harsh anti-abortion laws. Even sponsoring a bill to make abortion a felony, including cases of rape and incest. I want my daughter to have the same choices

as I do. Seriously. It's 2014. The only place that Cory Gardner will take women's rights is backwards."
https://www.youtube.com/watch?v=26sbLmONB2Y.

Abortion Uncivil (Female Candidate)
Title: "Backwards"; **State:** Michigan; **Candidate Attacked:** Republican Terri Lynn Land; **Script of the Commercial:** "Backwards. That's the direction that Terri Lynn Land would take Michigan women. Under Land's radical plan, common forms of birth control would be outlawed. Insurance companies could go back to charging women more. And Land would ban abortion, even for victims of rape and incest. Terri Lynn Land has it backwards on women's health. Michigan women just can't afford Republican Terri Lynn Land."
https://www.youtube.com/watch?v=YRYwH-rwuNE.

Abortion Civil (Female Candidate)
Title: "iPad"; **State:** Michigan; **Candidate Attacked:** Republican Terri Lynn Land; **Script of the Commercial:** Video on iPad of Terri Lynn Land: "But as a woman, I might know a little bit more about women then Gary Peters." A woman says, "Terri Lynn Land doesn't know me." Then iPad video of Terri Lynn Land saying "I might know a little bit more about women." Another woman, "Land doesn't think that women should have a right to choose, even in a case of rape or incest." Then iPad video of Terri Lynn Land saying "I might know a little bit more about women." A third woman said, "Terri Lynn Land said guaranteeing equal pay for women who do the same work as men is not a good idea." A fourth woman says, "Terri Lynn Land knows nothing about the Michigan women I know."
https://www.youtube.com/watch?v=k74TKNeLoOw.

Rubber Stamp Uncivil (Male Candidate)
Title: "Rubber Stamp"; **State:** Arkansas; **Candidate Attacked:** Democrat Mark Pryor; **Script of the Commercial:** "Mark Pryor has voted with Barack Obama at least ninety percent of the time. For the failed stimulus, for higher taxes, more spending, trillions more in debt, and more job-killing regulations. And Pryor cast the deciding vote for Obamacare. For more than five years, Mark Pryor has been Obama's rubber stamp. Not a fighter for us."
https://www.youtube.com/watch?v=KKj2uguGPj8.

Rubber Stamp Civil (Male Candidate)
Title: "Spelling Bee"; **State:** Arkansas; **Candidate Attacked:** Democrat Mark Pryor; **Script of the Commercial:** " 'Your next word is *Pryor*.' 'May I have the definition please?' 'Pryor: A Washington liberal out of touch with Arkansas, voted for the Obama agenda ninety percent of the time.' 'May I hear it in a sentence?' 'Mark Pryor was the deciding vote for Obamacare.' 'Pryor: O-B-A-M-A.' 'Close enough.' "
https://www.youtube.com/watch?v=xqHXks5Qjwc.

Rubber Stamp Uncivil (Female Candidate)

Title: "Respect"; **State**: Georgia; **Candidate Attacked**: Democrat Michelle Nunn; **Script of the Commercial**: "What kind of senator would Michelle Nunn be? [Video of Michelle Nunn:] 'I'm proud to have worked with President Obama.' Michelle Nunn. A rubber stamp for Obama's liberal values. [Video of Michelle Nunn:] 'I am very grateful for my service with President Obama.' Obamacare, higher taxes, billions in cuts to Medicare. That's the Obama-Nunn agenda. [Video of Michelle Nunn:] 'I defer to the president's judgment.' Michelle Nunn. She'll be Obama's senator. Not yours." https://www.youtube.com/watch?v=Bb8D3UPaLz4&list=UULpDIMhugAoYQ2t iSB1_8HA.

Rubber Stamp Civil (Female Candidate)

Title: "Nunn Says It All"; **State**: Georgia; **Candidate Attacked**: Democrat Michelle Nunn; **Script of Commercial**: "Because of President Obama's mismanagement, Georgia veterans died waiting for the care our country promised them. Yet, Michelle Nunn said, 'I defer to the president's judgment.' Georgia families are losing their coverage, yet Nunn would keep Obamacare. And Nunn even initially refused a travel ban to help stop Ebola. Michelle Nunn would be Obama's Senator. Not Georgia's. [Michelle Nunn:] 'I defer to the president's judgment.' " https://www.youtube.com/watch?v=6Dfox_eyGXA&feature=youtu.be.

Koch Brothers Uncivil (Male Candidate)

Title: "Agenda"; **State**: Louisiana; **Candidate Attacked**: Republican Bill Cassidy; **Script of the Commercial**: "Out-of-state billionaires, spending millions to rig the system and elect Bill Cassidy. Their goal: Another politician bought and paid for. Their agenda: protect tax cuts for companies that ship our jobs overseas, cut Social Security, and end Medicare as we know it. They even tried to kill relief for hurricane victims. Cassidy's billion-dollar backers, they've got a plan for him, and it's not good for Louisiana." https://www.youtube.com/watch?v=FUxj9Fun-Ko.

Koch Brothers Civil (Male Candidate)

Title: "Losses"; **State**: Louisiana; **Candidate Attacked**: Republican Bill Cassidy; **Script of the Commercial**: "Battered by hurricanes, lost everything to floods. And for thousands of Louisianans, flood insurance and hurricane relief were our only protection. But the out-of-state billionaire Koch brothers funded the fight to let flood insurance premiums soar, helping the insurance companies, and cut off hurricane relief for Louisiana families. Now their spending millions to buy a Senate seat for Bill Cassidy so he can fight for them. If the Kochs and Cassidy win, Louisiana loses." https://www.youtube.com/watch?v=PXSpPmDPO6Y.

Koch Brothers Uncivil (Female Candidate)

Title: "Dark Money"; **State:** Iowa; **Candidate Attacked:** Republican Joni Ernst; **Script of the Commercial:** "'Okay, who's next?' 'Iowa. Joni Ernst.' 'We got her to pledge?' Joni signed on the line.' 'Hmmmm. The tax breaks that pledge protects are gold. Green light. More outsourcing. China, Mexico, all the way. She isn't worried about Iowa jobs?' 'Oh—never mind that. Joni Ernst is with us.' 'Any chance she will back out?' 'When pigs fly.'"
https://www.youtube.com/watch?v=311bg6zIZSc&feature=youtu.be.

Koch Brothers Civil (Female Candidate)

Title: "Shared"; **State:** Iowa; **Candidate Attacked:** Republican Joni Ernst; **Script of the Commercial:** "Sure, Joni Ernst's campaign is pretty slick, but look behind it. The Koch brothers, out-of-state oil billionaires are buying the election for Joni Ernst because she shares their agenda. More tax breaks to billionaires and big corporations, cutting Medicare, privatizing Social Security. Joni Ernst went even further and voted to raise the gas tax. Joni Ernst. Right for the oil billionaires, wrong for the rest of us."
https://www.youtube.com/watch?v=PFVVOQLTWAU.

Coding Instructions for Original Content Analysis of Negative Advertisements

Civility (Cohen's Kappa = .74): scored on a scale from 1 (not very civil) to 3 (very civil).[3]

When coding civility, think about what the tone may seem like to the average citizen of the state. Regardless of someone's partisan view, would a viewer consider the tone of the advertisement to be courteous or polite? If so, the advertisement should receive a code of 3. If the tone seems somewhat civil but not overly harsh, the advertisement should receive a code of 2. If the advertisement contains some extremely pointed criticisms or ad hominem attacks, the advertisement should be coded as a 1. If words like "liar," for example, are used instead of "dishonest," the appropriate code is likely to be 1. When coding the civility of the advertisement, it is important to consider the music (threatening, sad, humorous) and the types of visuals (dark, unflattering). If you are not sure whether the advertisement is uncivil (1) or somewhat civil (2), you should give the advertisement a code of 2. Similarly, if you not sure whether the advertisement is somewhat civil (2) or very civil (3), you should give the advertisement a code of 2.

---

3. Reliability was assessed between two coders for 10% of the advertisements. We rely on Cohen's Kappa instead of percentage of agreement between coders since Cohen's Kappa corrects for the possibility of agreement occurring by chance (McHugh, 2012). McHugh suggests that scores of higher than .80 indicate strong agreement, while scores between .60 and .79 indicate moderate agreement. With this classification, all but one of our measures (civility) achieves strong agreement with the Cohen's Kappa coefficient.

Relevance (Cohen's Kappa = .84): scored on a scale from 1 (not very relevant) to 3 (very relevant).

When coding relevance, think about whether the content of the commercial would be relevant or important to the average citizens of the state. (Will they care about the content of the topic? Is it clear why they should care? Is it an issue or subject that the average person cares about in the state? Is it a topic that seems important for a senatorial campaign?) When considering the relevance of the advertisement, if most/all of the advertisement focuses on a relevant topic (e.g., focusing on a policy area or focusing on the candidate's personality characteristics), then the relevance coding should be 3. If the advertisement focuses on topics of questionable relevance (e.g., focusing on issues no longer on the nation's/state's agenda, on topics that most voters would think to be trivial, on content that does not seem relevant to the ongoing campaign), the relevance of the advertisement should be coded as a 1. Many advertisements will focus on topics that may appear to be somewhat relevant to the average person, or some part of the advertisement focuses on important issues, while other parts of the advertisement may discuss questionable topics. These types of advertisements should receive a code of 2. Also, if you are not sure whether an advertisement should be coded as a 1 or 2 (or 2 or 3), give the advertisement the middle code of 2.

Going Washington (Cohen's Kappa = .90): For incumbents or members of Congress seeking election to Senate. Anything about losing touch with the state, caring more about Washington than home. References to "Washington politician" should be coded here.

Negative Ties to Business (Cohen's Kappa = .88): Any negative ties to Wall Street, big business, special interests, corporate interests.

Ties to Koch Brothers (Cohen's Kappa = .94): Needs to mention Koch brothers. A commercial could have mention of Koch brothers as well as negative ties to business.

Rubber Stamp on Obama (Cohen's Kappa = .96): 90% plus voting record with Obama, Obama's senator.

Lack Independence (Cohen's Kappa = .91): "Rubber stamp" would also count here. "Does the bidding of corporate interests" would count here as well as in negative ties to business, blindly votes the party line, etc.

Too Liberal and Too Conservative (Cohen's Kappa = .93): Needs to be a pretty clear point of the advertisement, not your own reading of the issue stands.

Dishonest (Cohen's Kappa = .90): We are combining dishonest, untrustworthy and immoral together in this category. "You can't trust this person" should be coded as dishonest.

Not Smart (Cohen's Kappa = .88): We are combining not smart and uninformed.

Not Hardworking (Cohen's Kappa = .89): Absentee votes, not doing his or her job.

Not Empathetic (Cohen's Kappa = .92): Any specific reference to not caring about people or a group of people (i.e., doesn't care, insensitive, not compassionate). If the ad discusses how the candidate doesn't care about women or farmers or veterans, should be coded as not empathetic. But if the ad doesn't discuss people but only talks about the candidate cutting spending for veteran's health or supporting anti-abortion legislation or cutting spending for children's hospitals (without explicitly saying candidate doesn't care), these shouldn't be coded as not empathetic.

Erratic (Cohen's Kappa = .94): Votes both ways on the same issue; changes positions over time, etc. Code any reference to changing positions on issues or saying one thing and then doing something else later.

Inexperienced (Cohen's Kappa = .92): Anything about lack of experience, lack of qualifications, etc.

Not One of Us (Cohen's Kappa = .94): Not from the state, doesn't care about the state, doesn't know about the state. "Not one of us" and "Not ties to state" are being combined into this category.

Text of *14 Advertisements for ASU Focus Group Study*

1. **Title**: "Loan Sharknado"; **State**: Michigan; **Candidate Attacked**: Democrat Gary Peters; **Civility Rating**: 2; **Relevance Rating**: 1; **Script of the Commercial**: "Dark clouds are gathering and Gary Peters is in the eye of the storm. Funded by a convicted felon, connected to a loan shark ring, run by an international gangster, who also contributed to Peters's campaign. Gary Peters 'loan sharknado,' coming soon to a voting booth near you."
   https://www.youtube.com/watch?v=6ol7o3G9Q9E.

2. **Title**: "Bribery Scandal"; **State**: Kentucky; **Candidate Attacked**: Republican Mitch McConnell; **Civility Rating**: 2; **Relevance Rating**: 1; **Script of the Commercial**: "Kentucky U.S. senator is keeping quiet about the sudden resignation of his campaign manager. Senator Mitch McConnell is declining to answer questions about his former campaign manager who resigned during a federal investigation of a bribery scandal. He was linked to a federal investigation into a bribery scandal. Senator McConnell knew about the investigation or the details behind it when he hired Benton last year. McConnell refused to answer any more questions about Benton. Kentucky deserves answers."
   https://www.youtube.com/watch?v=u-QE1HANuec.

3: **Title**: "Backwards"; **State**: Colorado; **Candidate Attacked**: Republican Cory Gardner; **Civility Rating**: 2; **Relevance Rating**: 3; **Script of the Commercial**: "For Colorado's women and families. Congressman Gardner just doesn't get it. For some, it's Gardner's support for harsh anti-abortion laws. Even sponsoring a bill to make abortion a felony, including cases of rape and incest. I want my daughter to have the same choices as I do. For others, it's Gardner's eight-year crusade that would ban birth control. Seriously. It's 2014. The only place that Cory Gardner will take women's rights is backwards."

https://www.youtube.com/watch?v=26sbLmONB2Y.

4. **Title**: "Dark Money"; **State**: Iowa; **Candidate Attacked**: Republican Joni Ernst; **Civility Rating**: 1; **Relevance Rating**: 2; **Script of the Commercial**: " 'Okay, who's next?' 'Iowa. Joni Ernst.' 'We got her to pledge?' 'Joni signed on the line.' Hmmmm. The tax breaks that pledge protects are gold. Green light. More outsourcing. China, Mexico, all the way. She isn't worried about Iowa jobs?' 'Oh—never mind that. Joni Ernst is with us.' 'Any chance she will back out?' 'When pigs fly.' "

https://www.youtube.com/watch?v=311bg6zIZSc&feature=youtu.be.

5. **Title**: "Tom Cotton Helped Spread Ebola Virus"; **State**: Arkansas; **Candidate Attacked**: Republican Tom Cotton; **Civility Rating**: 1; **Relevance Rating**: 2; **Script of Commercial**: "The Ebola outbreak is worse than anyone expected; it's been vastly underestimated. Tom Cotton voted against preparing Americans for pandemics like Ebola. Congressman Cotton voted to cut billions from our nation's medical disaster and emergency program. He was the only Arkansas congressman to vote this way. Just like he was the only one to vote against children's hospital. Instead, Cotton voted for tax cuts for billionaires funding his campaign rather than protecting our families."

https://www.youtube.com/watch?v=c8xYDfwqNWk.

6. **Title**: "Spelling Bee"; **State**: Arkansas; **Candidate Attacked**: Democrat David Pryor; **Civility Rating**: 2; **Relevance Rating**: 2; **Script of Commercial**: " 'Your next word is *Pryor*.' 'May I have the definition please?' 'Pryor: A Washington liberal out of touch with Arkansas, voted for the Obama agenda ninety percent of the time.' 'May I hear it in a sentence?' 'Mark Pryor was the deciding vote for Obamacare.' 'Pryor: O-B-A-M-A.' 'Close enough.' "

https://www.youtube.com/watch?v=xqHXks5Qjwc.

7. **Title**: "The Deciding Vote for Obamacare"; **State**: Virginia; **Candidate Attacked**: Democrat Mark Warner; **Civility Rating**: 1; **Relevance Rating**: 2; **Script of Commercial**: "Mark Warner cast the deciding vote to make you live under Obamacare. But just a few days ago, he voted to shut down the government rather than give up his own special exemption from Obamacare. That's right. Congress gets its own special exemption. You get the worst of Obamacare and he gets a special subsidy. Call him today and tell him, 'Open the government, stop paying taxpayer money on Obamacare.' "

https://www.youtube.com/watch?v=IdtF2W9Pzr8.

8. **Title**: "Bermuda"; **State**: Minnesota; **Candidate Attacked**: Republican Mike McFadden; **Civility Rating**: 2; **Relevance Rating**: 1; **Script of Commercial**: "Bermuda: Known for its beauty, its pink beaches, and for businesses trying to avoid paying taxes. Meet investment banker Mike McFadden. He's running for Senate in Minnesota. But McFadden's business is based right here in Bermuda. That's right, McFadden's company uses a special tax loophole to list its headquarters off-shore and avoid paying millions of dollars in taxes in America. Mike McFadden: he is definitely not for you."
https://www.youtube.com/watch?v=Zg3rbEbrRqc.

9. **Title**: "Crime Scene"; **State**: Alaska; **Candidate Attacked**: Republican Dan Sullivan; **Civility Rating**: 1; **Relevance Rating**: 2; **Script of Commercial**: "I want to show you a crime scene. I was on the Anchorage police force for twenty years. I don't know how long Dan Sullivan lived in Alaska, but I know what he did as attorney general. He let a lot of sex offenders get off with light sentences. One of them got out of prison, and he's now charged with breaking into that apartment building, murdering a senior couple, and sexually assaulting their two-year-old granddaughter. Dan Sullivan should not be a U.S. Senator."
https://www.youtube.com/watch?v=sJLoGqt49Bw.

10. **Title**: "Absent"; **State**: Colorado; **Candidate Attacked**: Democrat Mark Udall; **Civility Rating**: 1; **Relevance Rating**: 3; **Script of Commercial**: "Down in the polls. Mark Udall's TV ads now talk tough on terrorism, but what was Senator Udall's record? Absent for more than half the public hearings in the Senate Armed Services Committee. Absent for all public hearing on emerging threats. Then Udall said, 'I said last week that ISIL does not present an imminent threat to this nation and it doesn't.' Not an imminent threat? Mark Udall's wrong and absent when it counts."
https://www.youtube.com/watch?v=6VCGgjdbxFI.

11. **Title**: "Chicken Dance"; **State**: Iowa; **Candidate Attacked**: Democrat Bruce Braley; **Civility Rating**: 1; **Relevance Rating**: 1; **Script of Commercial**: "The Chicken Dance. Bruce Braley claims he's a farmer. [Woman says:] 'We're farmers.' [Braley says:] 'So am I.' What? [Woman says:] 'We're farmers.' [Braley says:] 'So am I.' But he's really a trial lawyer. 'I spent twenty-four years of my life practicing law.' The Chicken Dance. Braley supported Obamacare. He wants to be our senator? No More Chicken Dance! Say no to Braley for Senate."
https://www.youtube.com/watch?v=2kEQA2O9rIw.

12. **Title**: "Apartment"; **State**: North Carolina: **Candidate Attacked**: Republican Thom Tillis; **Civility Rating**: 1; **Relevance Rating**: 1; **Script of Commercial**: "Thom Tillis shared an apartment with his chief of staff when North Carolina *News &*

Observer reported that the chief of staff was having an extramarital affair with a lobbyist. He was caught on camera and resigned. Then one week later, another Tillis staffer resigned for another sexual relationship with a lobbyist. Thom Tillis's reaction: he claims he was surprised by his roommate's affair but rewarded both aides with taxpayers paid bonuses. Thom Tillis: Spending our money to clean up his mess." https://www.youtube.com/watch?v=SPUY5vv5W-Q.

13. **Title**: "Spelling Bee"; **State**: New Hampshire; **Candidate Attacked**: Democrat Jean Shaheen; **Civility Rating**: 2; **Relevance Rating**: 2; **Script of Commercial**: " 'Your next word is *Shaheen*.' 'May I have a definition please?' 'Shaheen: A Washington liberal out of touch with New Hampshire, voted for the Obama agenda ninety-nine percent of the time.' 'May I hear it in a sentence?' 'Jean Shaheen was the deciding vote for Obamacare.' 'Shaheen: O-B-A-M-A.' 'Close enough.' " https://www.youtube.com/watch?v=VeASvCUOuMI.

14. **Title**: "The Deciding Vote for Obamacare"; **State**: Louisiana; **Candidate Attacked**: Democrat Mary Landrieu; **Civility Rating**: 1; **Relevance Rating**: 2; **Script of Commercial**: "Mary Landrieu cast the deciding vote to make you live under Obamacare. But just a few days ago, she voted to shut down the government rather than give up her own special exemption from Obamacare. That's right. Congress gets its own special exemption. You get the worst of Obamacare; she gets a special subsidy. Call her today and tell her, 'Open the government, stop paying taxpayer money on Obamacare.' " https://www.youtube.com/watch?v=1iXAzSMvAbo.

Focus Group Questionnaire Used to Assess Relevance and Civility of Advertisements

Some people don't pay much attention to political campaigns. How about you? Would you say that you are very much interested, somewhat interested, or not much interested in political campaigns?

    1   Very Much Interested
    2   Somewhat Interested
    3   Not Much Interested
    9   Don't Know

The following questions assess your views about negative advertisements, in general.

Please indicate how much you agree with the following statement:

Some negative advertisements are so nasty that I stop paying attention to what the candidates are saying.

    1   Agree strongly
    2   Agree somewhat
    3   Disagree somewhat
    4   Disagree strongly
    9   Don't Know

Please indicate how much you agree with the following statement:

Negative advertisements discussing a candidate's personal misbehavior are fair game.

1 Agree strongly
2 Agree somewhat
3 Disagree somewhat
4 Disagree strongly
9 Don't Know

Please indicate how much you agree with the following statement:

Hard-hitting commercials attacking the opponent are not helpful during election campaigns.

1 Agree strongly
2 Agree somewhat
3 Disagree somewhat
4 Disagree strongly
9 Don't Know

Please indicate how much you agree with the following statement:

I find negative political commercials attacking a candidate for conduct occurring long before the candidate entered public life as uninformative.

1 Agree strongly
2 Agree somewhat
3 Disagree somewhat
4 Disagree strongly
9 Don't Know

Generally speaking, do you usually think of yourself as a Republican, Democrat, an independent, or what? Where would you place yourself on the following scale?

1. Strong Democrat
2. Weak Democrat
3. Independent, Leaning toward the Democratic Party
4. Independent
5. Independent, Leaning toward the Republican Party
6. Weak Republican
7. Strong Republican
8. Don't Know

Where are you most likely to get news or current events?

1. Television/local news
2. Television/national news
3. Television/cable news (Fox, CNN, MSNBC)
4. Internet/news sites
5. Internet/social media
9. None of the above

How often do you pay attention to news about politics and government affairs in a typical week?

1. Every day
2. A few times a week
3. About once a week
4. A few times a month
5. Less than once a month
9 None of the above

The following is the first of several political advertisements. Please click on the link, watch the entire advertisement, and then answer the questions following the advertisement.
http://www.youtube.com/watch?v=Zg3rbEbrRqc.

Thinking about the content of the first advertisement, how useful do you consider the advertisement on a scale ranging from (1) Not useful at all to (5) Very useful?

1 Not Useful at All
2
3
4
5 Very Useful
9 Don't Know

Thinking about the tone of the first advertisement, how would you characterize the tone of the advertisement on a scale ranging from (1) Not hostile at all to (5) Very hostile

1 Not Hostile at All
2
3
4
5 Very Hostile
9 Don't Know

Thinking about the first advertisement, how much do you like the advertisement on a scale from 1 (Dislike the Advertisement a Great Deal) to 5 (Like Advertisement a Great Deal).

1 Dislike the Advertisement a Great Deal

2

3

4

5 Like the Advertisement a Great Deal

9 Don't Know

Name ONE thing that you LIKED about the first advertisement.

Name ONE thing that you DISLIKED about the first advertisement.

The following is the second political advertisement. Please click on the link, watch the entire advertisement, and then answer the questions following the advertisement. https://www.youtube.com/watch?v=sJLoGqt49Bw.

Thinking about the content of Advertisement #2, how useful do you consider the advertisement on a scale ranging from (1) Not useful at all to (5) Very useful?

1 Not Useful at All

2

3

4

5 Very Useful

9 Don't Know

Thinking about the tone of Advertisement #2, how would you characterize the tone of the advertisement on a scale ranging from (1) Not hostile at all to (5) Very hostile

1 Not Hostile at All

2

3

4

5 Very Hostile

9 Don't Know

Thinking about Advertisement #2, how much do you like the advertisement on a scale from 1 (Dislike the Advertisement a Great Deal) to 5 (Like Advertisement a Great Deal).

1 Dislike the Advertisement a Great Deal

2

3

4

5 Like the Advertisement a Great Deal

9 Don't Know

Name ONE thing that you LIKED about Advertisement #2.

Name ONE thing that you DISLIKED about Advertisement #2.
The following is the third political advertisement. Please click on the link, watch the entire advertisement, and then answer the questions following the advertisement. https://www.youtube.com/watch?v=6VCGgjdbxFI.

Thinking about the content of Advertisement #3, how useful do you consider the advertisement on a scale ranging from (1) Not useful at all to (5) Very useful?

1 Not Useful at All

2

3

4

5 Very Useful

9 Don't Know

Thinking about the tone of Advertisement #3, how would you characterize the tone of the advertisement on a scale ranging from (1) Not hostile at all to (5) Very hostile

1 Not Hostile at All

2

3

4

5 Very Hostile

9 Don't Know

Thinking about Advertisement #3, how much do you like the advertisement on a scale from 1 (Dislike the Advertisement a Great Deal) to 5 (Like Advertisement a Great Deal).

1 Dislike the Advertisement a Great Deal

2

3

4

5 Like the Advertisement a Great Deal

9 Don't Know

Name ONE thing that you LIKED about Advertisement #3.

Name ONE thing that you DISLIKED about Advertisement #3.
The following is the fourth political advertisement. Please click on the link, watch the entire advertisement, and then answer the questions following the advertisement. https://www.youtube.com/watch?v=2kEQA2O9rIw.

Thinking about the content of Advertisement #4, how useful do you consider the advertisement on a scale ranging from (1) Not useful at all to (5) Very useful?

    1 Not Useful at All
    2
    3
    4
    5 Very Useful
    9 Don't Know

Thinking about the tone of Advertisement #4, how would you characterize the tone of the advertisement on a scale ranging from (1) Not hostile at all to (5) Very hostile

    1 Not Hostile at All
    2
    3
    4
    5 Very Hostile
    9 Don't Know

Thinking about Advertisement #4, how much do you like the advertisement on a scale from 1 (Dislike the Advertisement a Great Deal) to 5 (Like Advertisement a Great Deal).

    1 Dislike the Advertisement a Great Deal
    2
    3
    4
    5 Like the Advertisement a Great Deal
    9 Don't Know

Name ONE thing that you LIKED about Advertisement #4.

Name ONE thing that you DISLIKED about Advertisement #4.

The following is the fifth political advertisement. Please click on the link, watch the entire advertisement, and then answer the questions following the advertisement. https://www.youtube.com/watch?v=SPUY5vv5W-Q.

Thinking about the content of Advertisement #5 how useful do you consider the advertisement on a scale ranging from (1) Not useful at all to (5) Very useful?

  1 Not Useful at All
  2
  3
  4
  5 Very Useful
  9 Don't Know

Thinking about the tone of Advertisement #5, how would you characterize the tone of the advertisement on a scale ranging from (1) Not hostile at all to (5) Very hostile

  1 Not Hostile at All
  2
  3
  4
  5 Very Hostile
  9 Don't Know

Thinking about Advertisement #5, how much do you like the advertisement on a scale from 1 (Dislike the Advertisement a Great Deal) to 5 (Like Advertisement a Great Deal).

  1 Dislike the Advertisement a Great Deal
  2
  3
  4
  5 Like the Advertisement a Great Deal
  9 Don't Know

Name ONE thing that you LIKED about Advertisement #5.

Name ONE thing that you DISLIKED about Advertisement #5.

The following is the sixth political advertisement. Please click on the link, watch the entire advertisement, and then answer the questions following the advertisement. https://www.youtube.com/watch?v=VeASvCUOuMI.

Thinking about the content of Advertisement #6, how useful do you consider the advertisement on a scale ranging from (1) Not useful at all to (5) Very useful?

  1 Not Useful at All
  2
  3
  4

5 Very Useful
9 Don't Know

Thinking about the tone of Advertisement #6, how would you characterize the tone of the advertisement on a scale ranging from (1) Not hostile at all to (5) Very hostile

1 Not Hostile at All
2
3
4
5 Very Hostile
9 Don't Know

Thinking about Advertisement #6, how much do you like the advertisement on a scale from 1 (Dislike the Advertisement a Great Deal) to 5 (Like Advertisement a Great Deal).

1 Dislike the Advertisement a Great Deal
2
3
4
5 Like the Advertisement a Great Deal
9 Don't Know

Name ONE thing that you LIKED about Advertisement #6.

Name ONE thing that you DISLIKED about Advertisement #6.

The following is the seventh political advertisement. Please click on the link, watch the entire advertisement, and then answer the questions following the advertisement. https://www.youtube.com/watch?v=1iXAzSMvAbo.

Thinking about the content of Advertisement #7, how useful do you consider the advertisement on a scale ranging from (1) Not useful at all to (5) Very useful?

1 Not Useful at All
2
3
4
5 Very Useful
9 Don't Know

Thinking about the tone of Advertisement #7, how would you characterize the tone of the advertisement on a scale ranging from (1) Not hostile at all to (5) Very hostile

   1 Not Hostile at All

   2

   3

   4

   5 Very Hostile

   9 Don't Know

Thinking about Advertisement #7, how much do you like the advertisement on a scale from 1 (Dislike the Advertisement a Great Deal) to 5 (Like Advertisement a Great Deal).

   1 Dislike the Advertisement a Great Deal

   2

   3

   4

   5 Like the Advertisement a Great Deal

   9 Don't Know

Name ONE thing that you LIKED about Advertisement #7.

Name ONE thing that you DISLIKED about Advertisement #7.

Now we would to ask you some more general questions.

Please indicate your level of agreement with the following statements.

Most men are better suited emotionally for politics than most women.

   1. Strongly Agree

   2. Agree

   3. Neither Agree nor Disagree

   4. Disagree

   5. Strongly Disagree

Women should run for public office and take part in the government just as men do.

   1. Strongly Agree

   2. Agree

   3. Neither Agree nor Disagree

   4. Disagree

   5. Strongly Disagree

Men are better qualified to be political leaders than women.

1. Strongly Agree
2. Agree
3. Neither Agree nor Disagree
4. Disagree
5. Strongly Disagree

We would like to ask you a few questions about the government in Washington. Many people are too busy to keep up with these topics, so if you don't know the answer, just skip the question.

What position or office does Elena Kagan hold today?

Do you happen to know which party has the most members in the House of Representatives in Washington, D.C., today?

Whose responsibility is it to determine if a law is constitutional or not—is it the president's, the Congress's, or the Supreme Court's?

Who is currently the U.S. secretary of defense?

How long is the term of a U.S. senator?

One way that people talk about politics in the United States is in terms of liberal, conservative, and moderate ideology. The political views people might hold are often arranged from extremely liberal (1) to extremely conservative (7). Where would you place yourself on this scale?

1. Extremely Liberal
2. Liberal
3. Somewhat Liberal
4. Moderate
5. Somewhat Conservative
6. Conservative
7. Very Conservative
8. Don't Know

Finally, we would like to ask you some questions about yourself.

What year are you in school?

1. Freshman
2. Sophomore

   3. Junior

   4. Senior

   5. Graduate Student

What is your major?

   1. Political science

   2. Global studies

   3. Social science major, other than political science and global studies

   4. Humanities major

   5. Natural science major

   6. Engineering major

   7. Business major

   8. Other major

In what year were you born?

Is your primary residence in the United States?

   1. Yes

   2. No

Please indicate your gender.

   1. Male

   2. Female

   3. Other

U.S. Senate Advertisements Examined in Emotions Focus Group Study

1. **Title**: "People Not Politics"; **State**: North Carolina; **Candidate Attacked**: Democrat Kay Hagan; **Civility Rating**: 3; **Relevance Rating**: 3; **Script of Commercial**: "People don't like political ads. I don't like them either. But healthcare isn't about politics. It's about people. It's not about a website that doesn't work. It's not about poll numbers or approval ratings. It's about people. And millions of people have lost their health insurance. Millions of people can't see their own doctors. And millions are paying more. And getting less. Obamacare doesn't work. It just doesn't work. Tell Senator Hagan to stop thinking about politics and start thinking about people."
https://www.youtube.com/watch?v=IWIvp9NIaQk&feature=youtu.be.

2. **Title**: "Shutdown"; **State**: Arkansas; **Candidate Attacked**: Republican Tom Cotton; **Civility Rating**: 1; **Relevance Rating**: 3; **Script of Commercial**: "'Are you prepared to shut down the government?' [Congressman Cotton:] 'I think we have to be.' 'Congressman Tom Cotton recklessly voted to shut down the government and threatened to default and harm the economy by depressing business and consumer confidence. Cotton hurt Arkansans by stopping loans to small business and farmers and would put social security benefits at risk. Reckless and irresponsible. That's Congressman Cotton.'"
https://www.youtube.com/watch?v=2GNDktIUjbw&feature=youtu.be.

3. **Title**: "Rubber Stamp"; **State**: Georgia; **Candidate Attacked**: Democrat Michelle Nunn; **Civility Rating**: 1; **Relevance Rating**: 3; **Script of Commercial**: "Because of President Obama's mismanagement, Georgia veterans died waiting for the care our country promised them. Yet Michelle Nunn said, 'I defer to the president's judgment.' Georgia families are losing their coverage, yet Nunn would keep Obamacare.

And Nunn even initially refused a travel ban to help stop Ebola. Michelle Nunn would be Obama's senator. Not Georgia's. [Michelle Nunn:] 'I defer to the president's judgment.'"

https://www.youtube.com/watch?v=6Dfox_eyGXA&feature=youtu.be.

4. **Title**: "Worst Day"; **State**: Kentucky; **Candidate Attacked**: Republican Mitch McConnell; **Civility Rating**: 1; **Relevance Rating**: 1; **Script of Commercial**: "McConnell told billionaires Charles and David Koch about the day the Senate passed a law to get big money out of politics. [A voice recording of Mitch McConnell:] 'The worst day of my political life.' Really, Mitch? Not 9/11? Not the day of the financial collapse? Nope. It was the day a law passed to make Washington a bit less corrupt that McConnell called 'The worst day of my political life.' Mitch McConnell: Standing up for big corporations and the Koch brothers at our expense. [A voice recording of Mitch McConnell:] 'Thank you, Charles and David.'"
https://youtu.be/MB949C2elfQ.

5. **Title**: "Good for the Goose"; **State**: Arkansas; **Candidate Attacked**: Democrat Mark Pryor; **Civility Rating**: 3; **Relevance Rating**: 3; **Script of Commercial**: "What's good for goose . . . ought to be good for the gander. But not in Washington. Mark Pryor cast the deciding vote to make you live under Obamacare. But Pryor votes himself and everyone in Congress special subsidies so they're protected from Obamacare. Exemptions and special subsidies for Mark Pryor. Higher insurance premiums for you. Mark Pryor. Voting with Obama, voting against Arkansans like you."
https://www.youtube.com/watch?v=-WakK_7v7aM&feature=youtu.be.

6. **Title**: "Torn Apart"; **State**: Colorado; **Candidate Attacked**: Republican Cory Gardner; **Civility Rating**: 2; **Relevance Rating**: 2; **Script of Commercial**: "Your whole world is torn apart. But Congressman Gardner would make it harder, pushing to outlaw a woman's right to choose. Even in cases of rape and incest. Worse. Gardner tried to redefine rape to mean only forcible rape. In Gardner's bill, victims who were drugged or minors who were victims of statutory rape would not be considered rape victims. Cory Gardner is just too extreme."
https://www.youtube.com/watch?v=9bjx2EJtl3A&feature=youtu.be.

7. **Title**: "Debate"; **State**: North Carolina; **Candidate Attacked**: Democrat Kay Hagan; **Civility Rating**: 1; **Relevance Rating**: 1; **Script of Commercial**: "While Obama let his guard down, the Islamic State Isis embarks on mass murder, beheads Americans, threatens terrorism on American soil. The Senate Armed Services Committee had a crucial hearing on threats from the Islamic State. [A video of Kay Hagan:] 'There was one. And what had happened at that hearing. It was scheduled early in the day. And then votes were scheduled. And then that hearing had to be postponed later that day. So, yes, I did miss that one.' Kay Hagan skipped the hearing for a fundraiser. FIRE Senator Kay Hagan."
https://www.youtube.com/watch?v=RnAQZxjwaaA.

8. **Title**: "Personhood"; **State**: Iowa; **Candidate Attacked**: Republican Joni Ernst; **Civility Rating**: 2; **Relevance Rating**: 2; **Script of Commercial**: "Joni Ernst pushed for the Personhood Amendment. What would that mean? It would ban many forms of birth control and would make all abortions illegal. Ernst would outlaw abortions even for victims of rape or incest. And would actually impose criminal penalties on doctors. [A video of Joni Ernst:] 'I think providers should be punished if there were a Personhood Amendment.' And that's just too extreme. Joni Ernst: Too extreme for Iowa."

https://www.youtube.com/watch?v=msIfrEHsOlU&feature=youtu.be.

Questionnaire Employed in Emotions Focus Group Study

Computer Number

Date

Time

Some people don't pay much attention to political campaigns. How about you? Would you say that you are very much interested, somewhat interested, or not much interested in political campaigns?

    1 Very Much Interested
    2 Somewhat Interested
    3 Not Much Interested
    9 Don't Know

Who did you vote for in the 2016 presidential election?

    Hillary Clinton
    Gary Johnson
    Jill Stein
    Donald Trump
    Other
    Didn't Vote

The following questions assess your views about negative advertisements, in general.

Please indicate how much you agree with the following statement:

Some negative advertisements are so nasty that I stop paying attention to what the candidates are saying.

   1 Agree strongly
   2 Agree somewhat
   3 Disagree somewhat
   4 Disagree strongly
   9 Don't Know

Please indicate how much you agree with the following statement:

Negative advertisements discussing a candidate's personal misbehavior are fair game.

   1 Agree strongly
   2 Agree somewhat
   3 Disagree somewhat
   4 Disagree strongly
   9 Don't Know

Please indicate how much you agree with the following statement:

Hard-hitting commercials attacking the opponent are not helpful during election campaigns.

   1 Agree strongly
   2 Agree somewhat
   3 Disagree somewhat
   4 Disagree strongly
   9 Don't Know

Please indicate how much you agree with the following statement:

I find negative political commercials attacking a candidate for conduct occurring long before the candidate entered public life as uninformative.

   1 Agree strongly
   2 Agree somewhat
   3 Disagree somewhat
   4 Disagree strongly
   9 Don't Know

Generally speaking, do you usually think of yourself as a Republican, a Democrat, an independent, or what? Where would you place yourself on the following scale?

1. Strong Democrat
2. Weak Democrat
3. Independent, Leaning toward the Democratic Party
4. Independent
5. Independent, Leaning toward the Republican Party
6. Weak Republican
7. Strong Republican
8. Don't Know

How often do you pay attention to news about politics and government affairs in a typical week?

1. Every day
2. A few times a week
3. About once a week
4. A few times a month
5. Less than once a month
9 None of the above

Please rate the following political figures on the feeling thermometer. Ratings between 50 degrees and 100 degrees mean that you feel favorable and warm toward the person. Ratings between 0 degrees and 50 degrees mean that you don't feel favorable toward the person and that you don't care too much for that person. You would rate the person at the 50-degree mark if you don't feel particularly warm or cold toward the person. If you come to a person whose name you don't recognize, you don't need to rate that person.

Donald Trump
Nancy Pelosi
Mitch McConnell
Hillary Clinton
Jeff Flake
John McCain
Mike Pence
Bernie Sanders

We are going to show you a series of political advertisements and ask you to answer some questions about each advertisement. The first set of advertisements were taken from the 2014 U.S. Senate campaigns. Please click on the link, watch the entire advertisement, and then answer the questions following the advertisement. https://youtu.be/IWIvp9NIaQk.

Thinking about the content of the first advertisement, how useful do you consider the advertisement on a scale ranging from (1) Not useful at all to (5) Very useful?

  1 Not Useful at All

  2

  3

  4

  5 Very Useful

  9 Don't Know

Thinking about the tone of the first advertisement, how would you characterize the tone of the advertisement on a scale ranging from (1) Not hostile at all to (5) Very hostile

  1 Not Hostile at All

  2

  3

  4

  5 Very Hostile

  9 Don't Know

Does the ad make you feel less likely to vote for the candidate targeted in the advertisement? (4 = much less likely, 3 = somewhat less likely, 2 = a little less likely, 1 = not less likely)

Again, thinking about this advertisement, please answer the following questions. Does the advertisement make you feel?

	Not at All	A Little	Somewhat	To a Great Extent
ANGRY?				
JOY?				
FEAR?				
SURPRISE?				
CONTEMPT?				
SAD?				
DISGUST?				
FRUSTRATION?				

The following is the second political advertisement. Please click on the link, watch the entire advertisement, and then answer the questions following the advertisement. https://www.youtube.com/watch?v=2GNDktIUjbw&feature=youtu.be.

Thinking about the content of the advertisement, how useful do you consider the advertisement on a scale ranging from (1) Not useful at all to (5) Very useful?

1 Not Useful At All

2

3

4

5 Very Useful

9 Don't Know

Thinking about the tone of the advertisement, how would you characterize the tone of the advertisement on a scale ranging from (1) Not hostile at all to (5) Very hostile

1 Not Hostile at All

2

3

4

5 Very Hostile

9 Don't Know

Does the ad make you feel less likely to vote for the candidate targeted in the advertisement? (4 = much less likely, 3 = somewhat less likely, 2 = a little less likely, 1 = not less likely)

Again, thinking about this advertisement, please answer the following questions. Does the advertisement make you feel?

	Not at All	A Little	Somewhat	To a Great Extent
ANGRY?				
JOY?				
FEAR?				
SURPRISE?				
CONTEMPT?				
SAD?				
DISGUST?				
FRUSTRATION?				

The following is the third political advertisement. Please click on the link, watch the entire advertisement, and then answer the questions following the advertisement. https://www.youtube.com/watch?v=6Dfox_eyGXA&feature=youtu.be.

Thinking about the content of the advertisement, how useful do you consider the advertisement on a scale ranging from (1) Not useful at all to (5) Very useful?

1 Not Useful at All
2
3
4
5 Very Useful
9 Don't Know

Thinking about the tone of the advertisement, how would you characterize the tone of the advertisement on a scale ranging from (1) Not hostile at all to (5) Very hostile

1 Not Hostile at All
2
3
4
5 Very Hostile
9 Don't Know

Does the ad make you feel less likely to vote for the candidate targeted in the advertisement? (4 = much less likely, 3 = somewhat less likely, 2 = a little less likely, 1 = not less likely)

Again, thinking about this advertisement, please answer the following questions. Does the advertisement make you feel?

	Not at All	A Little	Somewhat	To a Great Extent
ANGRY?				
JOY?				
FEAR?				
SURPRISE?				
CONTEMPT?				
SAD?				
DISGUST?				
FRUSTRATION?				

The following is the fourth political advertisement. Please click on the link, watch the entire advertisement, and then answer the questions following the advertisement. https://youtu.be/MB949C2elfQ.

Thinking about the content of the advertisement, how useful do you consider the advertisement on a scale ranging from (1) Not useful at all to (5) Very useful?

1 Not Useful at All

2

3

4

5 Very Useful

9 Don't Know

Thinking about the tone of the advertisement, how would you characterize the tone of the advertisement on a scale ranging from (1) Not hostile at all to (5) Very hostile

1 Not Hostile at All

2

3

4

5 Very Hostile

9 Don't Know

Does the ad make you feel less likely to vote for the candidate targeted in the advertisement? (4 = much less likely, 3 = somewhat less likely, 2 = a little less likely, 1 = not less likely)

Again, thinking about this advertisement, please answer the following questions.
Does the advertisement make you feel?

	Not at All	A Little	Somewhat	To a Great Extent
ANGRY?				
JOY?				
FEAR?				
SURPRISE?				
CONTEMPT?				
SAD?				
DISGUST?				
FRUSTRATION?				

The following is the fifth political advertisement. Please click on the link, watch the entire advertisement, and then answer the questions following the advertisement
https://www.youtube.com/watch?v=-WakK_7v7aM&feature=youtu.be.

Thinking about the content of the advertisement, how useful do you consider the advertisement on a scale ranging from (1) Not useful at all to (5) Very useful?

   1 Not Useful at All

   2

   3

   4

   5 Very Useful

   9 Don't Know

Thinking about the tone of the advertisement, how would you characterize the tone of the advertisement on a scale ranging from (1) Not hostile at all to (5) Very hostile

   1 Not Hostile at All

   2

   3

   4

   5 Very Hostile

   9 Don't Know

Does the ad make you feel less likely to vote for the candidate targeted in the advertisement? (4 = much less likely, 3 = somewhat less likely, 2 = a little less likely, 1 = not less likely)

Again, thinking about this advertisement, please answer the following questions. Does the advertisement make you feel

	Not at All	A Little	Somewhat	To a Great Extent
ANGRY?				
JOY?				
FEAR?				
SURPRISE?				
CONTEMPT?				
SAD?				
DISGUST?				
FRUSTRATION?				

The following is the sixth political advertisement. Please click on the link, watch the entire advertisement, and then answer the questions following the advertisement. https://youtu.be/9bjx2EJtl3A.

Thinking about the content of the advertisement, how useful do you consider the advertisement on a scale ranging from (1) Not useful at all to (5) Very useful?

1 Not Useful at All

2

3

4

5 Very Useful

9 Don't Know

Thinking about the tone of the advertisement, how would you characterize the tone of the advertisement on a scale ranging from (1) Not hostile at all to (5) Very hostile

1 Not Hostile at All

2

3

4

5 Very Hostile

9 Don't Know

Does the ad make you feel less likely to vote for the candidate targeted in the advertisement? (4 = much less likely, 3 = somewhat less likely, 2 = a little less likely, 1 = not less likely)

Again, thinking about this advertisement, please answer the following questions. Does the advertisement make you feel?

	Not at All	A Little	Somewhat	To a Great Extent
ANGRY?				
JOY?				
FEAR?				
SURPRISE?				
CONTEMPT?				
SAD?				
DISGUST?				
FRUSTRATION?				

The following is the seventh political advertisement. Please click on the link, watch the entire advertisement, and then answer the questions following the advertisement. https://www.youtube.com/watch?v=RnAQZxjwaaA.

Thinking about the content of the advertisement, how useful do you consider the advertisement on a scale ranging from (1) Not useful at all to (5) Very useful?

   1 Not Useful at All

   2

   3

   4

   5 Very Useful

   9 Don't Know

Thinking about the tone of the advertisement, how would you characterize the tone of the advertisement on a scale ranging from (1) Not hostile at all to (5) Very hostile

   1 Not Hostile at All

   2

   3

   4

   5 Very Hostile

   9 Don't Know

Does the ad make you feel less likely to vote for the candidate targeted in the advertisement? (4 = much less likely, 3 = somewhat less likely, 2 = a little less likely, 1 = not less likely)

Again, thinking about this advertisement, please answer the following questions. Does the advertisement make you feel?

	Not at All	A Little	Somewhat	To a Great Extent
ANGRY?				
JOY?				
FEAR?				
SURPRISE?				
CONTEMPT?				
SAD?				
DISGUST?				
FRUSTRATION?				

The following is the eighth political advertisement. Please click on the link, watch the entire advertisement, and then answer the questions following the advertisement. https://youtu.be/msIfrEHsOlU.

Thinking about the content of the advertisement, how useful do you consider the advertisement on a scale ranging from (1) Not useful at all to (5) Very useful?

  1 Not Useful at All
  2
  3
  4
  5 Very Useful
  9 Don't Know

Thinking about the tone of the advertisement, how would you characterize the tone of the advertisement on a scale ranging from (1) Not hostile at all to (5) Very hostile

  1 Not Hostile at All
  2
  3
  4
  5 Very Hostile
  9 Don't Know

Does the ad make you feel less likely to vote for the candidate targeted in the advertisement? (4 = much less likely, 3 = somewhat less likely, 2 = a little less likely, 1 = not less likely)

Again, thinking about this advertisement, please answer the following questions. Does the advertisement make you feel?

	Not at All	A Little	Somewhat	To a Great Extent
ANGRY?				
JOY?				
FEAR?				
SURPRISE?				
CONTEMPT?				
SAD?				
DISGUST?				
FRUSTRATION?				

Now, we would to ask you some more general questions.

We would like to ask you a few questions about the government in Washington. Many people are too busy to keep up with these topics, so if you don't know the answer, just skip the question.

What position or office does Elena Kagan hold today?

Do you happen to know which party has the most members in the U.S. Senate in Washington, D.C., today?

Whose responsibility is it to determine if a law is constitutional or not—is it the president's, the Congress's, or the Supreme Court's?

Who is currently the U.S. secretary of defense?

How long is the term of a U.S. senator?

One way that people talk about politics in the United States is in terms of liberal, conservative, and moderate ideology. The political views people might hold are often arranged from extremely liberal (1) to extremely conservative (7). Where would you place yourself on this scale?
    1. Extremely Liberal
    2. Liberal
    3. Somewhat Liberal
    4. Moderate
    5. Somewhat Conservative
    6. Conservative
    7. Very Conservative
    8. Don't Know

Please indicate your degree of agreement or disagreement with the following statements. (0) Disagree Strongly (1) Disagree Somewhat (2) Disagree Slightly (3) Agree Slightly (4) Agree Somewhat (5) Agree Strongly

I hate arguments.
I find conflicts exciting.
I feel upset after an argument.
I enjoy challenging the opinions of others.
Arguments don't bother me.

Below is a series of statements concerning men and women and their relationships in contemporary society. Please indicate the degree to which you agree or disagree with each statement using the following scale:

(0) Disagree Strongly (1) Disagree Somewhat (2) Disagree Slightly (3) Agree Slightly (4) Agree Somewhat (5) Agree Strongly

Many women are actually seeking special favors, such as hiring policies that favor them over men, under the guise of asking for "equality."

Most women interpret innocent remarks or acts as being sexist.

Women are too easily offended.

Feminists are not seeking for women to have more power than men.

Most women fail to appreciate fully all that men do for them.

Women seek to gain power by getting control over men.

Women exaggerate problems they have at work.

Once a woman gets a man to commit to her, she usually tries to put him on a tight leash.

When women lose to men in a fair competition, they typically complain about being discriminated against.

There are actually very few women who get a kick out of teasing by men by seeming sexually available and then refusing male advances.

Feminists are making entirely reasonable demands of men.

Finally, we would like to ask you some questions about yourself.

What year are you in school?

1. Freshman
2. Sophomore
3. Junior
4. Senior
5. Graduate Student

How old are you?

Please indicate your gender

1. Male
2. Female
3. Other

References

Abramowitz, A. I. 1980. A Comparison of Voting for US Senator and Representative in 1978. *American Political Science Review* 74(3): 633–640.

Abramowitz, Alan, and Jeffrey Allan Segal. 1992. *Senate Elections*. Ann Arbor: University of Michigan Press.

Abramson, Paul R., John H. Aldrich, Brad T. Gomez, and David W. Rohde. 2015. *Change and Continuity in the 2012 and 2014 Elections*. Washington, D.C.: Congressional Quarterly Press.

Anderson, Ashley, Dominque Brossard, Dietram Scheufele, Michael Xenos, and Peter Ladwig. 2014. The "Nasty Effect": Online Incivility and Risk Perceptions of Emerging Technologies. *Journal of Computer-Mediated Communication* 19(3): 373–387.

Ansolabehere, Stephen, and Shanto Iyengar. 1996. *Going Negative: How Political Advertisements Shrink and Polarize the Electorate*. New York: Free Press.

Ansolabehere, Stephen, Stephen Iyengar, Adam Simon, and Nicholas Valentino. 1994. Does Attack Advertising Demobilize the Electorate? *American Political Science Review* 88(4): 829–838.

Ansolabehere, Stephen, and Philip Edward Jones. 2010. Constituents' Responses to Congressional Roll-Call Voting. *American Journal of Political Science* 54(3): 583–597.

Ansolabehere, Stephen, and Brian Schaffner. 2015. Cooperative Congressional Election Study 2010–2014 Panel Study [Computer File]. Release 1: June 10, 2015. Amherst: University of Massachusetts, Amherst.

Ansolabehere, Stephen, and Brian Schaffner. 2017. *Cooperative Election Study 2016: Common Content [Compuer File]. Released 2: August 4, 2017*. Cambridge, MA: Harvard University.

Ansolabehere, Stephen, Erik C. Snowberg, and James M. Snyder Jr. 2006. Television and the Incumbency Advantage in US Elections. *Legislative Studies Quarterly* 31(4): 469–490.

Ansolabehere, Stephen, and James M. Snyder Jr. 2002. The Incumbency Advantage in US Elections: An Analysis of State and Federal Offices, 1942–2000. *Election Law Journal* 1(3): 315–338.

Avery, James M. 2009. Videomalaise or Virtuous Circle? The Influence of the News Media on Political Trust. *International Journal of Press/Politics* 14(4): 410–433.

Bafumi, Joseph, and Robert Y. Shapiro. 2009. A New Partisan Voter. *Journal of Politics* 71(1): 1–24.

Banda, Kevin K. 2014. Issue-Based Negativity and Candidate Assessment. *Public Opinion Quarterly* 78(3): 707–720.

Banda, Kevin K., and Jason H. Windett. 2016. Negative Advertising and the Dynamics of Candidate Support. Political Behavior 38(3): 747–766.

Bandura, Albert. 1977. *Social Learning Theory.* Englewood Cliffs, NJ: Prentice-Hall.

Bartels, Larry M. 2002. Beyond the Running Tally: Partisan Bias in Political Perceptions. *Political Behavior* 24(2): 117–150.

Benoit, William L. 2000. A Functional Analysis of Political Advertising Across Media, 1998. *Communication Studies* 51(3): 274–295.

Bettencourt, B., and Norman Miller. 1996. Gender Differences in Aggression as a Function of Provocation: A Meta-analysis. *Psychological Bulletin* 119(3): 422–447.

Bonanno, George A., and Dacher Keltner. 1997. Facial Expressions of Emotion and the Course of Conjugal Bereavement. *Journal of Abnormal Psychology* 106(1): 126–137.

Box-Steffensmeier, Janet M., David Darmofal, and Christian A. Farrell. 2009. The Aggregate Dynamics of Campaigns. *Journal of Politics* 71(1): 309–323.

Brader, Ted. 2005. Striking a Responsive Chord: How Political Ads Motivate and Persuade Voters by Appealing to Emotions. *American Journal of Political Science* 49(2): 388–405.

Brooks, Deborah J. 2006. The Resilient Voter: Moving toward Closure in the Debate over Negative Campaigning and Turnout. *Journal of Politics* 68(3): 684–696.

Brooks, Deborah Jordan. 2010. A Negativity Gap? Voter Gender, Attack Politics, and Participation in American Elections. *Politics & Gender* 6(3): 319–341.

Brooks, Deborah J., and John G. Geer. 2007. Beyond Negativity: The Effects of Incivility on the Electorate. *American Journal of Political Science* 51(1): 1–16.

Brooks, Deborah Jordan, and Michael Murov. 2012. Assessing Accountability in a Post–*Citizens United* Era: The Effects of Attack Ad Sponsorship by Unknown Independent Groups. *American Politics Research* 40(3): 383–418.

Brown, Calin. 2017. Grant to Trump: How Court Cases Influenced Campaign Finance. Open Secrets, October 6. https://www.opensecrets.org/news/2017/10/grant-to-trump-how-court-cases-influenced-campaign-finance/. Accessed November 19, 2017.

Campbell, Angus, Philip E. Converse, Warren E. Miller, and Donald Stokes. 1960. *The American Voter.* New York: John Wiley & Sons.

Cassese, Erin C., and Mirya R. Holman. 2017. Party and Gender Stereotypes in Campaign Attacks. *Political Behavior,* 40(3): 785–807.

Chavez, Paola, and Veronica Stracqualursi. 2016. From "Crooked Hillary" to "Little Marco": Donald Trump's Many Nicknames. ABC News, May 11. http:// abcnews.go.com/Politics/crooked-hillary-marco-donald-trumps-nicknames/ story?id=39035114. Accessed August 20, 2017.

Clinton, Joshua D., and John S. Lapinski. 2004. Targeted Advertising and Voter Turnout: An Experimental Study of the 2000 Presidential Election. *Journal of Politics* 66(1): 69–96.

Coe, Kevin, Kate Kenski, and Stephen A. Rains. 2014. Online and Uncivil? Patterns and Determinants of Incivility in Newspaper Website Comments. *Journal of Communication* 64(4): 658–679.

Collins, Michael. 2016. Fewer and Fewer U.S. House Seats Have Any Competition. *USA Today*, November 4. https://www.usatoday.com/story/news/politics/ elections/2016/11/04/fewer-and-fewer-us-house-seats-have-any-competition/ 93295358/. Accessed September 1, 2017.

Cohn, Jeffrey F., Zara Ambadar, and Paul Ekman. 2007. Observer-Based Measurement of Facial Expression with the Facial Action Coding System. In James A. Coen and John J. B. Allen (eds.), *The Handbook of Emotion Elicitation and Assessment*, 203–221. New York: Oxford University Press.

Cox, Gary W., and Jonathan N. Katz. 1996. Why Did the Incumbency Advantage in US House Elections Grow? *American Journal of Political Science* 40(2): 478–497.

Craig, Stephen C., and Paulina S. Rippere. 2014. Political Trust and Negative Campaigns: Two Tests of the Figure-Ground Hypothesis. *Politics & Policy* 42(5): 693–743.

Craig, Scotty D., Sidney D'Mello, Amy Witherspoon, and Art Graesser. 2008. Emote Aloud During Learning with AutoTutor: Applying the Facial Action Coding System to Cognitive–Affective States During Learning. *Cognition and Emotion* 22(5): 777–788.

Dahl, Robert. 1956. *A Preface in Democratic Theory*. Chicago: University of Chicago Press.

Damore, David F. 2004. The Dynamics of Issue Ownership in Presidential Campaigns. *Political Research Quarterly* 57: 391–397.

Delli Carpini, Michael X., and Scott Keeter. 1993. Measuring Political Knowledge: Putting First Things First. *American Journal of Political Science* 37(4): 1179–1206.

Dowling, Conor M., and Amber Wichowsky. 2014. Attacks without Consequence? Candidates, Parties, Groups, and the Changing Face of Negative Advertising. *American Journal of Political Science* 59(1): 19–36.

Druckman, James N., Donald P. Green, James H. Kuklinski, and Arthur Lupia. 2006. The Growth and Development of Experimental Research in Political Science. *American Political Science Review* 100(4): 627–635.

Eagly, Alice H. 2013. *Sex Differences in Social Behavior: A Social Role Interpretation*. Mahwah, NJ: Lawrence Erlbaum Associates.

Eagly, Alice H., and Valerie J. Steffen. 1986. Gender Stereotypes, Occupational Roles, and Beliefs about Part-Time Employees. *Psychology of Women Quarterly* 10(3): 252–262.

Ekman, Paul, and Wallace V. Friesen. 1976. Measuring Facial Movement. *Environmental Psychology and Nonverbal Behaviour* 1(1): 56–75.

Ekman, Paul, and Erika L. Rosenberg. 1997. *What the Face Reveals: Basic and Applied Studies of Spontaneous Expression Using the Facial Action Coding System (FACS)*. New York: Oxford University Press.

Finkel, Steven, and John G. Geer. 1998. Spot Check: Casting Doubt on the Demobilizing Effect of Attack Advertising. *American Journal of Political Science* 42(2): 573–595.

Fiorina, Morris. 1981. *Retrospective Voting in American National Elections*. New Haven, CT: Yale University Press.

Fowler, Erika, Michael Franz, and Travis Ridout. 2016. *Political Advertising in the United States*. Boulder, CO: Westview Press.

Fowler, Erika Franklin, Michael Franz, and Travis N. Ridout. 2017. Political Advertising in 2014. Version 1.0 [Dataset]. Middletown, CT: Wesleyan Media Project, Department of Government at Wesleyan University.

Fowler, Erika Franklin, and Travis N. Ridout. 2011. Advertising Trends in 2010. *The Forum* 8(4): 1–16.

Fowler, Erika Franklin, and Travis N. Ridout. 2012. Negative, Angry, and Ubiquitous: Political Advertising in 2012. *The Forum* 10(4): 41–61.

Fowler, Erika Franklin, Travis N. Ridout, and Michael M. Franz. 2016. Political Advertising in 2016: The Presidential Election as Outlier?" *The Forum* 14(4): 445–469.

Franklin, Charles H. 1991. Eschewing Obfuscation? Campaigns and the Perception of US Senate Incumbents. *American Political Science Review* 85(4): 1193–1214.

Franz, Michael M., Paul Freedman, Kenneth Goldstein, and Travis N. Ridout. 2008. Understanding the Effect of Political Advertising on Voter Turnout: A Response to Krasno and Green. *Journal of Politics* 70(1): 262–268.

Freedman, Paul, Michael M. Franz, and Kenneth Goldstein. 2004. Campaign Advertising and Democratic Citizenship. *American Journal of Political Science* 48(4): 723–41.

Freedman, Paul, and Kenneth Goldstein. 1999. Measuring Media Exposure and the Effects of Negative Campaign Ads. *American Journal of Political Science* 43(4): 1189–1208.

Freedman, Paul, William Wood, and Dale Lawton. 1999. Do's and Don'ts of Negative Ads: What Voters Say. *Campaigns & Elections* 20(9): 20–25.

Fridkin, Kim L., Jillian Courey, Samantha Hernandez, and Joshua Spears. 2016. Gender Differences in Reactions to Fact Checking of Negative Commercials. *Politics & Gender* 12(2): 369–390.

Fridkin, Kim L., and Patrick J. Kenney. 2004. Do Negative Messages Work? The Impact of Negativity on Citizens' Evaluations of Candidates. *American Politics Research* 32(5): 570–605.

Fridkin, Kim, and Patrick J. Kenney. 2008. The Dimensions of Negative Messages. *American Politics Research* 36(5): 694–723.

Fridkin, Kim L., and Patrick Kenney. 2011. Variability in Citizens' Reactions to Different Types of Negative Campaigns. *American Journal of Political Science* 55(2): 307–325.

Fridkin Kim L., and Patrick Kenney. 2012. The Impact of Negative Campaigning on Citizens' Actions and Attitudes. In Holli A. Semetko and Margaret Scammell (eds.), *The SAGE Handbook of Political Communication*, 173–185. Los Angeles: Sage.

Fridkin, Kim, Patrick J. Kenney, and Amanda Wintersieck. 2015. Liar, Liar, Pants on Fire: How Fact-Checking Influences Citizens' Reactions to Negative Advertising. *Political Communication* 32(1): 127–151.

Frodi, Ann, Jacqueline Macaulay, and Pauline R. Thome. 1977. Are Women Always Less Aggressive Than Men? A Review of the Experimental Literature. *Psychological Bulletin* 84(4): 634–660.

Funk, Carolyn L. 1996. The Impact of Scandal on Candidate Evaluations: An Experimental Test of the Role of Candidate Traits. *Political Behavior* 18(1): 1–24.

Funk, Carolyn L. 1999. Bringing the Candidate into Models of Candidate Evaluation. *Journal of Politics* 61(3): 700–720.

Furnham, Adrian, and Joseph Marks. 2013. Tolerance of Ambiguity: A Review of the Recent Literature. *Psychology* 4(9): 717–728.

Gabriel, Trip. 2016. Both Disliked, Hillary Clinton and Donald Trump Accentuate the Negatives. *New York Times*, May 10. https://www.nytimes.com/2016/05/11/us/politics/hillary-clinton-donald-trump-campaign-character-negative.html?_r=0. Accessed May 10, 2016.

Galician, Mary-Lou. 1986. Perceptions of Good News and Bad News on Television. *Journalism Quarterly* 63(Fall): 611–616.

Garramone, Gina M. 1984. Voter Responses to Negative Political Ads. *Journalism Quarterly* 61(2): 250–259.

Garramone, Gina M. 1985. Effects of Negative Political Advertising: The Roles of Sponsor and Rebuttal. *Journal of Broadcasting & Electronic Media* 29(2): 147–159.

Gearan, Anne, Abby Phillip, and Karen Tumulty. 2016. Clinton: Trump Is "Dangerously Incoherent," "Temperamentally Unfit" to Be President. *Washington Post*, June 2. https://www.washingtonpost.com/politics/clinton-trump-is-dangerously-incoherent-temperamentally-unfit-to-be-president/2016/06/02/577e5174-28db-11e6-b989-4e5479715b54_story.html?utm_term=.236e07864f38. Accessed January 15, 2018.

Geer, John G. 2006. *In Defense of Negativity: Attack Ads in Presidential Campaigns*. Chicago: University of Chicago Press.

Geer, John G. 2012. The News Media and the Rise of Negativity in Presidential Campaigns. *PS: Political Science & Politics* 45(3): 422–427.

Geer, John G. 2013. The News Media and the Rise of Negativity in Presidential Campaigns: A New Hypothesis. In Daniel M Shea and Morris P. Fiorina (eds.),

Can We Talk? The Rise of Rude, Nasty, Stubborn Politics, 171–187. New York, NY: Pearson.

Geer, John G., and Richard R. Lau. 2006. Filling in the Blanks: A New Method for Estimating Campaign Effects. *British Journal of Political Science* 36(2): 269–290.

Geer, John G., and Lynn Vavreck. 2014. Negativity, Information, and Candidate Position-Taking. *Political Communication* 31(2): 218–236.

Gerber, Alan S., James G. Gimpel, Donald P. Green, and Daron R. Shaw. 2011. How Large and Long-lasting Are the Persuasive Effects of Televised Campaign Ads? Results from a Randomized Field Experiment. *American Political Science Review* 105(1): 135–150.

Gerber, Alan S., and Donald P. Green. 2000. The Effects of Canvassing, Telephone Calls, and Direct Mail on Voter Turnout: A Field Experiment. *American Political Science Review* 94(3): 653–663.

Gerber, Alan S., Donald P. Green, and Ron Shachar. 2003. Voting May Be Habit-Forming: Evidence from a Randomized Field Experiment. *American Journal of Political Science* 47(3): 540–550.

Gervais, Bryan T. 2014. Following the News? Reception of Uncivil Partisan Media and the Use of Incivility in Political Expression. *Political Communication* 31(4): 564–583.

Gervais, Bryan T. 2015. Incivility Online: Affective and Behavioral Reactions to Uncivil Political Posts in a Web-Based Experiment. *Journal of Information Technology & Politics* 12(2): 167–185.

Globetti, Suzanne, and Marc J. Hetherington. 2000. The Negative Implications of Anti-Government Campaign Rhetoric. Paper presented at the annual meeting of the Midwest Political Science Association.

Goldstein, Kenneth, and Paul Freedman. 2000. New Evidence for New Arguments: Money and Advertising in the 1996 Senate Elections. *Journal of Politics* 62(4): 1087–1108.

Goldstein, Kenneth, and Paul Freedman. 2002. Lessons Learned: Campaign Advertising in the 2000 Elections. *Political Communication* 19(1): 5–28.

Goldstein, S. 1999. Construction and Validation of a Conflict Communication Scale. *Journal of Applied Social Psychology* 29(9): 1803–1832.

Grable, John E. 2000. Financial Risk Tolerance and Additional Factors That Affect Risk Taking in Everyday Money Matters. *Journal of Business and Psychology* 14(4): 625–630.

Grunau, Ruth V. E., and Kenneth D. Craig. 1987. Pain Expression in Neonates: Facial Action and Cry. *Pain* 28(3): 395–410.

Haddock, Geoffrey, and Mark P. Zanna. 1997. Impact of Negative Advertising on Evaluations of Political Leaders: The 1993 Canadian Federal Election. *Basic and Applied Social Psychology* 19(2): 205–223.

Hains, Tim. 2017. "Latino Victory Fund" Ad Depicts Ed Gillespie Supporter Terrorizing Minority Children. *Real Clear Politics*, October 30. https://www.realclearpolitics.

com/video/2017/10/30/latino_victory_fund_ad_depicts_ed_gillespie_sup-porter_terrorizing_minority_children.html. Accessed November 17, 2017.

Haselmayer, Martin, and Marcelo Jenny. 2014. Measuring the Tonality of Negative Campaigning: Combining a Dictionary Approach with Crowd-Coding. Paper prepared for presentation at Political Context Matters: Content Analysis in the Social Sciences Conference, October 10–11, Mannheim, Germany.

Hassell, Hans, and Kelly R. Oeltjenbruns. 2016. When to Attack: The Trajectory of Congressional Campaign Negativity. *American Politics Research* 44(2): 222–246.

Hayes, Danny. 2008. Party Reputations, Journalistic Expectations: How Issue Ownership Influences Election News. *Political Communication* 25(4): 377–400.

Hayes, Danny. 2010. Trait Voting in US Senate Elections. *American Politics Research* 38(6): 1102–1129.

Henderson, John A., and Alexander G. Theodoridis. 2017. Seeing Spots: Partisanship, Negativity and the Conditional Receipt of Campaign Advertisements. *Political Behavior* 40(4): 965–987.

Herbst, Susan. 2010. *Rude Democracy: Civility and Incivility in American Politics.* Philadelphia: Temple University Press.

Hill, Ronald Paul. 1989. An Exploration of Voter Responses to Political Advertisements. *Journal of Advertising* 18(4): 14–22.

Hill, Ronald Paul, Michael Capella, and Yoon-Na Cho. 2015. Incivility in Political Advertisements: A Look at the 2012 US Presidential Election. *International Journal of Advertising* 34(5): 812–829.

Hill, Seth J., James Lo, Lynn Vavreck, and John Zaller. 2013. How Quickly We Forget: The Duration of Persuasion Effects from Mass Communication. *Political Communication* 30(4): 521–547.

Hillygus, Sunshine. 2005. Campaign Effects and the Dynamics of Turnout Intention in Election 2000. *Journal of Politics* 67(1): 50–68.

Hillygus, Sunshine., Todd G. Shields. 2005. Moral Issues and Voter Decision Making in the 2004 Presidential Election. *PS:Political Science and Politics* 38(2): 201–209.

Hitchon, Jacqueline C., and Chingching Chang. 1995. Effects of Gender Schematic Processing on the Reception of Political Commercials for Men and Women Candidates. *Communication Research* 22(4): 430–458.

Hyde, Janet S. 1984. How Large Are Gender Differences in Aggression? A Developmental Meta-analysis. *Developmental Psychology* 20(4): 722–736.

Isaacowitz, Derek M., Eric S. Allard, Nora A. Murphy, and Mark Schlangel. 2009. The Time Course of Age-Related Preferences toward Positive and Negative Stimuli. *Journal of Gerontology Series B: Psychological Sciences and Social Sciences* 64B(2): 188–192.

Jackson, Robert A. 2002. Gubernatorial and Senatorial Campaign Mobilization of Voters. *Political Research Quarterly* 55(4): 825–844.

Jackson, Robert, and Thomas Carsey. 2007. US Senate Campaigns, Negative Advertising, and Voter Mobilization in the 1998 Midterm Election. *Electoral Studies* 26(1): 180–195.

Jackson, Robert A., Jeffrey J. Mondak, and Robert Huckfeldt. 2009. Examining the Possible Corrosive Impact of Negative Advertising on Citizens' Attitudes toward Politics. *Political Research Quarterly* 62(1): 55–69.

Jackson, Robert A., and Jason C. Sides. 2006. Revisiting the Influence of Campaign Tone on Turnout in Senate Elections. *Political Analysis* 14(2): 206–218.

Jacobs, Jennifer. 2014 . Here are Bruce Braley's "I Made a Mistake" Remarks In Full. *Des Moines Register*, April 3. https://www.desmoinesregister.com/story/news/politics/elections/2014/04/03/braley-iowa-farmer-gaffe/7265377/ Accessed February 11, 2017.

Jacobson, Gary C., 2013. Partisan Polarization in American Politics: A Background Paper. *Presidential Studies Quarterly* 43(4): 688–708.

Jacobson, Gary C., and Jamie L. Carson. 2015. *The Politics of Congressional Elections*. Lanham, MD: Rowman & Littlefield.

Jaffe, Alexandra. 2016. Donald Trump Has "Small Hands," Marco Says. NBC News, February 20. https://www.nbcnews.com/politics/2016-election/donald-trump-has-small-hands-marco-rubio-says-n527791 Accessed February 22, 2017.

Jamieson, Kathleen Hall, and Bruce W. Hardy. 2008. Will Ignorance and Partisan Election of Judges Undermine Public Trust in the Judiciary? *Daedalus* 137(4): 11–15.

Jamieson, Kathleen Hall, and Bruce W. Hardy. 2012. What is Civil Engaged Argument and Why Does Aspiring to it Matter? *PS: Political Science and Politcs* 45(3): 412–415.

Jasperson, Amy E., and David P. Fan. 2002. An Aggregate Examination of the Backlash Effect in Political Advertising: The Case of the 1996 US Senate Race in Minnesota. *Journal of Advertising* 31(1): 1–12.

Johannes, John R., and John C. McAdams. 1981. The Congressional Incumbency Effect: Is It Casework, Policy Compatibility, or Something Else? An Examination of the 1978 Election. *American Journal of Political Science* 25(3): 512–542.

Johnston, Anne, and Lynda Lee Kaid. 2002. Image Ads and Issue Ads in U.S. Presidential Advertising: Using Videostyle to Explore Styalistic Differences in Televised Potilital Ads From 1952 to 2000. *The Journal of Communication* 52(2): 281–300.

Kahn, Kim Fridkin. 1993. Incumbency and the News Media in US Senate Elections: An Experimental Investigation. *Political Research Quarterly* 46(4): 715–740.

Kahn, Kim Fridkin, and Patrick J. Kenney. 1999a. Do Negative Campaigns Mobilize or Suppress Turnout? Clarifying the Relationship between Negativity and Participation. *American Political Science Review* 93(4): 877–889.

Kahn, Kim Fridkin, and Patrick J. Kenney. 1999b. *The Spectacle of US Senate Campaigns*. Princeton, NJ: Princeton University Press.

Kahn, K. F. and P. J. Kenney. 2004. *No Holds Barred: Negativity in US Senate Campaigns*. Upper Saddle River, NJ: Pearson Prentice Hall.

Kaid, Lynda Lee, and John Boydston. 1987. An Experimental Study of the Effectiveness of Negative Political Advertisements. *Communication Quarterly* 35(2): 193–201.

Kamhawi, Rasha, and Maria Elizabeth Grabe. 2008. Engaging the Female Audience: An Evolutionary Psychology Perspective on Gendered Responses to News Valence Frames. *Journal of Broadcasting & Electronic Media* 52 (no. 1, March): 33–51.

Kern, Montague, and Marion Just. 1997. A Gender Gap among Viewers? In Pippa Norris (ed.), *Women, Media, and Politics*, 99–112. New York: Oxford University Press.

King, James D., and Jason B. McConnell. 2003. The Effect of Negative Campaign Advertising on Vote Choice: The Mediating Influence of Gender. *Social Science Quarterly* 84(4): 843–857.

Krasno, Jon S., and Donald P. Green. 2008. Do Televised Presidential Ads Increase Voter Turnout? Evidence from a Natural Experiment. *Journal of Politics* 70(1): 245–261.

Krupnikov, Yanna. 2011. When Does Negativity Demobilize? Tracing the Conditional Effect of Negative Campaigning on Voter Turnout. *American Journal of Political Science* 55(4): 797–813.

Krupnikov, Yanna. 2014. How Negativity Can Increase and Decrease Voter Turnout: The Effect of Timing. *Political Communication* 31(3): 446–466.

Krupnikov, Yanna, and Nichole M. Bauer. 2014. The Relationship between Campaign Negativity, Gender and Campaign Context. *Political Behavior* 36(1): 167–188.

Krupnikov, Yanna, and Spencer Piston. 2015. Accentuating the Negative: Candidate Race and Campaign Strategy. *Political Communication* 32(1): 152–173.

Lariscy, Ruth Ann Weaver, and Spencer F. Tinkham. 1999. The Sleeper Effect and Negative Political Advertising. *Journal of Advertising* 28(4): 13–30.

Lau, Richard. 1985. Two Explanations for Negativity Effects in Political Behavior. *American Journal of Political Science* 29(1): 353–377.

Lau, Richard, and Gerald M. Pomper. 2001. Effects of Negative Campaigning on Turnout in US Senate Elections, 1988–1998. *Journal of Politics* 63(3): 804–819.

Lau, Richard, and Gerald M. Pomper. 2002. Effectiveness of Negative Campaigning in US Senate Elections. *American Journal of Political Science* 46(1): 47–66.

Lau, Richard, and Gerald M. Pomper. 2004. *Negative Campaigning: An Analysis of US Senate Elections.* Lanham, MD: Roman & Littlefield.

Lau, Richard R., and David P. Redlawsk. 2015. The Effects of Advertising Tone on Information Processing and Vote Choice. In Alessandro Nai and Annemarie Walter (eds.), *New Perspectives on Negative Campaigning: Why Attack Politics Matters*, 247–264. ECPR Press (Studies in European Political Science), Colchester, United Kingdom.

Lau, Richard, and Ivy B. Rovner. 2009. Negative Campaigning. *Annual Review of Political Science* 12: 285–306.

Lau, Richard, Lee Sigelman, Caroline Heldman, and Paul Babbitt. 1999. The Effects of Negative Political Advertisements: A Meta-Analytic Assessment. *American Political Science Review* 93(4): 851–876.

Lau, Richard, Lee Sigelman, and Ivy B. Rovner. 2007. The Effects of Negative Political Campaigns: A Meta-Analytic Reassessment. *Journal of Politics* 69(4): 1176–1209.

Leshner, Glenn, and Esther Thorson. 2000. Overreporting Voting: Campaign Media, Public Mood, and the Vote. *Political Communication* 17(3): 263–278.

Lipsitz, Keena, and John G. Geer. 2017. Rethinking the Concept of Negativity: An Empirical Approach. *Political Research Quarterly* 70(3): 577–589.

Lodge, Milton, and Charles S. Taber. 2005. The Automaticity of Affect for Political Leaders, Groups, and Issues: An Experimental Test of the Hot Cognition Hypothesis. *Political Psychology* 26(3): 455–482.

Madison, James. [1788] 1981. Federalist 49. *The Federalist Papers*. Baltimore: Johns Hopkins University Press.

Manchester, Julia. 2017. Ad Uses Scalise Shooting against Ossoff in Georgia. *The Hill*, June 18. http://thehill.com/blogs/ballot-box/house-races/338370-ad-uses-scalise-shooting-against-ossoff. Accessed November 17, 2017.

Marcus, George E. 2000. Emotions in politics. *Annual Review of Political Science* 3(1): 221–250.

Markus, Gregory B. 1982. Political Attitudes During an Election Year: A Report on the 1980 NES Panel Study. *American Political Science Review* 76(3): 538–560.

Markus, Gregory B., and Philip E. Converse. 1979. A Dynamic Simultaneous Equation Model of Electoral Choice. *American Political Science Review* 73(4): 1055–1070.

Martin, Paul S. 2004. Inside the Black Box of Negative Campaign Effects: Three Reasons Why Negative Campaigns Mobilize. *Politcal Psychology* 25(4): 545–562.

Martinez, Michael D., and Ted Delegal. 1990. The Irrelevance of Negative Campaigns to Political Trust: Experimental and Survey Results. *Political Communication and Persuasion* 7(1): 25–40.

Massaro, Toni M., and Robin Stryker. 2012. Freedom of Speech, Liberal Democracy, and Emerging Evidence on Civility and Effective Democratic Engagement. *Arizona Legal Studies* 54: 12–12.

Mattes, Kyle, and David P. Redlawsk. 2015. *The Positive Case for Negative Campaigning*. Chicago: University of Chicago Press.

McDuff, Daniel, Rana El Kaliouby, Evan Kodra, and Rosalind Picard. 2013. Measuring Voter's Candidate Preference Based on Affective Responses to Election Debates. In *Affective Computing and Intelligent Interaction* (ACII), 2013 Humaine Association Conference, 369–374. Washington, DC: IEEE.

McHugh, Mary L. 2012. Interrater Reliability: The Kappa Statistic. *Biochemia Medica* 22(3): 276–282.

Merritt, Sharyne. 1984. Negative Political Advertising: Some Empirical Findings. *Journal of Advertising* 13(3): 27–38.

Mill, John Stuart. [1861] 1991. Considerations on Representative Government. In *On Liberty and Other Essays*. Oxford: Oxford University Press. 205–470.

Mölders, Christina, Niels Van Quaquebeke, and Maria Paola Paladino. 2015. Consequences of Politicians' Disrespectful Communication Depends on Social Judgment Dimensions and Voters' Moral Identity. *Political Psychology* 38(1): 119–135.

Mondak, Jeffery J., and Mary R. Anderson. 2004. The Knowledge Gap: A Re-examination of Gender-Based Differences in Political Knowledge. *Journal of Politics* 66(2): 492–512.

Muehling, Darrel D., Akshaya Vijayalakshmi, and Russell N. Laczniak. 2016. The Effects of Tolerance of Negativity on Consumers' Responses to Comparative Attack Advertising. *Journal of Marketing Communications* 703–719.

Mutz, Diane C. 2007. Effects of In-Your-Face Television Discourse on Perceptions of a Legitimate Opposition. *American Political Science Review* 101(4): 621–635.

Mutz, Diane C. 2015. *In-Your-Face Politics: The Consequences of Uncivil Media.* Princeton, NJ: Princeton University Press.

Mutz, Diana C., and Byron Reeves. 2007. The New Videomalaise: Effects of Televised Incivility on Political Trust. *American Political Science Review* 99(1): 1–15.

Nagourney, Adam. 2016. Going Dirty. *New York Times*, June 25. https://www.nytimes.com/2016/06/26/opinion/sunday/going-dirty.html?_r=0. Accessed March 18, 2017.

Neuman, W. Russell, George E. Marcus, and Michael B. MacKuen. 2013. Hardwired for News: Affective Intelligence and Political Attention. Paper presented at the American Political Science Association Annual Meeting, Chicago.

Niven, David. 2006. A Field Experiment on the Effects of Negative Campaign Mail on Voter Turnout in a Municipal Election. *Political Research Quarterly* 59(2): 203–210.

Painter, David Lynn. 2014. Collateral Damage: Involvement and the Effects of Negative Super PAC Advertising. *American Behavioral Scientist* 58(4): 510–523.

Pantic, Maja, and Ioannis Patras. 2006. Dynamics of Facial Expression: Recognition of Facial Actions and Their Temporal Segments from Face Profile Image Sequences. *IEEE Transactions on Systems, Man, and Cybernetics, Part B (Cybernetics)* 36(2): 433–449.

Peirce, Kate. 2001. What If the Energizer Bunny Were Female? Importance of Gender in Perceptions of Advertising Spokes-Character Effectiveness. *Sex Roles* 45(11–12): 845–858.

Petrocik, Jack R. 1996. Issue Ownership in Presidential Elections, with a 1980 Case Study. *American Journal of Political Science* 40: 825–850.

Pew Research Center for the People and the Press. 2004. News Audiences Increasingly Politicized. http://www.people-press.org/files/legacy-pdf/215.pdf. Accessed February 1, 2015.

Phillips, Todd. 2016. How Negative Political Campaigning Is Crippling America. *Huffington Post*, July 31. https://www.huffingtonpost.com/todd-phillips/negative-political-campaigning_b_1554744.html. Accessed July 21, 2012.

Pinkleton, Bruce E. 1998. Effects of Print Comparative Political Advertising on Political Decision-making and Participation. *Journal of Communication* 48(4): 24–36.

Pinkleton, Bruce E., Nam-Hyun Um, and Erica Weintraub Austin. 2002. An Exploration of the Effects of Negative Political Advertising on Political Decision Making. *Journal of Advertising* 31(1): 13–25.

Prinz, Timothy S. 1995. Media Markets and Candidate Awareness in House Elections, 1978–1990. *Political Communication* 12(3): 305–325.

Prior, Markus. 2006. The Incumbent in the Living Room: The Rise of Television and the Incumbency Advantage in US House Elections. *Journal of Politics* 68(3): 657–673.

Prior, Markus, and Arthur Lupia. 2008. Money, Time, and Political Knowledge: Distinguishing Quick Recall and Political Learning Skills. *American Journal of Political Science* 52(1): 169–183.

Rawls, John. 1971. *A Theory of Justice.* Cambridge, MA: Harvard University Press.

Redlawsk, David P. 2002. Hot Cognition or Cool Consideration? Testing the Effects of Motivated Reasoning on Political Decision Making. *Journal of Politics* 64(4): 1021–1044.

Redlawsk, David P., Andrew J. W. Civettini, and Karen M. Emmerson. 2010. The Affective Tipping Point: Do Motivated Reasoners Ever "Get It"? *Political Psychology* 31(4): 563–593.

Reed, Andrew E., and Laura L. Carstensen. 2012. The Theory behind the Age-Related Positivity Effect. *Frontiers in Psychology* 3: 251–259.

Ridout, Travis N., Erika Franklin Fowler, Michael M. Franz, and Kenneth Goldstein. 2018. The Long-Term and Geographically Constrained Effects of Campaign Advertising on Political Polarization and Sorting. *American Politics Research* 46(1): 3–25.

Ridout, Travis N., Michael M. Franz, and Erika Franklin Fowler. 2015. Sponsorship, Disclosure, and Donors: Limiting the Impact of Outside Group Ads. *Political Research Quarterly* 68(1): 154–166.

Ridout, Travis N., and Jenny L. Holland. 2017. The Effects of Political Advertising. In Christina Holtz-Bacha and Marion R. Just (eds.), *Routledge Handbook of Political Advertising,* 81–92. New York: Routledge.

Rogowski, Jon C. 2014. Electoral Choice, Ideological Conflict, and Political Participation. *American Journal of Political Science* 58(2): 479–494.

Rosenstone, Steven J., and John Mark Hansen. 1993. *Mobilization, Participation, and Democracy in America.* New York: Macmillan.

Rudman, Laurie A., and Peter Glick. 2001. Prescriptive Gender Stereotypes and Backlash toward Agentic Women. *Journal of Social Issues* 57(4): 743–762.

Sapiro, Virginia. 1999. Considering Political Civility Historically: A Case Study of the United States. Paper presented at the annual meeting of the International Society for Political Psychology, Amsterdam.

Sayette, Michael A., Jeffrey F. Cohn, Joan M. Wertz, Michael A. Perrott, and Dominic J. Parrott. 2001. A Psychometric Evaluation of the Facial Action Coding System for Assessing Spontaneous Expression. *Journal of Nonverbal Behavior* 25(3): 167–185.

Schaffner, Brian, and Stephen Ansolabehere. 2017. 2016 CCES—American National Election Study Parallel Survey. doi:10.7910/DVN/YDGQMQ. Harvard Dataverse, V1.

Shea, Daniel M., and Morris P. Fiorina. 2013. *Can We Talk? The Rise of Rude, Nasty, Stubborn Politics.* New York: Pearson Education.

Shea, Daniel M., and Alex Sproveri. 2012. The Rise and Fall of Nasty Politics in America. *PS: Political Science & Politics* 45(3): 416–421.

Sides, John, Keena Lipsitz, and Matthew Grossmann. 2010. Do Voters Perceive Negative Campaigns as Informative Campaigns? *American Politics Research* 38(3): 502–530.

Simon, Jeffrey, and Raluca M. Gaher. 2005. The Distress Tolerance Scale: Development and Validation of a Self-Report Measure. *Motivation and Emotion* 29: 83–102.

Skaperdas, Stergios, and Bernard Grofman. 1995. Modeling Negative Campaigning. *American Political Science Review* 89(1): 49–61.

Sobieraj, Sarah, and Jeffrey M. Berry. 2011. From Incivility to Outrage: Political Discourse in Blogs, Talk Radio, and Cable News. *Political Communication* 28(1): 19–41.

Soroka, Stuart, Elisabeth Gidengil, Patrick Fournier, and Lilach Nir. 2016. Do Women and Men Respond Differently to Negative News? *Politics & Gender* 12(2): 344–368.

Squire, Peverill. 1989. Challengers in U.S. Senate Elections. *Legislative Studies Quarterly* 14(14): 531–547.

Steenbergen, Marco R., and Bradford S. Jones. 2002. Modeling Multilevel Data Structures. *American Journal of Political Science* 46(1): 218–237.

Stevens, Daniel. 2012. Tone versus Information: Explaining the Impact of Negative Political Advertising. *Journal of Political Marketing* 11(4): 322–352.

Stevens, Daniel, Barbara Allen, John Sullivan, and Eric Lawrence. 2015. Fair's Fair? Principles, Partisanship, and Perceptions of the Fairness of Campaign Rhetoric. *British Journal of Political Science* 45(1): 195–213.

Stewart III, Charles, and Mark Reynolds. 1990. Television Markets and US Senate Elections. *Legislative Studies Quarterly* 15(4): 495–523.

Strach, Patricia, Katherine Zuber, Erika Franklin Fowler, Travis N. Ridout, and Kathleen Searles. 2015. In a Different Voice? Explaining the Use of Men and Women as Voice-Over Announcers in Political Advertising. *Political Communication* 32(2): 183–205.

Stryker, Robin, J. Taylor Danielson, and Bethany Conway. 2015. Who Is More Tolerant of Political Incivility? The Role of Gender, Political Ideology, and Media Use. Paper presented at the 111th annual meeting of the American Political Science Association, San Francisco, September.

Sullivan, Denis G., and Roger D. Masters. 1988. "Happy Warriors": Leaders' Facial Displays, Viewers' Emotions, and Political Support. *American Journal of Political Science* 32(2): 345–368.

Sydnor, Emily. 2015. Fighting Words and Fiery Tone: The Interaction of Political Incivility and Psychological Conflict Orientation. Ph.D. dissertation, University of Virginia.

Sydnor, Emily. 2018. Platforms for Incivility: Examining Perceptions across Different Media Formats. *Political Communication* 35(1): 97–116.

Taber, Charles S., and Milton Lodge. 2006. Motivated Scepticism in the Evaluation of Political Beliefs. *American Journal of Political Science* 50(3): 755–769.

Teinowitz, Ira. 2008. Political Ads Hit $1 Billion Mark; Spending, Negativity Up in Battle for Senate; Boon for Spot TV. *Advertising Age*, November 4.

Teixeira, Thales, Michel Wedel, and Rik Pieters. 2012. Emotion-Induced Engagement in Internet Video Advertisements. *Journal of Marketing Research* 49(2): 144–159.

Teven, Jason J., James C. McCroskey, and Virginia P. Richmond. 1998. Measurement of Tolerance for Disagreement. *Communication Research Reports* 15(2): 209–217.

Tocqueville, Alexis de. [1835] 1956. *Democracy in America*. Edited and abridged by R. D. Heffner. New York: Mentor Books.

Ulbig, Stacy G., and Carolyn L. Funk. 1999. Conflict Avoidance and Political Participation. *Political Behavior* 21(3): 265–282.

Vandewalker, Ian. 2015. Election Spending 2014: Outside Spending in Senate Races Since *Citizens United*. Brennan Center for Justice at New York University School of Law, New York. https://www.brennancenter.org/sites/default/files/analysis/Outside%20Spending%20Since%20Citizens%20United.pdf. Accessed November 17, 2017.

Vavreck, Lynn. 2009. *The Message Matters: The Economy and Presidential Campaigns*. Princeton, NJ: Princeton University Press.

Verba, Sidney, Kay Lehman Schlozman, and Henry E. Brady. 1995. *Voice and Equality: Civic Voluntarism in American Politics*. Cambridge, MA: Harvard University Press.

Villa, Dana R. 1992. Postmodernism and the Public Sphere. *American Political Science Review* 86(3): 712–721.

Wallace, Gregory. 2016. Negative Ads Dominate in Campaign's Final Days. CNN, November 8. http://www.cnn.com/2016/11/08/politics/negative-ads-hillary-clinton-donald-trump/index.html. Accessed September 2, 2017.

Wattenberg, Martin, and Craig Leonard Brians. 1999. Negative Campaign Advertising: Demobilizer or Mobilizer? *American Political Science Review* 93(4): 877–890.

Wesleyan Media Project. 2016a. Over 2 Million Political Ads Aired This Cycle. Press Release, August 24. http://mediaproject.wesleyan.edu/wp-content/uploads/2016/09/2016Release4_FINAL-6.pdf. Accessed October 27, 2018.

Wesleyan Media Project. 2016b. Special Report on Outside Group Activity, 2000–2016: Super PACs Dominate 2016; "Dark Money" a Consistent but Growing Presence since 2000. http://mediaproject.wesleyan.edu/wpcontent/uploads/2016/08/DisclosureReport_FINAL-5.pdf. Accessed November 18, 2017.

Wesleyan Media Project. 2017. Political Advertising in 2014. March. http://mediaproject.wesleyan.edu/wp-content/uploads/2017/03/WMP-2014-releasecodebook_v1.0-1.pdf. Accessed October 27, 2018.

Wesleyan Media Project. N.d. Project Background. Accessed http://mediaproject.wesleyan.edu/about/project-background/. October 27, 2018.

Westlye, Mark. 1991. *Senate Elections and Campaign Intensity*. Baltimore, MD: Johns Hopkins University Press.

Wolf, Michael, J. Cherie Strachan, and Daniel M. Shea. 2012. Incivility and Standing Firm: A Second Layer of Partisan Division. *Political Science & Politics* 45(3): 428–434.

Wolfinger, Raymond E., and Steven J. Rosenstone. 1980. *Who Votes?* New Haven, CT: Yale University Press.

Wood, Wendy, and Alice H. Eagly. 2002. A Cross-Cultural Analysis of the Behaviour of Women and Men: Implications for the Origins of Sex Differences. *Psychological Bulletin* 128(5): 699–727.

Youngman, Sam. 2014. Alison Lundergan Grime Holds a Slim 4-Point Advantage over Mitch McConnell in Kentucky. *Lexington Herald Leader*, February 6. http://www. kentucky.com/news/politics-government/article44470230.html. Accessed July 10, 2016.

Index

Figures, notes, and tables are indicated by *f*, *n*, and *t* following the page number.